WHAT PRICE PREJUDICE?

Studies in Judaism and Christianity

Exploration of Issues in the Contemporary Dialogue Between Christians and Jews

Editor in Chief for
Stimulus Books
Helga Croner

Editors
Lawrence Boadt, C.S.P.
Helga Croner
Rabbi Leon Klenicki
Rev. Dr. John Koenig
Kevin A. Lynch, C.S.P.
Dennis McManus
Dr. Susan Shapiro

A STIMULUS BOOK

WHAT PRICE PREJUDICE?

Christian Antisemitism in America

Frank E. Eakin, Jr.

A STIMULUS BOOK
PAULIST PRESS ◆ NEW YORK ◆ MAHWAH, N.J.

Appreciation is expressed to Augsburg Fortress Press for permission to reprint from *Luther's Works,* volume 47, edited by Franklin Sherman, copyright © 1971 by Fortress Press, used by permission of Augsburg Press; to HarperCollins Publishers Inc. for permission to quote from *Faith and Fratricide,* by Rosemary Ruether; to the Episcopal Church for permission to include in its entirety "Guidelines for Christian-Jewish Relations," as adopted by the General Convention, 1988; to the Presbyterian Church, U.S.A., for permission to include "A Theological understanding of the Relationship Between Christians and Jews" as adopted by the 199th General Assembly (June, 1987) of the Presbyterian Church, U.S.A.; and to the Evangelical Lutheran Church in America for permission to include "The Declaration of the Evangelical Lutheran Church in America to the Jewish Community," as adopted by the Church Council of the Evangelical Lutheran Church in America on April 18, 1994. Scriptural quotations are taken from the *New Revised Standard Bible,* copyright 1989 by the Division of Christian Education of the National Council of the Churches of Christ in the United States of America.

Artwork by Frank Sabatté, C.S.P.

Cover design by John Murello.

Library of Congress Cataloging-in-Publication Data

Eakin, Frank E., 1936–
    What price prejudice? : Christian antisemitism in America / Frank E. Eakin, Jr.
        p.   cm.—(Studies in Judaism and Christianity) (A Stimulus book)
    Includes bibliographical references and index.
    ISBN 0–8091–3822–0 (alk. paper)
    1. Antisemitism—History. 2. Christianity and antisemitism. 3. Antisemitism—United States—History. 4. Judaism—Relations—Christianity. 5. Christianity and other religions—Judaism. I. Title. II. Series.
DS145.E35   1998
261.2′6′09—dc21   98–26299
                                                                                        CIP

Published by Paulist Press
997 Macarthur Boulevard
Mahwah, New Jersey 07430

www.paulistpress.com

Printed and bound in the
United States of America

Contents

For supporters exemplar,
Carole and Marcus
Fannie and Gilbert

**What Spectacle
Can Be More Edifying
Or More Seasonable,
Than That Of
Liberty and Learning,
Each Leaning On The Other
For Their Mutual
& Surest Support?**
James Madison*

**Inscription carved outside the entrance to the James Madison
Memorial Building of the Library of Congress in Washington, D.C.*

Preface

Neither an individual nor a corporate body can be devoid of conditioning influences. As a case in point, regardless of how open we consider ourselves to be on the issue of Jewish-Christian relations, we cannot respond as though we are primeval individuals acting in a vacuum. Both Jews and Christians carry the baggage of almost two thousand years of collective interaction. As much as we desire an unbiased and unqualified acceptance of another human being, we are individually encapsulated within the shells of our own experiences. This is reality, but it is not an admission that relationships are unalterably bound by the confinements of our social, economic, political, psychological, or religious milieu.

As one deals with this subject, there must be a referent point. For our concern, it is the American Christian experience in the United States, a quite diverse situation as regards both Jews and Jewish-Christian relations. It makes a tremendous difference whether one addresses the richness of metropolitan New York, where approximately one of every three Jews residing in the United States lives; or the Newport, Rhode Island community, which has been historically significant but is now statistically unimportant; or Nebraska, where Jews have been neither historically nor statistically of consequence. Bottom line—where one is located does make a difference!

It is difficult for us to recognize that a problem in Jewish-Christian relations exists when we do not know any Jews or anyone who is a blatant antisemite. But the responsibility is still ours—it is incumbent upon us to read and understand our history, and for one who does so the role of the church in antisemitism is a clear, albeit difficult issue with which to deal. What can be done? This is the focus of our concern. It derives out of

1

both personal and professional interest, and as a result it is both academically focused and at the same time intensely experiential and existential.

Where date designations are helpful, I have characteristically used B.C.E. (Before the Common Era) and C.E (Common Era) rather than B.C. (Before Christ) and A.D. (Anno Domini). Although this book will likely be read primarily by Christians, an issue throughout is the importance of sensitivity. Without any personal offense, Christians may use B.C.E. and C.E. Understandably, however, Jews prefer not to use B.C. and A.D., both of which imply an affirmation they do not make. This is a situation where Christians may take the first step in encouraging meaningful Jewish-Christians relations.

As is always true, one is assisted in countless ways in a project of this type. I am deeply indebted to Father Lawrence Boadt, C.S.P, editor at Paulist Press, for his assistance and guidance as this project progressed. I am especially appreciative of his careful reading of the manuscript, which resulted in numerous suggestions for improvement. While his comments greatly improved the finished product, any omissions or errors are, of course, my responsibility.

It was Father Boadt's suggestion that the book be published under the Stimulus imprint. I express here my gratitude to Helga Croner, Editor in Chief for Stimulus Books, and to the Stimulus Foundation Board for their acceptance of the manuscript.

This book is dedicated to three groups who have been especially meaningful to me in this study. First, Carole and Marcus Weinstein and Fannie and Gilbert Rosenthal have endowed the Chair in Jewish and Christian Studies that I hold at the University of Richmond. Through this Chair I have been encouraged to examine issues of greatest import to me and have been able to bring outstanding speakers to the university to address issues associated with Jewish-Christian relations; the endowment has also provided significant support for my research, with this volume being a witness to that assistance. Both families know individually of my continued gratitude to them for what they do, and the primary dedication necessarily resides with them. Second, for those of us who have the luxury of life in the Academy, one reason above all draws us to this endeavor—the students. Thus, I also dedicate this book to those students through the years, both Jewish and Christian, who have helped to sensitize me to the importance of this study. Thirdly, I have been privileged over the years to have many opportunities to speak before both Jewish and Christian groups. The subject addressed has usually focused around issues of Jewish-Christian relations, and I express my appreciation to these groups for what they have done to enhance my own perceptions. I know more assuredly because of them just how open people are to the investigation of truth and how much more capable laypersons are of dealing with difficult theological issues than is often thought to be the case. So, thirdly, this book is dedicated to these inquiring individuals who have been so helpful to me in shaping my own perspectives.

I express sincere appreciation to my wife, Frances, who has always been available to assist as the research and writing of this project was pursued. She has often shared vacation times with trips to nearby libraries to further the "research project"! Shirley Ann Fisk, the Department of Religion secretary, has assisted in countless ways, most especially in preventing my being consumed by the computer. Individuals in various libraries have made my task so much more simple: Boatwright Library at the University of Richmond; The American Jewish Archives on the Cincinnati campus of the Hebrew Union College-Jewish Institute of Religion; the American Jewish Historical Society, located on the campus of Brandeis University; the Jewish Section of the New York Public Library; the various libraries and archives of Harvard University; and the Library of Congress.

Introduction

Prejudice. Discrimination. Antisemitism. These words chronicle the order of development as the covert thought becomes overt expression. These are words that for most individuals conjure up distaste, and yet unfortunately they address the reality of the human condition. None of us is exempt from prejudice, regardless of how subtle its expression or how much we try to mask it. Nonetheless, most of us do not have a first-hand acquaintance with the insidious evil associated with prejudice enacting itself in the discriminatory deeds of antisemitism.

Individuals who are not Jewish are often impatient with what is perceived as a Jewish obsession with antisemitism. After all, almost everyone has experienced situations where an invitation to a certain club or social event was not forthcoming, or perhaps a desired appointment did not materialize. We have perhaps concluded that these personal slights resulted from our not being thought to be on a social parity with the invitees or perhaps that special appointment went to a "competitor" who had the "proper" family background and attended the "right" university. But this type of prejudice and discrimination is of a different genre from the blackness of antisemitism.

In the United States an environment has generally existed in which, relatively speaking, antisemitism has not been widely evident. One says "relatively" because the general European environment at the time Jews began to enter the Colonies was extraordinarily hostile to the Jews. It is also true that antisemitism has been a factor in the American Jewish experience since their initial arrival on these shores in 1654, although the experience of antisemitism was never as excessive as in the European and Hispanic countries. Antisemitism has been sufficiently manifest, however, that books have been written focusing exclusively on the U.S. experience of antisemitism (see selected books listed in the bibliography).

From the perspective of an individual raised as a Christian, or for that matter one who is simply not Jewish, it is difficult to understand fully the problems of antisemitism for Jews. Be assured, however, that even in this relatively non-hostile environment, such problems do exist. There are two levels at which Jewish people necessarily must respond. On the one hand, one must relate to the present and to the areas of life where Jews are fully integrated.[1] On the other hand, the present can never be seen in a historical vacuum. What is presently experienced must be evaluated against history. It must be acknowledged that what has been earlier experienced can indeed be repeated, and thus all of the acceptance and integration of the moment, whether authentic or superficial, must be seen against the possibility that the future may not be characterized by a continuing sense of openness.

The basic problem is that we can even talk about acceptance and integration as if there were other options! Many Jews can attest that our society does indeed operate as though acceptance and integration were choices among options. They are often treated as though *being Jewish* makes one in some way different or unusual when compared with the rest of the population. In Protestant Christian circles, there is generally no substantive distinction made, for example, among Episcopal, Methodist, and Presbyterian denominations. Increasingly we draw fewer distinctions between an individual's being Protestant or Catholic; the person is simply Christian. And that is the position that we must embrace in terms of the Jewish and Christian issue—no distinction can or should be made between two individuals, one of whom is Christian while the other is Jewish. Both individuals are citizens who differ in that they have chosen or been born into differing faith affirmations.[2] This should not impact at all the evaluation of the merit of either individual as a potentially productive citizen and certainly should offer to neither individual the prerogative to coerce the other into conformity with personal views. But this is precisely the problem faced by the Jew—he or she is judged to be different because of being Jewish, and there are many Christians who in good conscience seem compelled to convert Jews to Christianity.

This monograph is an attempt by one individual who happens to stand within the life of the church to address antisemitism. While reading Stuart E. Rosenberg's book entitled *The Christian Problem: A Jewish View,* I noted a reference to his book's putting the ball in the Christian's court. This is precisely the intent of this book. Rosenberg made a significant contribution, but it is probably true that only a Christian can place this issue squarely within Christendom's court!

The problem is approached historically by letting some of the events of history speak to us and by entering into open and honest interpretation of selected New Testament passages. What is investigated rationally is not so easily used in a twisted or derogatory fashion. How shall we proceed?

We address initially the phenomenon of antisemitism. What is antisemitism and how does it manifest itself? As we address such issues, it becomes increasingly clear that antisemitism has found some of its firmest roots in New Testament passages. We need to investigate some of the Biblical statements to understand both what is and is not conveyed. Finally, we shall indicate some concrete manifestations of antisemitism, especially during the medieval and ultimately in the New World eras. Finally, we shall evaluate some of the responses that ecclesiastical bodies have made to the Shoah (Holocaust), because in these responses we see the hope or tragedy of Jewish-Christian relations.

From this type of historical reflection, we shall ultimately turn our attention to some suggestions for improving Jewish-Christian relations. Given the fact that the relationship of Jews and Christians has suffered for almost two thousand years from misperceptions and misplaced emphases, there is obviously no quick fix available. It is important, however, to understand what has been and to investigate what might be done. It is equally crucial to recognize the dangers for both Jew and Christian of simply continuing with business as usual!

It should be noted that since World War II a plethora of books and articles focusing on antisemitism and Jewish and Christian relations have emerged (see the Bibliography for a partial list of these). The thrust of these writings has varied from instructional to polemical. Particularly from the Christian perspective it is easy for an element of self-flagellation to creep into the material.

My concerns seek to avoid both the polemical and self-flagellation and to focus on the instructional. From my working with university students, I have become convinced that the collective memory becomes truncated in a relatively short time. Today's students, unless they are

Jewish, are essentially unaware of that distant phenomenon called World War II and the horrendous actions visited upon world Jewry. During the Third Reich, centuries of history focused upon the relationship of two communities of faith and how seeds of distrust, hatred, and violence inevitably came to full bloom. How to deal with this horrendous reality is the focus of the material to follow.

I. Searching for Roots

INTRODUCTION

Post-World War II Christian concern about antisemitism has been awakened by the horrors of the Holocaust. This is an important issue, for Christians must recognize their historical complicity in anti-semitism, which helped to make possible the Holocaust. Antisemitism was able to flourish during the Third Reich because the Christian church, the one group which should have refuted all manifestations of antisemitism throughout its approximate two millennia of history, frequently encouraged, and too often participated in, its continuation.

ROOTS AND BRANCHES

The analogy to a tree with roots and branches is helpful when seeking to understand antisemitism. It is not one thing but many, and it does not have a single manifestation but indeed multiple incarnations. When one views the trunk of a massive tree, there is a monolithic quality to what is viewed. But, if one could gaze into the earth, one would see an extensive root system feeding the trunk. So it is with antisemitism. Just as an extensive root system comes from all directions to nourish the life of the trunk, so antisemitism derives from many points of causation, which come together in the manifestation of hatred. Even in the most "polite" manifestations of antisemitism, where this hatred is veiled, it is nonetheless damaging to the recipients. In the most blatant manifestations of antisemitism, the expression is open for all to observe, often encouraging emulation by others in this hideous activity!

MODERN ANTISEMITISM

Modern antisemitism had its rise in nineteenth-century Central and Eastern Europe, with the first antisemitic political parties arising in the 1870s and 1880s. Hannah Arendt points to the trial of Alfred Dreyfus, held in Paris in 1894, as a crux for understanding the antisemitism that would develop in the twentieth century. The Dreyfus case became a cause célèbre for those who would struggle with the causes and effects of antisemitism.[1]

Alfred Dreyfus (1859–1935), a French army Captain, was falsely accused of transmitting military secrets to the Germans, and he was brought to trial in late 1894 amidst scandalous antisemitism. Theodor Herzl was assigned to cover the trial for Vienna's *Neue Freie Presse.* And even though he was originally convinced of Dreyfus's guilt, he rather quickly began to question his earlier conclusion. As Dreyfus's innocence emerged more and more clearly, Herzl became convinced that if a Jew could be so abysmally maltreated in France, the country that gave birth to democratic government through the French Revolution, then a Jew was not safe anywhere. It was not that the trial radically changed Herzl; rather, as stated by Amos Elon, "the Dreyfus affair was merely the last straw."[2]

In spite of the fact that the charges were clearly concocted, Captain Dreyfus was convicted in 1894 and imprisoned on Devil's Island. Fortunately, the injustice of his conviction was recognized, and he was pardoned in 1899. It was not, however, until 1906, again amidst divisive controversy and flagrant antisemitism, that he was finally cleared of all charges against him. Two factors stand out most clearly in this sordid affair. The first is the lasting impact the trial and its attendant circumstances had on Herzl, generally understood as the father of modern political Zionism. His proposed solution to the Jewish problem, *Der Judenstaat (The Jewish State),* was published in 1896, just two years after Dreyfus's conviction. The first Zionist congress, for which Herzl was the prime mover, was held in Basel, Switzerland, August 29–31, 1897; and ultimately six international congresses were orchestrated and convened by Herzl prior to his untimely death in 1904. The second factor is that no Jew who heard the antisemitic slurs of the crowds or observed Dreyfus's degradation ceremony prior to being sent to Devil's Island could ever falsely evaluate the tenuous position of Jews throughout all of Europe. Sadly, one hundred years following the French revolution, circumstances had not changed very much the historical role to which the Jews were accustomed!

Melvin M. Tumin, in *Antisemitism in the United States,* has addressed in as clear and concise a manner as possible the nature and major ingredients of antisemitism. Although he deals with it primarily as a U.S. phenomenon, his emphasis on the ludicrous nature of stereotypes, which Tumin suggests to be at the base of antisemitism, is universally applicable. Undergirding antisemitism, he suggests, is the conviction that a Jew may be clearly identified:

> This belief in the identifiability of Jews need not concern us. But, if and when this belief is accompanied by some kind of fear of Jews—a feeling that they ought to be kept at a distance, and a desire to deny them certain rights enjoyed by others—then we have the phenomenon called anti-Semitism.[3]

With this statement Tumin has concisely identified the nature of incipient antisemitism. In summary, then, he would designate the four primary ingredients of antisemitism as follows:

1. a belief that Jews are different, that they can be identified and distinguished from non-Jews;
2. some kind of fear of them;
3. a desire to keep them at a distance;
4. a willingness to discriminate against them—in schools, jobs, housing, social clubs, resorts, and other such places.[4]

TERMINOLOGY

One of the problems we confront when speaking about antisemitism is terminology. "Semite," as first used in 1781 by A. L. Schlözer, designated the various descendants of Shem, one of the three sons of Noah (with Ham and Japheth) in the genealogical listing of Genesis 10. Properly used the word designates peoples who share a common linguistic base. Usually three Semitic language divisions are referenced: the Eastern, Northwestern (in which Hebrew is listed), and Southern.[5]

"Antisemitism" as a specific category seems to have been first promulgated in 1873 by Wilhelm Marr, a German journalist, who published a pamphlet entitled "The Victory of Judaism over Germanism," in which he conveyed the charge that would become standard, namely that the Jews were corrupting German society. Marr, along with others, was basically advocating a policy toward Jews based on "racism," with racism in quotation marks because it is clear that being Jewish has nothing to do with race. This racist theory "proclaimed that humans were divided into clearly distinguishable races and that the intellectual, moral, and social conduct and potential of these races were biologically determined."[6] From this type of misconceived "scientific" view, "antisemitism" came to designate a hatred of the Jews in general and of their religious practices and so-called basic personality type in particular. The former aspect is often reinforced by a special brand of antisemitism, designated theological antisemitism, which adds religious grounds to those based on culture and politics.

Popular use has so distorted the word *Semite* that a dictionary definition describes the "antisemite" as "one who is hostile to or discriminates against Jews."[7] The more appropriate definition, however, is "one who is anti-Judaism and anti-Jew." We may accede to popular use with the term antisemitism, but its true referent should not be forgotten. As it is characteristically employed, antisemitism refers to any ideology that attempts minimally to impose disabilities or maximally to annihilate the Jews, based upon misconstrued racial grounds.[8] This much, however, is clear: under no circumstances should the word *Semite* be understood to have racial connotations. However much we think Jewishness may be identifiable in a person, ultimately to be a Jew is to embrace a faith and/or a culture but has nothing to do with race.

While the operative rationale for antisemitism differs from situation to situation, James Parkes noted that there are at least three factors, religious, political, and economic, in antisemitism.[9]

To these elements one should add at least the sociological and psychological perspectives.[10] The brake within a society to prevent the manifestation of antisemitism in any of these forms depends on the humaneness of that society. Particularly telling is the seriousness with which the hopes and aspirations of minorities are viewed by the majority and the degree to which it is assumed that all participants in a society not only contribute to its welfare but have a reasonable expectation to derive from it a degree of fulfillment. The Declaration of Independence describes this as the right to "life, liberty, and the pursuit of happiness," while the Bible presents this as the choice of a full "life" (Dt 30:19).

The Deuteronomistic perspective is especially concerned that the Israelite not forget that the Israelites were once sojourners in a foreign land, that God redeemed them, and that now they had a responsibility toward those who dwelt in their land as strangers.[11] The Book of Deuteronomy accordingly contains numerous injunctions to care for the stranger (see, for example, Dt 10:18–19, 14:29, *et al.*).

Antisemitism is the antithesis of the right to "life, liberty, and the pursuit of happiness," of the option to choose "life" in a Biblical sense, or of a caring, humanitarian concern for the stranger in your midst. Ida Jacobs has correctly noted that antisemitism, however ill conceived, acts as a poisonous agent within a society:

> That anti-Semitism finds its stronghold in the mediocre, in the superficial, in those suffering from a sense of inferiority, does not lessen the potential damage. The idea of inequality poisons the air of a democracy—it is harmful both to those who believe in it and act accordingly, and to their victims.[12]

THE ORIGINS OF ANTISEMITISM

Antisemitism has a long history that began before the Christian era but was redefined and intensified with the emergence of Christianity. But if antisemitism existed prior to Christianity, when, where, and how? Rosemary Ruether has spoken to this issue helpfully in *Faith and Fratricide*.[13] Several examples will suffice to make the point.

Egypt plays a significant role in the history of antisemitism.[14] The Egyptian bondage-release narrative found in the book of Exodus was a pivotal story for Israelite self-perception because it was woven into Israel's covenant experience. In this narrative, Egypt was the nation that potentially could preclude fulfillment of the salvation promise made to father Abraham. Later, some of the Ptolemaic rulers settled large numbers of Jews in Alexandria, using this minority as liaison between the rulers and subject populations.[15] The inevitable result was suspicion and hatred of the Jew by the Egyptian. For the Jew, the Egyptian experience recounted not only the nature of their God as a redeeming, community-creating God, but it also served as the prototype for the inhumanity that they as a people must be able to endure.

There was also generally a negative reaction to Judaism in Hellenistic societies, a phenomenon also true of the developed Greco-Roman environment. Particularly indicative was the attempt by Antiochus IV [Epiphanes] (175–163 B.C.E.) to eliminate all traces of Jewish practice in Israel, which led to the Maccabean Revolt.[16] From a different vantage point, such Hellenistic antipathy led Philo of Alexandria to present Judaism to a Greek-speaking audience in Greek philosophic dress.[17]

Rome and the Jews had their problems, as is indicated by the Jewish revolts for independence in 66–73 C.E. and 132–135 C.E. (Bar Kokhba). Nonetheless, Rome was much more willing to work with the Jews in bringing peace and stability to the Palestinian portion of the Roman Empire. Importantly, "it was a pagan Rome that found formulae of special accommodation of Jewish ways within Greco-Roman society, while it was Christian Rome that gradually repealed this protected status of the Jews and began to create the legal instruments of the ghetto."[18]

BIBLICAL AUTHORITY AND THE NEW TESTAMENT

The Achilles' heel for Christian relationships with Jews is the bipartite issue of the Christian view of Biblical authority along with the apparent negation of the Jews as found in the New Testament. These, in turn, give rise to a myriad of other issues, each of which could be independently developed.

Several observations are in order. First, the relational problem is more often on the Christian than the Jewish side; thus it is appropriate to approach this as a *Christian* problem. Second, it is proper to refer to this as one issue rather than as several issues because the Christian view of Biblical authority and the message of the New Testament are so interwoven as to be inseparable.

Each of these statements can be developed further. Although it is asserted that the relational problem is more often a Christian issue than a Jewish issue, individuals will often raise questions such as the following: Were not the Jews violently opposed to the followers of Jesus when this movement first emerged?…Was it not the Jews who persecuted the followers of Jesus long before there was persecution of the Jews by Christians?…From a modern perspective, does not the

Holocaust, with all of the charges of Christian complicity, if not responsibility, make the problem of relationships more a Jewish than a Christian issue?

It should be noted that the very phrasing of the issues predetermines the outcome. For example, the phrasing of the first two questions above, that is, about the Jews being violently opposed to the followers of Jesus and the Jews persecuting the followers of Jesus prior to any persecution of Jews by Christians, presupposes a mode of reading the Bible. It presupposes that precisely what is recorded is what occurred. Would it not be better in this instance to recognize that the New Testament writings were written long after the occurrence of the events recorded and thus record events the way they were, or would have been perceived, in the time of the recorder rather than in the time of the actual occurrence. This leads us to the possibility that Jesus' relationship with the Jews was much more positive than that indicated by at least some of the scriptures, especially the Fourth Gospel. Looking at the New Testament through such a historical lens enables us to understand the hostility and the problems that it presents, but it also allows us to acknowledge that the problem between the Jews and the followers of Jesus is more likely a post-Jesus problem rather than one characteristic of Jesus' time. To take the material too literally can encourage and propagate antisemitism. Unfortunately, it is just this sense of literal historicity that too often governs the understanding of scripture, even among those who are generally more enlightened in their Christian faith.

It was earlier suggested that this is primarily a Christian issue because, for almost two thousand years, it has been the Christians rather than the Jews who have been the aggressors in this relationship. To put this another way, it is the Christians who should be charged with antisemitism throughout history. It is Christians who have developed the view that there is only one way for an individual to relate meaningfully with God; it is Christians who have developed a view of supersession which affirms the negation of and fulfillment of Judaism within Christianity; it is Christians who have taken over the Jewish scriptures and treated them as exclusively a Christian property. As we later investigate some of the specifics of Christian interpretation of scripture, these points will be elaborated. At this juncture, it seems accurate to conclude that this is primarily a Christian issue.

JEWISH AND CHRISTIAN INTERACTION

Christians often raise the issue of Jewish opposition to the followers of Jesus when the movement first emerged, essentially claiming that the Christians were acting in self-defense! To be sure, the Biblical text does indicate official unhappiness with what was perceived as a perversion of the Jewish message by Jesus and his followers, and the attempt to control and eliminate that perversion. Paul was himself engaged in fighting the early church according to the Book of Acts (8:1–3; 9:1–2). Negatively, this was the same kind of activity in which the church would later be involved as it sought to preserve orthodoxy within its ranks. With the church this would lead to councils, especially from the fourth through the sixth centuries. These councils sought to impose a belief structure through creedal formulations that were often backed up by force when individuals sought to disrupt this ideal. From a more positive perspective, however, one cannot claim that Jewish oppression and harassment of Christians continued over the duration of the relationship of Judaism and Christianity. It also does little good to argue that the Jews would have continued such persecution had the opportunities been available, that is, had the political circumstances developed differently. We must work with history the way it happened!

Finally, meaningful relationships with Christians are sometimes difficult for Jews in light of Christian complicity with the Holocaust. Nonetheless, most Jews have been able to rise above this issue, in part because they recognize that it serves Judaism better not to get mired in issues of culpability; rather, Judaism and its ultimate concerns are best served by taking the high road on this issue and doing what is possible to bring about positive Jewish-Christian relations in the present, whatever the past may have held. What would be extremely meaningful to Jews would be the various ways that Christians and the official arms of Christendom might acknowledge a recognition of Christian complicity with or responsibility for the Holocaust. That acknowledgement would work wonders in healing wounds that have refused to heal over the last half century. In Chapter 6 we will discuss some of the statements formulated by ecclesiastical bodies in response to the Holocaust and the impact that historical period has had on Jewish and Christian relations. The fact that most of these statements admit to Christian culpability, to participation in the "teaching of contempt," has indeed had a positive impact on Jewish and Christian relations.

ANTISEMITISM AND ITS CONTINUATION

Another Jewish writer, Jules Isaac, who himself experienced radically the pains of antisemitism during the Third Reich, accused Christianity of propagating against the Jews "the teaching of contempt" and a "system of degradation." These created, according to Isaac, a new type of antisemitism. He suggested that "the teaching of contempt" was forged primarily in the fourth century and encompassed such themes as degenerate Judaism, regarding the Jews as a sensual people; a people who misunderstood and rejected the Christ; a people reproved, degraded, and denounced by God; a people guilty of deicide; a people divinely despised; and the Synagogue of Satan.[19] Isaac suggested that the "system of degradation" emerged particularly in the eleventh century with the First Crusade. Resultant to the "system of degradation," Jews were excluded from most professions and thereby reduced to money lending and ultimately relegated to a ghetto existence. In addition, Isaac noted that they also experienced "spoliations, mass expulsions, burning of holy books, forced baptisms, children torn from their parents, calumnious denunciations of the profanation of the host, ritual crimes (accusations of the murder of Christian infants), tortures, corporeal punishments, autodafes of the Inquisition, innumerable and frightful massacres later given the Russian name of *pogroms*."[20]

Unfortunately, antisemitism continues to be a problem within the contemporary church. Of course this attitude demonstrated itself most clearly in this century during the Third Reich in Germany. Significant portions of the church masterfully deceived itself, convincing itself of Jewish guilt and thus of the merit of their difficulties. In 1939 Konrad Grober, the Roman Catholic Archbishop of Freising, Germany, sent a pastoral letter in which he "advised his flock that the Jews were entirely responsible for the Crucifixion of Christ and that 'their murderous hatred [of Him] has continued in later centuries.'"[21] Examples of this type could be multiplied almost endlessly; unfortunately, the listing on this side of the ledger would be much greater than on the side of those publicly renouncing such blatant antisemitism.

If one be tempted to excuse such reactions as wartime mania, the Glock-Stark research in the 1960s in the United States indicates that antisemitism is not conditioned primarily by war fever. In one of their questions, participants were asked "What group do you think was most responsible for crucifying Christ?" A total of 2,326 persons responded,

58 percent saying "The Jews" and 26 percent "The Romans." Of the 545 Catholics responding, 61 percent said "The Jews" while 22 percent said "The Romans."[22] This is only a part of this valuable research, but clearly it demonstrates that at the time it was done, an antisemitic spirit existed among those claiming ties to various Christian denominations. Statistical data are not available for the present decade. Since the time of the Glock-Stark study, however, the United States has experienced an oil embargo, the energy crisis intensified, the problems in the Middle East have continued to vacillate between mild and harsh conflict, peace treaties have been signed between Israel and Egypt and between Israel and Jordan, with the United States being the guarantor of oil for Israel, and there has been considerable resurgence of fundamentalist and/or conservative, evangelical Christianity. We acknowledge that it is from this branch of Christendom that the greatest negativity toward the Jews emanates.[23] It is partially conjecture, therefore, to suggest that such a survey conducted today would yield about the equivalent relative results toward Jews and Judaism. Support for this conclusion, however, does come from evidence gathered by the Anti-Defamation League of B'nai B'rith, which is discussed in Chapter 5 below.[24]

NEW TESTAMENT: BACKGROUND DATA

Antisemitism clearly existed prior to and apart from Christianity.[25] At the same time, it is clear that with the emergence of Christianity a new genre of antisemitism arose, rooted in Christianity's Christological dispute with Judaism. As Rosemary Ruether indicates, "The sad truth of religious history is that one finds that special virulence, which translates itself into diabolizing and damnation, only between groups that pose rival claims to exclusive truth within the same religious symbol system."[26] Thus, the stage was set with Christianity's emergence for an intensified antisemitism to erupt because of this shared religious symbol system and the resultant injection of new prejudicial venom.

The new historical element, Christianity's exclusive affirmation that Jesus was the Christ (Messiah), which was faith's reaction by Jesus' closest followers to the traumatic cross-resurrection event, served to ignite antisemitism on several fronts. Christian writings, later to be accorded the status of authoritative scripture, declared Jesus' condemnation of those to whom much had been entrusted and little returned, charged the Jews with obduracy in responding to Jesus' call to commitment, and ultimately held the Jews responsible for the death of Jesus. All of these factors would be conjoined to stimulate overt anti-semitism once Christians gained sufficient political strength to do so.

It should be noted that contemporary Jewish concern is not with Jesus, who indeed can be acknowledged as a significant first-century teacher who zealously sought to institute reforms in the people's under-standing of Judaism. This acknowledgement does not indicate agree-ment with all of his actions and teachings, of course, but the problem for Judaism lies more with Jesus' followers than with Jesus. Whereas we cannot at this point enter into an involved theological argument, it can be argued that from a Jewish perspective, it was the followers who altered the perception of what the Messiah was to be and in the process deified a man, assuredly a sacrilege for Jewish thought. In like fashion, it was the followers who too often turned an ethic of love to one of hatred and bigotry. Christians need desperately to study their history and to recognize the historical impact of Christianity upon Judaism, for too often Christianity and the church are understood only on a vertical plane, that is, as existing where we stand now. We have less recognition of the horizontal plane, that is, of the impact of Christianity's develop-ment over a span of almost two millennia.

Some Christians have demonstrated themselves to be amazingly nondiscriminating as regards what from the past should be preserved. James Daane's *The Anatomy of Anti-Semitism and Other Essays on Religion and Race* takes the position that the New Testament is inher-ently antisemitic based on historical grounds:[27]

> According to the New Testament records, Jews desired, plotted, and promoted the execution of Jesus (Matthew 27:1). No rewriting of history by those interested in freeing the Jews from responsibil-ity for the crucifixion, or by script writers of modern movies, dis-pels these claims of the New Testament historical records.... All this is not a fabric of prejudice against the Jews but the claims of the historical record of the New Testament.[28]

A helpful antidote to such a book is Gregory Baum's excellent study, *Is the New Testament Anti-Semitic?,* which sees this anti-semitism as a historically conditioned interpretive understanding.[29] One could only wish that this prescription might be disseminated broadly!

THE NATURE OF THE NEW TESTAMENT RECORD

One of the obvious problems associated with the position assumed by Daane, as well as countless others, is the loose way in which the term "historical" is attached to the Gospel writings. We could learn much from the nature of interpretation among Jews of New Testament times.

The Torah was constantly studied by Israel's learned men, and interpretations did not always agree. Some of the more influential of these orally transmitted interpretations were brought together into written form by Rabbi Judah about 200 C.E., creating what is known as the *Mishnah* ("repetition"). Differing interpretations continued to emanate from distinguished rabbis, however, and these were brought together to form the *Gemara* ("completion"). When the *Mishnah* and *Gemara* were brought together about 499 C.E., the Babylonian Talmud was the result. But, again, the Talmud did not cut off divergent views. Thus, beginning even before the Talmud's birth and continuing until about 1200 C.E., scribal and rabbinic commentaries and notes constituted a special body of literature designated *Midrash* ("explanation"). This material was essentially sermonic and sought to apply Jewish teachings to situations confronted in daily life.

The New Testament writings constitute a type of midrashic commentary directed to the community that grew up following the death and resurrection of Jesus of Nazareth. Certainly such homiletical, or sermonic, material is not the type to which the adjective "historical" would normally be applied. Nor is the literary genre "Gospel" meant to be biographical but rather a conscious attempt to express the truth of God's act among men. Consciously, therefore, it is not biographical. This does not mean that it is either antihistorical or ahistorical; rather, it simply acknowledges that the mere recording of historical events was not the purpose of the Gospel writers. Moreover, one should recognize that it is only within the last several centuries that the modern historical methodology has developed, with its insistence upon testing of hypotheses and verification of conclusions, critical evaluation of sources, and the clear delineation between factual data and opinion. Rather than dealing critically with verifiable events within history (German *Historie*), these writers, as virtually all ancient writers, were concerned to delineate the significance of history (German *Geschichte*). The Gospel of Mark, generally acknowledged to be the earliest written of the canonical Gospels, begins by stating: "The beginning of the good news of Jesus Christ, the Son of God" (1:1, NRSV). A clearer *Geschichtlich* approach would be difficult to delineate!

Viewing the New Testament in this midrashic sense opens many new and exciting avenues of interpretation. Once the view limiting the New Testament to a purely historical record is expurgated, the interpreter is free to learn from Jewish and Christian perceptions, to set the New Testament more squarely in its historical and theological context, and to let the material freely speak from within in an unmuzzled fashion (exegesis rather than eisegesis).

Even as one seeks to correct the popular Christian perception of the New Testament, it should be recalled that a part of the problem relates directly to the misuse of the Hebrew scriptures. Passages from the Hebrew scriptures were frequently used out of context, whether these were incorporated into the New Testament scriptures or simply reiterated constantly from Christian pulpits. All of this emphasis reinforced the idea that the Jews were stubborn, rebellious people who had rejected the Messiah, crucifying God's messenger.[30]

Any serious student of the New Testament recognizes the problematical exegetical ground upon which antisemitism rests. The historical-critical approach to the New Testament raises numerous issues: How accurately do the early chapters of the Acts of the Apostles reflect the emerging Christian community?...How authentically does the kerygmatic proclamation (as in Acts 2) portray the primitive believer's stance?...Within the Gospels, what is the historic relationship between the Synoptics and the Fourth Gospel?...How does one separate the Christ of faith affirmed by the post-resurrection believers from the Jesus of history who performed a first-century ministry, primarily in Galilee?...To what degree has the contextual setting of the early church determined the form of the Gospel narratives?...To what extent did Jesus authentically envision himself as Israel's Messiah?...If he so understood himself, how did he define the messianic role, and at what point in his brief career did he begin thus to perceive himself? Such questions could be asked endlessly; and, while all of the issues cannot be addressed, brief comment to several areas will be instructive for understanding the problems associated with using the New Testament as a justification for antisemitism.[31]

JESUS: MESSIAH?

Jesus' self-perception will never be assuredly known. It is probable that Jesus did not originally identify himself with the Messiah. As his ministry progressed, however, it is possible that he began to view himself as Israel's Messiah whose proclamation would assist in ushering in the Kingdom of God. To what extent he thought his words and deeds would accomplish his goal and precisely which messianic role he understood himself fulfilling will continue to be debated.[32] According to Vincent Martin, Jesus' problem, whatever his self-perception, was that he was not able to win over the religious leadership. Martin notes that the common people did not reject him, although they "wondered at his teaching, shared his hope for the imminent coming of God's Kingdom, and were disappointed by his miserable end."[33] Jesus' problems with the religious leadership were essentially twofold: he failed to win the support of the Pharisees, both because he was an "autodidact" and because of his attitude toward sinners; and in like fashion, he failed to win over the Sadducees because of his attitude toward the Temple.[34]

Although the church's perception of Jesus as the Christ is clearer, it is not definitive. Note that we must talk about "the church's perception," which by definition refers to the body of gathered believers in the period following the cross-resurrection event. While it is unclear whether the disciples who followed Jesus of Nazareth thought of him as a/the Messiah, most scholars would agree that they did not think of him as divine (see Mark 8:32). Much clearer is the fact that, very rapidly, the post-Easter believers did conclude that Jesus was the Messiah, whether messianism be associated with the new Moses, Son of Man, suffering Servant, Davidic warrior-king, or other concept. Furthermore, this messianism also developed a divine association, perhaps most overtly in John's Logos doctrine (see Jn 1:1–18). Because this messianic sect was so unalterably absolute in its affirmation, it was set on an inevitable collision course with traditional Judaism, which continued to anticipate the Messiah's arrival.

IS THE NEW TESTAMENT ANTISEMITIC?

Significant problems arise from a surface reading of New Testament texts. It would be relatively simple to prove a church-synagogue antagonism, an anti-Jew bias,[35] or a law-grace controversy by interpreting uncritically the material. The date of writing for the Gospels (Mark, 64–69 C.E.; Matthew and Luke, 80–85 C.E.; and John, 90–110 C.E.) must be evaluated seriously, for necessarily the concerns at the time of the recording influenced the material's written form. Thus, the interpreter must enter into dialogue with the record to determine its faithfulness to the events recorded or to the time recorded. Some resolution to this issue is important, for example, when dealing with passages in which Jesus is depicted as being apparently anti-Jewish. The Christ of faith as understood by the church of the first century often so obscured the Jesus of history that the latter became practically lost to historical recovery and certainly lost if one seeks unequivocal knowledge of the historical figure.

This consideration, of course, raises the issue of accountability. It is unlikely that Jewish disciples[36] who were responsible for the writing of the New Testament would be so obsessed with self-hatred that they condemned their own to eternal perdition.

Craig Evans, in *Anti-Semitism and Early Christianity,*[37] begins with the assumption that the New Testament is a Jewish rather than a Gentile record, and thus the rubric of in-house prophetic criticism needs to be carefully considered. He notes that such in-house criticism is neither racist nor bigoted,[38] and he gives some particularly poignant examples from the canonical prophets. Accepting his premise, this does not preclude, as Evans indicates, the possibility that later generations might misconstrue the nature of the New Testament criticism of the Jews and thus misinterpret the intention of the writers. This could lead to a perception that indeed the New Testament is antisemitic and its words may be used to bolster both the teaching and enactment of antisemitism.[39]

It is likely that culpability for New Testament antisemitism is to be found jointly in authors who authentically judged the Jews guilty of Jesus' death, and in later interpreters who were all too ready both to accept Jewish guilt and to use the text as justification for heinous deeds. Roy Eckardt has been one of those forcefully affirming this culpability of interpreters within the later church:

> There can be little serious doubt that Christendom's traditional antipathy to "the Jews" is the major historical root of antisemitism

in the Western World. Historically speaking, antisemitism derives from "the conflict of the church and the synagogue."[40]

As painful as the reckoning may be for Christians, Eckardt expressed perhaps most clearly what others have also thought: "Anti-semitism is…the war of Christians against Jesus the Jew."[41]

Such a reaction to the church should not be discounted as a heretical statement. If the church is the foundation of antisemitism, it has at that point ceased to be the church. D. D. Runes, from a Jewish perspective, has written a stinging indictment of the church for the historical wrongs committed against the Jews.[42] Clearly an encompassing cleansing catharsis is needed for the church, for the problem rests not with Jesus but with the followers.

THE NEW TESTAMENT IN THE ROMAN CONTEXT

The Jews, while tolerated by Rome, were not among Rome's favorite subjects.[43] Particularly noteworthy in this regard is the early Christian attempt to delineate clearly between themselves and the Jews. In the Gospels the Christians sought specifically to dissociate themselves from Judaism: "In their accounts of the trial of Jesus—and these accounts supply the basis for the traditional definition of the Jews as 'the people who killed Christ'—the evangelists were concerned to convince the Romans that adherence to the Christian faith did not imply hostility to the imperial authorities."[44] Thus, as a political statement, the Gospels, and surely one should add Luke's second volume, The Acts of the Apostles, serve to affirm an apologetic for Christianity within the empire.

As a particular way of dealing with the political problem, the Gospel writers used the person of Pontius Pilate. It is a recognized fact that Pilate was a cruel and oppressive figure, "certainly the worst of the Roman procurators of Judea."[45] In spite of this, as Heer states:

All four evangelists go out of their way to leave the question open as to whether the death sentence was imposed by the Roman governor. The historic Pontius Pilate, a cruel persecutor of the Jews, is transformed into a hesitant, vacillating man, becoming gentler and more amiable with each successive Gospel. The "Christian" career of Pontius Pilate ended with Constantine, for then the church had no more need of Roman witnesses to testify to its political innocuousness.[46]

The Gospels also indicate the continuing problems between early Christians and the Jews, or the church and the synagogue. A part of this is the desire mentioned earlier for dissociation on the part of the Christian. Numerous parables and activities of Jesus could be chronicled to support the idea that the later emerging church-synagogue problem was read back into the life and ministry of Jesus to indicate that the problem was already existent. They suggest that Jesus sided with Rome because, already during his ministry, he was in constant open conflict with the Jews. In no Gospel is this portrayal more clearly and blatantly expressed than in the Fourth Gospel, where "the Jews" constantly thwart the fulfillment of Jesus' ministry.[47]

Thus, many problems need to be considered prior to making authoritative pronouncements about the New Testament. One usually discovers that the more thorough the study, the less authoritative will be our utterances![48]

One of the characteristic features of the Synoptic Gospels is Jesus' conflict with the Pharisees. That such conflict existed is probably accurate; that the struggle was intensified in the Gospel records because of the escalating hostility between Christianity and Judaism is also probable. Whereas some would judge the following statement by Ruether to be overly harsh, she forces us to look anew at the relationship of early Judaism and Christianity:

> The real clash between Christianity and Pharisaic teachers was not over spiritualizing interpretations of the temple or the law or even the belief that Jesus was the Messiah. Rather, the crux of the conflict lay in the fact that the Church erected its messianic midrash into a *new principle of salvation.* For Christianity, salvation was found no longer in any observance—ritual or ethical—founded on the Torah of Moses, representing the covenant of the past. Rather, salvation was now found solely through faith in the messianic exegesis of the Church about the salvic role of Jesus as Prophet-King-Son of man, predicted by the prophets. Only that community gathered around this cornerstone is God's true people.[49]

Christians in the Diaspora confronted Judaism in the synagogue, which was the essential Pharisaic contribution to Jewish observance. More importantly, the Pharisees were the primary representatives of Judaism in the period following the revolt of 66 C.E. The conflict between the Christians and the Pharisees in this period was read back into the Jesus-of-history era in paradigmatic fashion and so distorted the degree of conflict during Jesus' life.[50] Ruether correctly indicates that "Christianity confronted Judaism with a demand for a conversionist relation to its own past that abrogated that past, in the sense that that past itself no longer provided a covenant of salvation."[51] But it should be noted that this type of either-or stance was characteristic of a later period, and it would be inaccurate to assign such an attitude to Jesus of Nazareth. It seems entirely possible that some type of Jewish-Christianity might have survived even into the present had not such animosity erupted between the followers of Jesus as the Christ of faith and the Jews. In any case, the conflict between Jesus and the Pharisees as portrayed in the Gospels reflects an important aspect of the deteriorating relationship between the church and the synagogue as the first Christian century progressed.

CONCLUSION

The subtitle of this book is *Christian Antisemitism in America,* and the thrust of this chapter has been to explore the importance of a Christian's grappling with the historical data relevant to an understanding of antisemitism. Generally speaking the church has not done a very effective job of helping Christians to understand this phenomenon, but one needs to recognize that antisemitism, while it definitely precedes the emergence of Christianity, has assumed both new forms and a new vitality since Christianity's emergence. Moreover, until Christians are willing to deal with the nature of the documents comprising the New Testament, it will be virtually impossible to deal therapeutically with the causes and ramifications of antisemitism. We turn our attention, therefore, to some of the New Testament passages that have been used to undergird historical antisemitism.

Suggested Questions

1. Read carefully Melvin Tumin's description of the ingredients present in explicit antisemitism. Think about your general environment, where you go

to school or work, and identify any examples of antisemitism that you observe. How might these manifestations be combatted?

2. In a dictionary, check the definitions for Jew, Semite, and antisemite. Discuss the difference between designating a given act as anti-Jewish or antisemitic.

3. How do you relate to the idea that the New Testament does not contain a historical record such as one would expect from a twentieth-century historian? Does the identification of the New Testament as a "midrashic text" offer any assistance in helping you to understand better the nature of the New Testament record?

4. What would you identify as the "teaching of contempt" as found in the New Testament? Do you believe this type of material to be indigenous to the New Testament text or to result from a particular approach to the interpretation of that text?

5. It has often been suggested that the Pharisees have been dealt with unfairly in the New Testament record, that they have become convenient scapegoats to counter some obvious early Christian failures. Go to a recognized Bible dictionary and read the section on the Pharisees. From what you read there, do you think the Pharisees were quite so negative a group as their portrayal in the Gospels? If it seems likely that they were more favorable representatives of first-century Judaism than their portrayal in the Gospels, what would have precipitated their negative portrayal as recounted in the Gospels?

II. The New Testament Bases

INTRODUCTION

Interpreting the New Testament in an objective and open fashion is frequently one of the most difficult assignments for the Christian. This should not surprise us because, like any attempt to understand the phenomenon of religion, the interpretation of the Christian scriptures inevitably involves the totality of the individual in terms of beliefs, emotions, and actions. The New Testament undergirds all that one holds sacred as a Christian. As one begins to look critically at that text, there is an internal fear that a rejection, rephrasing, or reinterpretation of parts of the New Testament carries the possibility or probability of losing that undergirding structure. Intellectually, we know something not to be true; emotionally, we are not nearly so certain!

We turn then to focus on a limited number of passages in the New Testament. This review of passages seeks neither to bolster confessional faith nor to undermine religious conviction. Let us simply open the text and let that text speak to us as openly and objectively as possible.

NEW TESTAMENT: GENERAL

It is important to acknowledge that the interpretation of New Testament passages in such fashion as to encourage antisemitism is not always the result of antisemitic intent. It is possible that one so reads a text simply because of the tradition with which one is associated, because one accepts unquestioningly traditional views, or because one has never thought seriously about New Testament interpretation from a critical perspective. Laypersons often fall into this latter category; but it is also true that, once introduced to some critical views, these individuals are remarkably able to come to their own conclusions regarding the text. However, it must also be acknowledged that some antisemitic interpretation is done with conscious intent to bolster antisemitism.

NEW TESTAMENT: PAUL

Paul's attitude toward Judaism will continue to be debated, for his writing is frequently quite enigmatic. One cannot ignore either Paul's personal relationship to Pharisaism (Phil 3:5) or his concern for the Jews, which expressed itself constantly, as he went first to the Jewish community in each city that he visited. Nonetheless, some of Paul's letters have formed an essential foundation for one pillar of Christian antisemitism, namely God's rejection of the Jews in favor of those who follow Jesus as the Christ.

Friedrich Heer is a good example of one who takes an extremely negative view of Paul and his contribution to the problems of anti-semitism. He argues forcefully that it was Paul who denied Judaism its continuing messianic heritage and served as the spiritual mentor for St. Augustine, who completed "the process of turning the 'true church' into a religion of celibates...."[1] Emphasizing the impact of Paul, he states:

> Jewish festivities retain to this day this note of joy. Early Christian love-feasts basked in a similar joy. Christianity after St. Paul denounced the fleshly, earthbound hope of the Jews and branded the Jews as lascivious, fleshly and sexually obsessed—right up to the trials of the Third Reich.[2]

Because Paul's thought is often so cryptic, throughout Christian history he has been either greatly esteemed as the architect of the early Christian church, or conversely assailed as the figure who helped to forge so many of those issues that have continued to plague the church, such as antisemitism and antifeminism. No matter which way one judges that issue, it appears to be minimally true that Paul was a Diaspora Jew who initially reacted negatively to the message of the early post-Resurrection followers of Jesus. He later became equally as committed a follower of the movement as he had been its assailant. Paul is often viewed as a pendulum-type personality who moved from one extreme to the other, and it would be natural to conjecture that Paul totally rejected Judaism when he accepted the Way. But a reading of the Letter to the Galatians and especially Romans 9–11 does not seem to confirm this. Even in the Book of the Acts, we note Paul's constant returning to Jerusalem, his concern with the needs of the Jerusalem church, and his constant reaffirmations of his Jewishness. Michael Cook seems quite on target when he asserts that he is confident that Paul, had he a son, would have seen to the circumcision of his male child on the eighth day.[3] This is simply to affirm a preference for the view that understands Paul to have remained consistently self-identified as a Jew, albeit a Jew who accepted Jesus of Nazareth to be the Christ.[4]

It has been argued that Paul understood the Torah to be composed of two distinctly differing demands upon the individual. On the one hand he perceived the ritual and on the other hand the ethical requirements. According to this position, the Jew must observe both the ritual and ethical stipulations, because the entirety of the Torah was God's revelation to the Jews. They are not free, therefore, to pick and choose. All of the *mitzvoth* found in the Torah must be observed to the extent possible even if one affirms the resurrected Lord to be the Christ. On the other hand, Paul maintained that the Gentile should not envision oneself as being bound by all of the traditions of Judaism, because the Torah was not given for all people but only for the Jews. For the Gentile, it was necessary only to keep the ethical portion of the Torah, not the ritual.[5]

One may postulate a relationship to the Noachide laws, which were understood to be seven laws given to the sons of Noah. Since Abraham, a later figure, was understood to be the father of all Hebrews and, according to tradition, the first Jew, this meant that the Noachide laws were God's expectation of all human beings. These seven laws included belief in the one God; prohibitions against blasphemy, killing, stealing, sexual immorality, and eating of the flesh of an animal while the animal was yet alive; and the injunction to set up certain law courts. While a direct correlation is not suggested, and indeed one cannot argue definitively that this sense of the applicability of the Noachite laws to the Gentiles was understood during the first century C.E., one might envision Paul's injunction that the Gentile no less than the Jew is to abide by the ethical injunctions of the Torah as a type of application of the Noachide laws.[6]

It is not difficult to see that Paul's attempt to be all things to all people (1 Cor 9:22) was a direct route to relational difficulties for Jewish and Gentile Christians. Let us assume that two first-century people, one a Jew and the other a Gentile, decide mutually that Jesus is the Messiah/Christ. They both embrace Christianity. According to Paul, however, the Jewish Christian must observe ritual and ethical Torah, while the Gentile Christian is bound only by the ethical Torah. This dual approach means that the most significant symbol of acceptance in the ancient world, table fellowship, was precluded to these two individuals. The Jew could not sit at meal with the Gentile because the Torah instructions regarding *kashrut* (kosher) not only instruct as to what can be eaten and how to prepare the foods consumed, they also relate to how one lives all of one's life, so that it would be a defiling experience to sit at table with an individual who did not observe *kashrut.* Such sharing at table was tantamount to giving sanction to ignoring the Torah-based instructions. To turn the phrase of Acts 10:15, how can you decree pure what God has declared impure?

This wall of separation between the Jewish and Gentile Christian meant that, as the church moved beyond Palestine and into the predominantly Gentile Greco-Roman world, the church would and did become increasingly Gentile and concomitantly the hostility against the Jews intensified. Paul's attempt to embrace all human beings within the arms of Christianity, while seeking at the same time to affirm his Judaism, led to a compromise that ultimately fed the fires of antisemitism. Paul would certainly reject such a suggestion, for assuredly that was not his intention. Nonetheless, division and the presumption of degrees of righteousness resulted, and such a thought pattern fed ultimately the prejudice of antisemitism.[7]

Romans 9–11 exemplifies a Pauline passage that has encouraged Christian antisemitism.[8] This is Paul's clearest statement regarding the role of the Jews in the divine *Heilsgeschichte* (salvation history). Paul had an abiding concern for the salvation of the Jew (10:1), but at the same time he was convinced that faith was the only way to a proper relationship between God and humanity (10:5–11). Because faith is the essential ingredient, he could affirm that "there is no distinction between Jew and Greek..." (10:12). Did this mean, therefore, that any special role for the Jew was rejected? Not according to Paul's ultimate conclusion, for he argued that Jewish obduracy to the Christian proclamation was divinely implanted (11:8–10). It was only because the Jews refused to hear the Gospel that the message was delivered to the Gentiles (11:26–32). Rosemary Ruether, suggesting that Paul was authentically referring to a "conversion of the Jews," has argued that Paul did not mean this to apply indiscriminately to all of Judaism:

> This "mystery" in Paul does not suggest in any way an ongoing validity of the Mosaic covenant as a community of salvation in its own right. Contemporary ecumenists who use Romans 11 to argue that Paul does not believe that God has rejected the people of the Mosaic covenant speak out of good intentions, but inaccurate exegesis. For Paul, there is, and has always been, only one true covenant of salvation. This is the covenant of the promise, given *apart from the Law,* to Abraham and now manifest in those who believe in Abraham's spiritual son, Christ. The people of the Mosaic covenant do not now and never have had any way of salvation through the Torah itself. God never intended to save his people through the Law.[9]

Ruether's position needs to be acknowledged, because popular opinion often agrees. Nonetheless, it does not seem that this is what Romans 9–11 is seeking to convey. Traditional Judaism and the Torah continue to be significant factors, a position with which Paul would likely agree.

Thus, for Paul the salvation of the Jew rested not upon traditional Judaism but upon the Jew's assuming the faith garb of Christianity. Ruether's quotation raises an issue addressed also in the Galatian correspondence, namely, does Judaism *per se* have a continuing rationale for being? The majority of expositors would respond affirmatively. Taking the contrary position, Gregory Baum, in the introduction to Ruether's *Faith and Fratricide,* states:

> All attempts of Christian theologians to derive a more positive conclusion from Paul's teaching in Romans 9–11 (and I have done this as much as others) are grounded in wishful thinking. What Paul and the entire Christian tradition taught is unmistakably negative: the religion of Israel is now superseded, the Torah abrogated, the promises fulfilled in the Christian Church, the Jews struck with blindness, and whatever remains of the election of Israel rests as a burden upon them in the present age.[10]

Will Herberg, along with others, has emphasized the centrality of the covenant for Biblical thinking.[11] Contrary to Ruether, however, Herberg did not envision the Christian covenant as one supplanting the Israelite covenant. He stated that the "Christian faith thus brings into being and defines a new covenant, which is new not in the sense of supplanting the old but in the sense of extending and enlarging it...."[12] C. H. Dodd, writing specifically about Romans 9–11, noted that the issue of Israel's rejection presented a serious difficulty "to all who accepted the historic revelation in Hebrew Scriptures as the starting-point of Christianity (as Paul did, and all Christians at the time, so far as we know)...."[13]

To the contrary, Rosemary Ruether emphasized that Paul envisioned two distinct aeons. She suggests that the "Mosaic and the Christian covenants have no common inheritance,"[14] and that there are two aeons as represented in Paul's *Galatian correspondence* (4:21–31) by Abraham's two wives: Sarah represents the aeon of freedom found in the Christ, while Hagar represents the aeon of slavery characteristic of the Mosaic covenant. According to Reuther, therefore, the real issue is whether Israel completed its raison d'être when it gave birth to Jesus. This would be a complete rejection of the *Heilsgeschichte* concept, which this writer finds difficult to accept as the Pauline position. Since the data is open to either interpretation, namely ongoing continuity or total breach, most indicators would align Paul with a sense of continuity existent between the historic faith of Judaism and the faith community finding expression in Jesus as the Christ. While personal preference would be given to this interpretation, it is the total breach or absolute supplanter view that most clearly stands behind antisemitism. Ruether's judgement would be absolutely correct were one to accept her interpretation that "Paul's position was unquestionably that of anti-Judaism."[15] The words of Will Herberg remind us, however, of the problems inherent in drawing too finely the distinctions between Judaism and Christianity:

> In respect to the covenant, the Jew's characteristic peril is the pride of exclusive possession—God's election was his from the beginning and his to keep for himself; the Christian's is the pride of supersession—the election is now his alone, the Jew having been disinherited. Again in respect to the covenant, but now negatively: the Jew who revolts against the "yoke of the Kingdom"

expresses it in the so-called self-hatred that reflects both rejection of his vocation and bitter resentment at having been "separated" by God and forced to be "different"; the Christian, on the other hand, expresses his resentment against the claim of God through anti-Semitism. "Whenever the pagan within the Christian soul rises in revolt against the yoke of the cross," Rosenzweig points out, "he vents his fury on the Jew" as Christ-bringer.[16]

This strange dialectic is one that the Christian community has inadequately addressed but one that it must understand if it is to comprehend itself and its role within the divine economy. Reading Paul in terms of two aeons, of the Christian faith supplanting the Jewish, of God's having rejected Judaism—all such hermeneutical orientation serves to encourage, indeed to foster antisemitism within the Christian community.

NEW TESTAMENT: THE LETTER TO THE HEBREWS

The Letter to the Hebrews, a treatise penned by an anonymous author probably prior to the fall of Jerusalem in 70 C.E., has long been valued within Christendom as one of the more astute interpretations of Jesus and his mission. At the same time, the approach of this author has been a major source for theological antisemitism.

Hebrews was apparently written to a young Hebrew Christian community on the brink of reverting to many of their Jewish ways. This letter served to encourage their steadfastness to the way of the Christ. This writing exhorted the superiority of Jesus to the prophets (1:1–3), to the angels (1:5–2:18), and to Moses (3:1–6). Furthermore, Jesus' role as the ultimate high priest is affirmed, stressing the superiority of his priesthood to that of the Levitical priesthood (4:14–7:28) as well as the superiority of his ultimate sacrifice to all of the sacrifices offered by the many priests (8:1–10:39).[17] As is apparent, little functional space was left for traditional Judaism by virtue of this absolute usurpation fulfilled by Jesus as the Christ. Although it is debatable whether or not one can demonstrate that Paul thought Jesus superseded the Torah, there is little question that the author of Hebrews understood Jesus' priesthood and sacrificial offering to supersede, indeed to abrogate, the Temple cultus. Is it possible that such a clearly delineated expression of supersession in one book of the New Testament helped to encourage supersessionist interpretation in other portions of the New Testament, especially the letters of Paul and the Gospels?

Again, the ultimate issue is Christological. There is in the Letter to the Hebrews a use of the Logos interpretation of the Christ (2:6–7), which is paralleled in Paul's Colossian letter (1:5ff.) and the Prologue to the Fourth Gospel (1:1–18). Further, the author, in his concern to prevent "apostasy" to Judaism by new Christians, drew an analogy between the vocation of Jesus and his follower:

> Therefore Jesus also suffered outside the city gate in order to sanctify the people by his own blood. *Let us then go to him outside the camp* and bear the abuse he endured. For here we have no lasting city, but we are looking for the city that is to come (Heb 13:12–14, NRSV, emphasis added).

In clear fashion the distinction is drawn between the Mosaic covenant, with its temporal and perishable associations, and the new covenant in the Christ with its heavenly and imperishable reality.

Given the likelihood that this letter pre-dates the 70 C.E. fall of Jerusalem, one can imagine how the writer's reaction to Judaism helped to intensify a negative reaction by the Jews toward the Christians. This would be especially true once the Jews had to deal with the reality of Rome's suppression of the 66–73 C.E. revolt. Fratricidal rejection has to be among the most traumatic of experiences. This Christian reaction portrayed in the Letter to the Hebrews might not have been so difficult in the period prior to Jerusalem's fall to Rome. Once Jerusalem fell in 70 C.E., this Letter not only encouraged supersessionism; eventually, it would foster antisemitism.[18]

NEW TESTAMENT: THE SYNOPTIC GOSPELS

The Synoptic Gospels[19] also contain numerous passages frequently interpreted to encourage antisemitism. It would be impossible to investigate this material extensively, but several passages indicate the often transparent anti-Jewish elements included.[20]

Mark 12:1–12 (parallel in *Mt 21:23–46* and *Lk 20:9–19*) records the *parable of the wicked tenants*. While this parable makes strong use of allegory, both C. H. Dodd and J. Jeremias argue for the authenticity of the parable rather than for its being an allegory constructed by the church.[21] The parable, which has some striking similarities to Isaiah 5, describes an individual who planted and cared for a vineyard. Traveling to a far country, however, he let out the vineyard to tenant farmers. On several occasions the owner sent back servants to check on the vineyard and to seek return of the portion of the harvest that was his rightful due. When the tenants repeatedly dealt harshly with the servants, the owner finally sent his son, thinking that the tenants would respect the owner's own flesh and blood. Unfortunately, thinking that perhaps the owner was dead and seeing the possibility of taking the vineyard for themselves if the son were dead too, the tenants killed him. Jesus' question was "What then will the owner of the vineyard do?" (Mk 12:9, NRSV). The response was that the owner would come to the vineyard, kill the tenants, and give the vineyard to others. This conclusion was supported by Psalm 118:22–23, NRSV:

> The stone that the builders rejected
>   has become the chief cornerstone.
> This is the LORD's doing;
>   it is marvelous in our eyes.

The obvious application of this parable was God's rejection of the Jews because of their maltreatment of the Christ. F. W. Beare states:

> The primary motif of the parable, then, is the warning that the leaders of Israel, who have abused their trust, will be called to a terrible accounting. Allied to this is the secondary theme, that the owner will "give the vineyard to others."[22]

In Matthew the parable "has become wholly an allegory of the history of salvation from the covenant of God with Israel, through the coming and rejection of Christ, to the transference of the kingdom to the Gentile."[23] With this reading, as symbolized in Matthew 21:43, the divine rejection of the Jew is clearly focused. Regarding Matthew 21:43, Hare states:

> Matthew sees both Jesus' mission and the mission of his messengers as having the purpose of exhibiting and bringing to completion the already existing guilt of Israel. Although this is not clearly articulated with respect to Jesus' own mission, it is implied in the allegory of the Wicked Tenants, in which the sending of the Son

serves only to demonstrate conclusively the guilt which has characterized the Tenants from the beginning.[24]

While in the Gospel of Mark only the religious leadership is indicted, in the Gospel of Matthew it is clearly the whole of Israel that stands under condemnation.[25] Thus, "In Matthew's gospel the rejection of Israel is permanent and complete."[26] It was this divine rejection of the Jews together with the sense of Christian superiority, as well as the guilt of the tenants because of their treatment of the son, which encouraged antisemitism. The next step, to the concept of deicide, was relatively easy. Here is found the clear rationale for dealing with those who have rejected the son, regardless of the methods used.

Another passage, outside of the Synoptic Gospels, which records a reaction similar to that of the wicked tenants, is the statement by Stephen recorded in the Book of Acts:

> You stiff-necked people, uncircumcised in heart and ears, you are forever opposing the Holy Spirit, just as your ancestors used to do. Which of the prophets did your ancestors not persecute? They killed those who foretold the coming of the Righteous One, and now you have become his betrayers and murderers....(Acts 7:51–52, NRSV).

A pattern of depicting the Jews as the stubborn rejectors of God and his way was emerging. The Christians developed two primary conclusions from this: (1) that the guilty people (the Jews) must pay for their obduracy, and (2) that Christians must deal with the associated problem of Jesus' having been born of Judaism. How does he indeed avoid the historical stigma attached to the people?

In the Synoptic Gospels there are three distinct predictions of suffering as Jesus made his way to Jerusalem. The first is set at Caesarea Philippi (Mk 8:27–33, paralleled in Mt 16:13–23 and Lk 9:18–22) as Jesus withdrew from the Galilean ministry, apparently contemplating his future mission on the basis of past reactions and present perceptions that he elicited from his closest followers. The second Passion prediction is set in Galilee as Jesus passed through there on his way toward Jerusalem (Mk 9:30–32, paralleled in Mt 17:22–23 and Lk 9:43b–45). The final prediction of the Passion depicts Jesus with his followers on the road approaching Jerusalem (Mk 10:32–34, paralleled in Mt 20:17–19 and Lk 18:31–34). It seems transparent that these three predictions of the Passion are integrally linked, with each prediction becoming more specific and explicit than the former. By the third prediction, the narrative reads like a clairvoyant, predicting with preciseness exactly what will occur.[27] That the three versions stem from a single saying from Jesus given in considerably less detail than this highly developed form is likely. Unfortunately, it is also the case that recovery of that precise word of the Jesus of history is now lost to us!

Notice that in Mark and Luke the reference in the third prediction is simply to the fact that Jesus was killed. In Matthew the reference became explicit—crucifixion, surely an indication that it was not only recorded *post eventum* but that indeed it was even constructed *post eventum.*

The importance for our concern is the fact that the Passion Narrative was the earliest developed written material relating to Jesus. In these predictions of the passion one has a synopsis of the Passion Narrative, and in such abbreviated form the guilt is clear: "...the Son of Man will be handed over to the chief priests and the scribes, and they will condemn him to death...." (Mk 10:33, NRSV). Jewish guilt is clearly affirmed, becoming one of the pillars upon which Christendom's view of Judaism and individual Jews would be based. While these predictions do not quote the Servant Poems of Deutero-Isaiah, especially Isaiah 52:13–53:12, the association within the minds of the early Christians seems apparent: Jesus, the servant, the Son of Man, has been rejected by Israel; indeed, as the ultimate sign of rejection, they have put him to death.

It is clear that the early church was not of one mind as regards the mission of Christianity. Even in the Synoptics this concern arises, as in the *parable of light* (Mt 5:14–16 and Lk 11:33). The distinctive use of this parable by Matthew, who sets the light on a stand to give light "to all *in the house,*" is quite different from Luke's concern that the light be so set "that *those who enter* may see the light." The difference between internal and external focus indicates the continuing conflict within early Christendom regarding its mission.

Christianity's real problem with Pharisaism lay in the fact that Christianity developed a *new principle of salvation* that asserted that "salvation was now found solely through faith in the messianic exegesis of the Church about the salvic role of Jesus as Prophet-King-Son of man, predicted by the prophets."[28] Ruether suggests that it was this emphasis, clarified in the preaching of Stephen, which precipitated Judaism's rejection of the Christian apologists in the Diaspora. There, unexpectedly, the Christians discovered a Jewish rejection even more vehement than that experienced in Jerusalem. The Gentile, however, was a fruitful mission field:

"For these Gentiles, the principle that was so offensive to the synagogue—namely the Church's insistence that one attaches oneself to the one community of the covenant, not by integrating oneself into the covenanted history of a people, but by attaching oneself to a redemptive *figure*—was no problem, since this was the customary principle of initiation into the mystery religions."[29]

This entrée provided by the mystery religions was also noted by Martin Buber, although specifically from the perspective of resurrection. He stated that the "resurrection of the individual is incredible to Jews, that of the mass ('the resurrection of the dead' Acts xvii.32) to Greeks; for them [that is, the Greeks] resurrection is an affair of the gods of the Mysteries and their kind—one only needs to make the Christ the God-man to make him credible to them [that is, the Greeks]."[30] Regardless, once the Christian "Way" moved beyond Palestine it rapidly became predominantly Gentile. Inevitably problems arose at that point, resulting ultimately in a breach separating Judaism and Christianity.

Is it possible to suggest anything about Jesus' attitude regarding the continuing impact of Judaism? An often quoted statement is "Do not think that I have come to abolish the law or the prophets; I have come not to abolish them but to fulfill" (Mt 5:17, NRSV). Even more significant regarding Jesus' attitudes are Mt 10:5–6 and 15:24. The former passage is associated with Jesus' sending out of the Twelve, where he instructed them, "Go nowhere among the Gentiles, and enter no town of the Samaritans, but go rather to the lost sheep of the house of Israel." The latter passage is set in the district of Tyre and Sidon where a Canaanite woman appealed to Jesus to heal her daughter. In response Jesus stated "I was sent only to the lost sheep of the house of Israel." The Matthean preservation of the passages, while neither Mark nor Luke include them, may be explained on the basis that such statements did not correlate with the Gentile thrust that both Mark and Luke were projecting.[31] Nonetheless, it is significant that these passages were preserved at all, given the rapid orientation of Christendom toward the Gentiles. While they are apparently countermanded by Matthew

28:19–20, these statements seem to indicate Jesus' perception of his own ministry as oriented exclusively to the Jews. One way to correlate the passages as transmitted with what apparently was intended is to assume that Israel was lost and that Jesus therefore gave them the authority "to be his assistants in the gathering together of his flock in his kingdom...."[32] Rather than interpreting this approach as indicating an immediate separation between Jews and Christians, however, it seems more appropriate to recognize that first-century Judaism had a strong concern to reach the non-Jew with the truths of Judaism. Many Gentiles converted to Judaism, while numerous others, categorized as "God-fearers," found the morality and monotheism associated with the synagogues quite appealing, although they did not ritually become Jews. It is quite possible, therefore, that Jesus, in his concern for the Jew, simply acknowledged the limitations of space and time upon his humanity. Necessarily, he restricted his ministry to the Jew; and if the Jew would truly serve as "a light to the nations" (Is 42:6), then Jesus' ultimate mission of opening the way of Yahweh to all persons would be accomplished.[33] This passage, which could have served as an indication of Jesus' alignment with Israel's historical covenantal purpose, has been rejected by Mark and Luke and generally played down by commentaries on Matthew's Gospel.

NEW TESTAMENT: THE ACTS OF THE APOSTLES

Although we will only briefly look at the Acts of the Apostles, the roots of antisemitism in this book are clear. Several examples suffice.

Professor Ruether makes a strong case for three distinct "churches" during Christendom's early existence. To the radical left was Paul with the basic idea that the Jewish Torah has no continuing salvic importance for the Jew or the Gentile. To the conservative right was James, the brother of Jesus, who apparently became a follower either just before or immediately following the Crucifixion and who became the leader of the Jerusalem church by mid-first century. In the middle, as a type of mediating element, stood Peter. "This Petrine church, represented by the Gospel tradition, had from the beginning created a salvation principle that relativized the Mosaic covenant to a mere predictive status."[34] Had the type of Christianity associated with James become dominant, Jesus would likely have been accorded the role of Messiah-designate with the church, awaiting his triumphal return as Israel's redeemer. Even the Petrine brand might have retained the option of the coexistence of Judaism and Christianity, but neither of those belief structures prevailed. It was Pauline Christianity that survived, and with its survival the possibilities either for a Jewish-Christianity being maintained or some type of compatible relationship between the two faith structures being effected was lost. With this loss the seeds for antisemitism were implanted, and eventually those seeds brought forth an abundant harvest.

Attention should also be directed anew to Stephen's defense before the council as recorded in Acts 7:2–53. Stephen used the usual methodology of discussing Israel's faith by relaying her history. He concluded with a statement, however, which so angered the council that he was taken out and stoned to death:

> You stiff-necked people, uncircumcised in heart and ears, you are forever opposing the Holy Spirit, just as your ancestors used to do. Which of the prophets did your ancestors not persecute? They killed those who foretold the coming of the Righteous One, and now you have become his betrayers and murderers. You are the ones that received the law as ordained by angels, and yet you have not kept it (Acts 7:51–53, NRSV).

Accusation that ultimately reaches the crescendo of rejection portrays Judaism in a posture from which there is no negotiation possible. The following statement derived from *The Bible as Literature* sets the Stephen incident in an appropriate perspective for our Jewish-Christian relationship concern:

> [Luke] was drawing the closest of parallels between Stephen and Christ as victims of religious bigotry. Like Jesus, Stephen works miracles and produces "signs" during his ministry. Stephen makes converts but arouses the hatred of the orthodox, as did Jesus. Like Jesus, Stephen is an opponent of the Temple cult. He is tried by the Jewish Council, as was Jesus. Stephen's charge that the Jews have always persecuted their prophets echoes that of Jesus in Luke 11:49–51. Stephen calls Jesus the "Son of Man," Jesus' own term—the only time this usage occurs in the New Testament outside the four gospels. As Jesus did in Luke 23:34, Stephen asks forgiveness for his murderers (though the authenticity of the earlier passage is in some dispute), and Stephen's prayer, "Lord Jesus, receive my spirit," parallels Jesus' own

words in Luke 23:46. It is clear that for Luke the martyrdom of Stephen was a decisive event second in importance only to the Crucifixion, for *it marked the beginning of the Church's destined mission toward the Gentiles and away from the Jews.*[35]

NEW TESTAMENT: THE GOSPEL OF JOHN

The most vitriolic of the New Testament writings in terms of anti-semitic quality is the Gospel of John.[36] In this Gospel the separation between the old and the new, with the Jews characterizing the old, is complete. Professor Ruether stated well the situation:

> In the Gospel of John, the philosophical incorporation of anti-Judaic midrash reaches its highest development in the New Testament. Here the antithesis between the old and the new, the temporal and the eschatological, the outward and the inward, the carnal and the spiritual have been so completely sublimated into an antithesis between a fulfilled spiritual universe poised over against a fallen universe of darkness, symbolized by "the Jews," that the language of the "two aeons," drawn from apocalyptic futurism has been almost entirely absorbed into the language of vertical and inward transcendence. Instead of "two aeons," we have "two worlds": the spiritual world of light "above" and the dark world of alienation from the divine "below." "The Jews" are programmatically identified with this false principle of existence of the world of darkness below.[37]

The Prologue (1:1–18) sets the anti-Jewish tone clearly: the Word as "light shines in the darkness, and the darkness did not overcome it" (1:5, NRSV); the Word was in the world, "yet the world did not know him" (1:10, NRSV). More specifically, "He came to what was his own, and his own people did not accept him" (1:11, NRSV). Lest there be any confusion, "The law indeed was given through Moses; grace and truth came through Jesus Christ" (1:17, NRSV). The ideas of Jewish rejection, supersession, and obduracy are emphasized.[38]

Each of the *seven signs* of the Fourth Gospel stresses fulfillment of the Jewish expectations for the "Christ, the Son of God" (20:31). Jesus is the "new wine," which far surpasses any yet tasted by Israel (2:1–11). Akin to Paul's emphasis on faith as the proper response of man to God, the second sign (4:46–54) depicts Jesus' healing an official's son. It is faith that results in life, not a response that must be vindicated by signs and wonders. The third sign revolves around Jesus' healing a man on the Sabbath at the pool in Jerusalem by the Sheep Gate (5:1–18). True life was derived from one who healed on the Sabbath in contradistinction to Jewish law. When the 5,000 were fed (6:1–14), the food that satisfies with superabundance was tasted. It would not be the Torah that would meet man's needs, but the new Way. It is Jesus who is the true bread of life, satisfying all who believe in him. Sign five depicts Jesus walking on the water (6:16–21) and would necessarily remind the Jew of the tradition's affirmation of the one who caused the firmament to "separate the waters from the waters" (Gn 1:6, NRSV) and who was the architect of the Fathers' escape at the Sea (Ex 14).[39] Who is Jesus? He is the same one who is offered by the tradition—"It is I" (probably to be associated with revealing of the divine name in Ex 3:14). The sixth sign returns the reader to a healing element, healing a man born blind (9:1–7). Not the old Way but the new is emphasized, with Jesus as the "light of the world" being the ultimate source of judgment. The final sign depicts Jesus as the true source of life in the raising of Lazarus (11:1–44). Furthermore, the crucifixion of Jesus, which now began to emerge, occurred because the Jews, refusing to acknowledge the giver of life, in fact took his life! As is evident, the anti-Jewishness of the writer rings clearly through the presentation of the signs.

It is also true that the Fourth Evangelist is clearer in his accusation that the Jews are responsible both for Jesus' death and for his inability to accomplish all that was potentially possible in his ministry. The Synoptics use the expression "the Jews" a total of sixteen times, while the Fourth Evangelist used it almost seventy times. Often this expression is used sarcastically (see 5:16, 18; 6:41; 7:1; 8:52; 10:31; 19:12 and 20:19 for examples), making the distinction clear between "the Jews" and the followers of Jesus.[40] It is this conflict of the old and the new that fills so much of the Fourth Gospel. The great sin of the Jews, therefore, was their refusal to recognize and receive Jesus as God's revelation (14:9). It was inevitable, therefore, that they would continue to walk in the darkness in which they are depicted in the Prologue (1:4–5).

The Christology of the Fourth Gospel has been a major influence in Christian thought. The Logos theology, with its preexistent divinity associated with Jesus, characterizes the way most Christians perceive Jesus.[41] Concomitant with this is the Fourth Evangelist's depiction of the crucifixion. More than in the Synoptics, this writer make clear that Pilate did not envision Jesus as guilty of any Roman crime. The guilt for Jesus' death is placed squarely upon the Jews—Jesus' death was requested on the basis of his having broken Judaism's crime of blasphemy (19:7). Although deicide would not emerge as a specific accusation against the Jews until the second century, it is obvious that the Fourth Evangelist moved dangerously close to this charge. It was because of "the Jews" and their actions that the death of Jesus occurred!

A SUMMARY AND PROJECTION

This brief investigation of some Biblical roots of antisemitism, beginning with Paul as the earliest New Testament author and concluding with the Fourth Evangelist, has emphasized selectively numerous concepts and expressions that have been used to support antisemitism. It should be acknowledged that sometimes proper interpretation is uncertain, as with Paul. On the other hand, it is clear that in the struggle that developed between Jews and Christians the latter tended to look negatively on the former whenever the possibility presented itself.[42]

Christian writings, ultimately to be affirmed as canonical, began to be formulated approximately two decades after Jesus' death (the writings of Paul). Professor Ruether suggests that the church sensed a need to legitimate as the proper reading of Jewish scripture its Christological midrash. She notes:

> It is not enough for the Christian tradition to hold this opinion. Nor is it enough to convince "a few Jews"…that this is the case. As long as "the Jews," that is, the Jewish religious tradition itself, continues to reject this interpretation, the validity of the Christian view is in question. The "wrath upon the Jews," poured out by Christianity, represents this ever unsatisfied need of the Church to prove that it has the true content of the Jewish Scriptures by finally making "the Jews"…"admit" that this is the true interpretation. Until Jewish religious tradition itself accepts this as the "real meaning" of its own Scriptures, "the Jews" must be kept in the status of the "enemies of God"….[43]

Professor Ruether contends, and probably accurately, that this anti-Jewish sentiment, coupled with the church's need to legitimate itself, manifested itself in the early church writers and continues to the present day.[44] This simply means that antisemitism cannot and will not disappear so long as Christians think that Christian scripture abrogates, supersedes, and fulfills Jewish scripture and that Jewish scripture is incomplete and ineffectual apart from Christian scripture—in short, that Judaism is an inferior religion incapable of bringing the Jew into a meaningful relationship with God. The inevitable corollary to this belief is that the Jew must be made over in the Christian's image!

THE EARLY CHURCH

As the sixties decade of the first Christian century arrived, the components for the deterioration of Jewish-Christian relations multiplied.[45] In 62 C.E. James, the brother of Jesus and the leader of the Jerusalem church, was martyred at the instigation of the Zealots. Following his death, the Christians, fearing for personal security, departed Jerusalem. Of notable importance, however, was the resultant Christian absence when the Jewish revolt against Rome erupted in 66 C.E. This absence must be coupled with the Bar Kokhba ("Son of the Star") revolt of 132–35, when this Jewish leader was heralded as the Messiah by no less a Rabbi than Aqiba. Christians did not participate in this revolt, both because of their self-imposed exile and because they already had their Messiah, Jesus of Nazareth. Especially since this was such a sanguinary defeat for the Jews, the Christians' refusal to participate significantly impacted Jewish-Christian relations. Many years would pass before there would be any possibility of reaffirming a sense of unity for Jews and Christians.[46]

The charge of deicide, literally the killing of God, is one of the major contributors to antisemitism. In his book *Has God Rejected His People?* Clark M. Williamson noted the relatively recent recovery of a sermon by Bishop Melito of Sardis in Syria. Melito, active during the latter part of the second century,[47] wrote a "Sermon 'On the Passover,'" and Williamson suggests that "Melito's work may well have been the real origin of the idea of deicide."[48] Melito expressed the supersession of Christianity over Judaism:

> so also the law was finished
> when the gospel was revealed.

Furthermore, the equation of Jesus with God provided grounding to the deicide charge, as in passages such as the following:

> He who hung the earth was hung;
>
> …
>
> he who sustained all was suspended on the tree;
>
> …
>
> God has been murdered;
> the king of Israel slain by an Israelite hand.

It is clear that very early in the life of the church issues were being raised and theological positions assumed that virtually made impossible the meaningful relationship of Jews and Christians.

This theological separation assumed sociopolitical overtones in 312 when Constantine, Emperor of the Roman Empire (306–337), embraced Christianity. Whatever his reasons and however one resolves the issue of precisely when Constantine did embrace Christianity, the exaltation of Christianity would now follow. The Council of Nicaea (325), with its creedal affirmation of Jesus' being "Very God of Very God" and "of one substance with the Father" undergirded the ultimate Christian charge of deicide against the Jews. Jesus of Nazareth, affirmed to be the Christ, was now viewed as divine. This meant that putting Jesus to death was the equivalent of putting God to death. This background, and this alone, makes understandable, though not acceptable, the church's actions during the Middle Ages.

Even as the Arian controversy raged, the struggle to establish the canon of the New Testament was in process. That struggle culminated in the latter part of the fourth century, as the Councils of Laodicea (363), Hippo (393), and Carthage (397) made the determinations that established the New Testament canon of scripture. This determination of canonical status added selected writings derived from the Christian community alongside existent writings from within the Jewish community. This process of affirmation of two parts of the canon contributed also to the slow, inexorable separation of the Christians from the Jews.

An individual who serves as a model for this growing separation is John Chrysostom (ca. 345–407[49]). He prepared for a legal career, but in his mid-twenties he was baptized and "in 386 he was advanced to the priesthood."[50] As a priest he was celebrated for his oratorical abilities, thus the designation "the golden-mouthed" (a name by which people often referred to him following his death),[51] and in 398 he was elevated to be the bishop of Constantinople. Ultimately, he was accused of theological improprieties, deposed, recalled, deposed again, and banished to small communities.[52]

Prior to becoming the bishop of Constantinople, he was for twelve years a preacher in Antioch (386–98), focusing upon the exegetical approach to the scriptures coupled with an emphasis upon the practical living of the Christian life. Chrysostom had many followers who would have acclaimed him the greatest preacher of the Eastern Church.[53]

While a presbyter in Antioch, Chrysostom preached a series of eight sermons directed against the Jews, or Judaizers.[54] While the dates are somewhat disputed, the sermons were apparently preached between the autumn of 386 and the autumn of 387. Meeks and Wilken conclude that "Chrysostom's aim in these homilies is not an attack on the Jews as such, but the deterrence of Christians from participating in Jewish rites."[55] According to the two authors, far from representing a popular hostility toward Judaism among Christians in Antioch, Chrysostom's imprecations reveal the exact opposite, "a widespread Christian infatuation with Judaism."[56] Their point is that Christians were finding many of the rites and festivals of Judaism fulfilling to the point of observing same and/or attempting to consolidate them into Christian worship practices. Thus, Chrysostom attacked more the Judaizing Christians who were rather naively and openly absorbing the Jewish rituals than he did the Jews or Judaism per se. Even if Meeks and Wilken are correct, however, the result of such a position would be the encouragement of antisemitism. This is precisely what happened, but let us permit Chrysostom to speak for himself (quotations taken from Homily 1, "Against the Jews"):

> What is this sickness? The festivals of the wretched and miserable Jews which follow one after another in succession—Trumpets, Booths, the Fasts—are about to take place.[57]

> Do not be surprised if I have called the Jews wretched. They are truly wretched and miserable for they have received many good things from God yet they have spurned them and violently cast them away....The Jews were branches of the holy root, but they were lopped off.[58]

...the synagogue is not only a house of prostitution and a theater, it is also a hideout for thieves and a den of wild animals....No Jew worships God....If they are ignorant of the Father, if they crucified the son, and spurned the aid of the Spirit, can one not declare with confidence that the synagogue is a dwelling place of demons? God is not worshipped there. Far from it! Rather the synagogue is a place of idolatry.[59]

One thing only [the Jews] know—how to stuff themselves and get drunk, to come to blows over dancers, and to get beat up in brawls over chariot drivers.[60]

...a synagogue is less honorable than any inn. For it is not simply a gathering place for thieves and hucksters, but also of demons; indeed, not only the synagogue, but the souls of Jews are also the dwelling places of demons.[61]

Where Christ-killers gather, the cross is ridiculed, God blasphemed, the father unacknowledged, the son insulted, the grace of the Spirit rejected.[62]

Such harshness and belligerence assuredly encouraged expressions of overt antisemitism. The intention of Chrysostom, therefore, becomes a somewhat academic question, for the reality of Christian hostility toward the Jews speaks for itself.

Sadly, the stage was clearly set during this period of the early church for the atrocities that would characterize the medieval church. Antisemitism was clearly manifest, and during the medieval period these manifestations would become both more numerous and more vitriolic!

CONCLUSION

Thus, we have come full circle. Christianity began as a community of believers, a community whose scripture was the scripture of Judaism. Only later did the writings emanating from the Christian community gradually assume a type of authority that, by the latter part of the fourth Christian century, was judged by church councils to be canonical alongside the scriptures of Judaism.

These writings, however, derived from specific contextual settings and displayed those emotions and motivations characteristic of their authors. Moreover, what was written about Jesus of Nazareth necessarily manifested an amalgamation of remembered aspects of the Jesus of History coupled with perceptions associated with the Christ of Faith. Inevitably, therefore, many of the conflicts and issues characteristic of a later time of writing were read back into the time and upon the lips of Jesus of Nazareth.

It is this end result that has helped to undergird a continuing antisemitic attitude on the part of Christendom, indeed has become the foundation stone of theological antisemitism. It is incumbent upon Christians that we deal honestly and openly with the problems of the New Testament text; namely, how it was derived and transmitted as well as what factors precipitated its emergence. It is simply not satisfactory or honest to treat this body of literature as *sui generis,* as has been the church's inclination in the past. This literature, as all literature, can only be enhanced through the application of literary and historical tools of interpretation. Let us permit the text to speak out of itself to us (exegesis), rather than forcing our preconceived views upon the text (eisegesis).

Suggested Questions

1. Paul's role in the development and propagation of theological antisemitism will continue to be debated. Read Romans 9–11 and formulate arguments that this writing does/does not support antisemitism.

2. The parable of the wicked tenants in Mark 12:1–12 (and parallel passages) is discussed in the text. In your Bible, read Mark 12:1–12 (and Matthew 21:23–46 and Luke 20:9–19) and Isaiah 5:1–7 and compare/contrast these two parables. What new and different ingredients are found in the Gospel materials? What changes in perspective would the Gospel's "new and different ingredients" likely engender?

3. One may argue either that the Gospel of John is the most antisemitic of the Gospels or that passages from the Gospel of John have been used more extensively than those from the Synoptic gospels to undergird antisemitism. What is the basic difference in these two perspectives?

4. John 10:30 quotes Jesus as saying that "The Father and I are one" (NRSV). Linking this statement to the usual "I am" sayings of the Fourth Gospel, why did this Gospel emerge as a particularly difficult block to meaningful Jewish-Christian relations?

5. It is always difficult "to turn back the clock," but it may be that this is precisely what needs to be done relative to the Christian understanding of the New Testament if meaningful Jewish and Christian relationships are to exist.

How might Christians approach and understand the New Testament so as to meet dual objectives: on the one hand to uphold their personal affirmation of Christianity and on the other not to place unalterable obstacles to meaningful relationships before their Jewish brethren?

III. The Medieval Church and Antisemitism

INTRODUCTION

Drawing upon the various manifestations of antisemitism in the early church, the medieval church continued and exacerbated the ugliness of antisemitism. Only selected evidence of this continued activity is discussed here, but it nevertheless gives a sense of the continuing deterioration. A careful reading of church history, or better yet a Jewish historian's recounting of the period, will multiply significantly the incidences with which one must wrestle.[1]

Once the medieval era and Christendom emerged, the impact upon Judaism is best clarified by focusing upon church councils and ecclesiastical decrees. At the conclusion of the medieval era, a reforming spirit that ultimately produced the Protestant Reformation turned officialdom on its head. Martin Luther is one of the chief spokesmen for this reform activity, but here our concern with the man and his thought has to do with his impact upon the Jews.

The church is not only officialdom, however, for equally important in the long-term is the way the common people thought. Cathedral iconography is important in this regard because it was used to instill into the common people the basic theological perspectives of the church. In the era prior to the moveable-type printing press, this iconography was for many the only Bible they "read." Thus, we focus upon some of this iconography for a better understanding of what encouraged the continuation and propagation of antisemitism, even during periods when other factors would suggest that it should have died.

51

EDICTS AND COUNCILS

Pope Gregory the Great (590–604) issued an edict that forbade the forced conversions of the Jews, a practice that was common until that time. Nonetheless, this edict also reaffirmed the Jews' second-class citizenship. For example, the Jews could build no new synagogues, Jewish physicians could not be in the employment of Christians, and it was forbidden for Jews to hold Christian slaves.

At the Fourth Council of Toledo, held in 633, the antipathy between the two faith communities was again clearly expressed, for the Council legalized the wresting of Jewish children from their parents in order to raise the children in Christian homes. Of course the highest motivations for such activity were claimed, namely the salvation of the soul of the child![2]

The medieval church fostered the Crusades, the national expulsions, the Spanish Inquisition, and the ghettos.[3] On November 26, 1095, Pope Urban II preached a sermon at the Council of Clermont exhorting Christians to recapture the Holy Land from the infidel. This led to a series of eight crusades from 1096 to 1291, resulting in what Heer designates the "first epoch of popular mass anti-Semitism."[4] While the Muslim was the avowed target of the Crusades, the Jew, the infidel nearer at hand, was often the victim of the Crusaders' wrath. Countless thousands of Jews lost their lives to the Crusaders' zeal. On occasion entire Jewish communities were murdered by these zealous Crusaders, most of whom never saw Jerusalem. The Crusades had additional negative effects on Jewish life as well. For example, because of restrictions imposed by a Christian society on how Jews could earn their living, many coordinated and facilitated trade between cities. The Crusades now made even this vocational pursuit impossible, since certain death would follow if the traveling Jew fell into the hands of the Crusaders. Mobility and vocational choice were therefore further reduced for the Jews during the Crusades.

In 1179 the Third Lateran Council mandated that Christians were not to dwell among the infidel. Although the establishment of a ghetto would not occur until 1516 in Venice, the mandate of the Third Lateran Council was the empowering legislation for the ghettos. Clearly, if the majority are not to live among the minority, it will not be the majority who change their residence! The Fourth Lateran Council, convened in 1215, decreed that Jews must wear a distinguishing badge. This badge took the form of either the six-pointed Star of David or a circle, symbolizing either the coinage for which Judas betrayed Jesus or the moneylending with which Jews had become associated. On November 30, 1215, the decree of the Fourth Lateran Council was implemented.

Jewish literacy apparently posed problems for the medieval church. The practice of Judaism requires a knowledge of Torah, and that level of learning made it more difficult for Christians to impose their will upon the Jews. Unfortunately, Christians on occasion responded to this issue by burning Jewish writings. On June 17, 1242, Pope Gregory IX issued a Papal Bull that required the gathering of all manuscripts from the synagogues of Paris. This resulted in the burning of twenty-four cartloads of manuscripts in the streets of Paris!

In 1278 Pope Nicholas III issued a decree that permitted Christians the freedom of Jewish pulpits. This meant that, whenever Jews were gathered in their synagogues, a Christian could enter the synagogue, assume the pulpit, and preach for the conversion of the Jews. Although no one can force another individual to listen to such a diatribe, nonetheless the Jews were required to remain seated as long as the Christian harangued them.

Jewish expulsions from west European countries began to occur in the thirteenth century. Excessive taxes had been exacted from the Jews over the years, until many now lived in poverty. Finally, in 1290, King Edward I of England ordered all Jews to leave the country in three months. Expulsions continued with Philip the Fair's decree in 1306 mandating all Jews in France to be arrested simultaneously. Their physical property was confiscated, and they were ordered to depart France within one month. Because of significant Jewish involvement in practically every aspect of Spanish life, however, the ultimate tragedy came in 1492 when Queen Isabella and King Ferdinand ordered all Jews to leave Spain within four months. Curiously, the order to equip a fleet for Christopher Columbus was issued on the same day as the Jewish expulsion decree, April 30, 1492, and the execution of this decree occurred on August 2, 1492, one day before he set sail.[5] These expulsions disrupted Jewish life, enforced Christian prejudices, and precipitated an eastward movement that removed from western Europe most of the Jewish people who had made significant cultural contributions to these countries.

The Spanish Inquisition,[6] which was initiated in 1480 and not abolished until 1834, was a device to "purify" the realm religiously. It was aimed primarily against apostate Christians and thus also against the *marranos,* who continued to practice Judaism secretly.[7] As Cecil Roth indicates, the first individuals to die (1481) as a result of the Inquisition were "six men and women of Jewish extraction...(who were)...burned alive for the crime of fidelity to the faith of their fathers."[8]

MARTIN LUTHER AND THE REFORMATION

Given the harsh treatment endured by the Jews during the medieval era, one might hope that the period heralded by Martin Luther's nailing of his ninety-five theses to the door of the castle church in Wittenberg on October 31, 1517, would have inaugurated a period of greater tolerance toward the Jews. After all, there had been earlier periods where strange alliances were formed, as when the Jews aligned with and benefitted from the Muslim conquest of Spain in the eighth century.[9] It might have been anticipated that the zeal of the reformers would bring about an internal division in the church and that the Jews might have found a comfortable alliance with one party to this intrafraternal strife.

When Martin Luther initially began his activity, he had a positive attitude toward the Jews. This is indicated in his essay of 1523, *That Jesus Christ Was Born a Jew,* in which he spoke against Jew-haters. He stated his position, however, in such a way as to indicate the ambivalence of his thought:

> If I had been a Jew and had seen such dolts and blockheads govern and teach the Christian faith, I would sooner have become a hog than a Christian....I hope that if one deals in a kindly way with the Jews and instructs them carefully from Holy Scripture, many of them will become genuine Christians and turn again to the faith of their fathers....[10]

In this same essay of 1523 Luther also stated the following:

> I would request and advise that one deal gently with them and instruct them from Scripture; then some of them may come along. Instead of this we are trying to drive them by force, slandering them, accusing them of having Christian blood if they don't stink, and I know not what other foolishness. So long as we thus treat them like dogs, how can we expect to work any good among them?[11]

These statements clearly demonstrate that Luther desired the conversion of the Jews. But this desire unfortunately contained the seeds of radical persecution to accomplish its goal. By the time Luther wrote *On the Jews and Their Lies* in 1543, twenty years later, his overt attitude toward the Jews had become remarkably hostile. It may be that his later attitude was only a clearer indication of his deepest reactions, that the overt and the covert have become synchronized, or it may simply result from the intense resistance of the Jews to the Christian proclamation. He did apparently believe that the Jews would respond to his "proper preaching" of the Gospel, but he rather quickly discovered that the Jews reacted no more favorably to his proclamation than they had to the earlier traditional utterances of the church. Thus, once Luther's breach with the church was effected, his initial positive response to the Jews turned vehemently against the Jews.[12]

Several of Luther's comments from *On the Jews and Their Lies* are especially instructive. He began by stating the following:

> I had made up my mind to write no more either about the Jews or against them. But since I learned that these miserable and accursed people do not cease to lure to themselves even us, that is, the Christians, I have published this little book, so that I might be found among those who opposed such poisonous activities of the Jews and who warned the Christians to be on their guard against them.[13]

Luther stated later in the writing that "you"[14] should "be on your guard against the Jews, knowing that wherever they have their synagogues, nothing is found but a den of devils in which sheer self-glory, conceit, lies, blasphemy, and defamy of God and men are practiced most maliciously...."[15]

Luther's deepest response to the Jew is portrayed in stating, "dear Christian, be advised and do not doubt that next to the devil, you have no more bitter, venomous, and vehement foe than a real Jew who earnestly seeks to be a Jew."[16]

At one point, Luther asked, "What shall we Christians do with this rejected and condemned people, the Jews?"[17] He goes on to give what he calls his "sincere advice":

> First, to set fire to their synagogues or schools and to bury and cover with dirt whatever will not burn, so that no man will ever again see a stone or cinder of them....Second, I advise that their

houses also be razed and destroyed....Third, I advise that all their prayer books and Talmudic writings, in which such idolatry, lies, cursing, and blasphemy are taught be taken from them....Fourth, I advise that their rabbis be forbidden to teach henceforth on pain of loss of life and limb....Fifth, I advise that safe-conduct on the highways be abolished completely for the Jews....Sixth, I advise that usury be prohibited to them, and that all cash and treasure of silver and gold be taken from them and put aside for safekeeping....Seventh, I recommend putting a flail, an ax, a hoe, a spade, a distaff, or a spindle into the hands of young, strong Jews and Jewesses and letting them earn their bread in the sweat of their brow, as was imposed on the children of Adam....[18]

Later, in the same writing, he slightly rephrased his "advice":

First, that their synagogues be burned down.... Second, that all their books—their prayer books, their Talmudic writings, also the entire Bible—be taken from them, not leaving them one leaf....Third, that they be forbidden on pain of death to praise God, to give thanks, to pray, and to teach publicly among us and in our country....Fourth, that they be forbidden to utter the name of God within our hearing.[19]

In a display of radical bitterness, Luther stated that "if I had power over them, I would assemble their scholars and their leaders and order them, on pain of losing their tongues down to the root, to convince us Christians within eight days of the truth of their assertions and to prove this blasphemous lie against us, to the effect that we worship more than the one true God."[20]

Thus, one can see that from Luther, especially the older Luther, the Reformation held no positive hope for the Jews. While Calvin was not as antisemitic as Luther,[21] he nonetheless did not serve as a Reformation antidote to Luther's often venomous spirit. Both men were ultimately the children of their intellectual and spiritual climates.

When the discriminatory actions against the Jews began to be removed, little credit could be claimed by the church, the institution that had been the primary agent of those actions. Roland de Corneille, in a brief study, summarized the situation:

While history will not permit us to lay the blame upon the doorsteps of medievalism, it also refuses to permit us the scapegoat of the papacy or the Roman Catholic Church. The temptation to lay the responsibility there is made all the more attractive by the fact that the plight of the Jews was gradually ameliorated during the centuries which followed the Protestant Reformation. Therefore, it has occurred to some people that Protestantism provided a kind of driving force toward the establishment of tolerance and more humane attitudes toward Jews. As a matter of historical fact, however, Protestantism did nothing of the kind...nothing positive emerged from it to change the persistent negative stereotypes by which the Christian habitually judged them. Any opportunity which Protestantism had to rectify the past, or at least to establish a segment of the Church on a new footing, was lost.[22]

As de Corneille concludes, it was not the church that championed the cause of the Jews. "It was only when movements outside the Church such as Humanism, Capitalism and Nationalism, brought their influence to bear that the situation improved at all."[23] This situation surrounding the Protestant Reformation was a bitter reality with which the Jew had to live. Christendom must reckon with the fact that the breakdown of the ghettos and the gradual removal of Jewish disabilities were primarily the result of an eighteenth-century Enlightenment mentality rather than a burst of enlightened Christendom that suddenly exposed the historical failures of the church and prompted it to treat the Jews humanely and with unconditional love, *agape,* the real message of the New Testament.

CHURCH AND CATHEDRAL ICONOGRAPHY

It is clear that various councils of the medieval church made decisions that propagated the antisemitism of the church. But one might question the impact of such decisions upon the general populace, since church councils involved primarily the bishops of the church or, even if viewed most inclusively, the bishops and certain priests. Just how much did this hateful attitude of the hierarchy filter down to the level of the common populace?

Clearly the filtering process did take place in every realm of human interrelationships. One means by which these antisemitic decisions of the councils found their way into the broader church was through the antisemitic iconography of medieval churches and cathedrals. The importance of this iconography should not be minimized, because this was the real mode of instruction for a large segment of the basically illiterate populace. Doubtlessly, the priests often used this visual iconography as the basis for sermons. Even today we recognize how powerful an aid to learning is this combination of hearing and seeing!

Henry Kraus has stated: "As the tide of anti-Semitism swept through Western Europe during the twelfth and thirteenth centuries, it was reflected in all media of religious art and liturgy."[24] Thus, the impact of the church's antisemitic spirit might be approached from numerous perspectives—among them paintings, dramatic portrayals, ecclesiastical liturgy, and cathedral/church iconography. The result is clear and unfortunately monolithic. The venom of antisemitism associated with "official" or "establishment" Christianity permeated the church through the clergy, who were trained in the antisemitism of medieval Biblical interpretation, and this perspective in turn was transmitted and translated into the "popular" Christianity of the masses.

Medieval artists were dependent for survival upon the patronage of Christians. Such patronage inevitably was reflected in the artists' work. For example, near the conclusion of the medieval era, Hieronymus Bosch (ca. 1450–1516) painted a scene depicting Jesus carrying his cross to the place of crucifixion. Jesus is portrayed as the noble victim of an angry Jewish mob, with the Jews depicted as having grotesque, monster heads. Only Jesus was painted as a "normal" being.[25] This is but one example of many that could be used to illustrate the artistic propagation of antisemitism.

It is interesting to speculate about the personal motivation of the artisan in the portrayal of such evil as antisemitism. Should it surprise one to suggest that these artists were probably "morally upright" individuals, persons who accepted a cultural perspective without questioning? Today we would refer to this as 'polite' antisemitism, and their lemming-like activity stands as a constant reminder to each of us to look seriously at all of the "givens" of our culture, to make certain that there is congruity between cultural practices often influenced by the church and the profession of the church.

The antisemitism of the church was unfortunately "canonized" in the iconography of the medieval churches and cathedrals, and the churches and cathedrals of France demonstrate this fact. Four of the more poignant examples of this "canonization" process will be

Hieronymus Bosch (c. 1450–1516). Jesus carrying the cross amidst Jewish mob.

discussed: Rheims Cathedral, Chartres Cathedral, the Church of La Madeleine at Vezelay, and Le Mans Cathedral. The iconography presented for each of these structures was unfortunately undergirded by Biblical understandings.

Located on the south portal of *Rheims Cathedral,* a thirteenth-century structure, is a larger-than-life piece of statuary[26] portraying the synagogue, that is, Judaism, as a beautiful but blindfolded and thus unseeing woman. Similar images often portray a vanquished Judaism as a woman holding a broken staff, that is, an instrument no longer viable or usable.[27] Such depictions of the Jewess are found at numerous sites in both stone and stained-glass iconography.[28] Simply stated, it is a portrayal of the Jews/Judaism as unable to recognize and to accept truth,[29] and thus doomed to eternal damnation. The ultimate end of such thinking is the Christian obsession to convert Jews, in order to save their souls, and when the ultimate goal is so lofty there are no limitations! In an oftentimes harsh environment, unbelievably cruel means were used to convert the Jews, but apparently little attention was given to the means because their end loomed so important.

Illiterate Christians looked often at these diverse but common portrayals of the blindfolded and ineffectual Jewess, and saw there, to be sure, the positive beauty of the figure. But this only led to the compulsion to bring this beautiful woman into the embracing arms of the church. Looking at these depictions and hearing them used as the basis of proclamations from the pulpits inevitably impacted the psyche of the medieval Christian.

Chartres Cathedral, a thirteenth-century structure dedicated to the Assumption of Mary (graphically represented in the Cathedral's high altar), has a series of five lancet windows located beneath the south rose window. In the center of the rose is the Christ as the apocalyptic one, thus portraying a crucial medieval perception of Jesus. And since the Cathedral is dedicated to Mary, the center lancet window directly below depicts Mary, who is crowned, holding the infant Jesus in her left arm. Two prophets stand on each side in the adjoining lancet windows.

The significant aspect of these four prophetic windows, however, is the fact that astride the shoulders of each of these four prophets sits one of the four evangelists. To Mary's far left stands Daniel, with Mark astride, and to her immediate left is Ezekiel carrying John. To Mary's

Rheims Cathedral, *Synagogue.* Judaism represented as a
blindfolded woman with a broken staff.

immediate right is Isaiah with Matthew, and to the outside right is Jeremiah with Luke.[30]

The unknown aspect of this interpretive equation is the intent of the glaziers in the framing of these lancet windows (and many similar depictions elsewhere). Clearly the interpretation that conveys the greatest sense of harmony between Judaism and Christianity is the idea of Christianity's building upon Judaism. This is expressed well in the following:

> Like dwarfs upon the shoulders of giants, the evangelists are smaller yet see further, but only because the prophets have lifted them up. The Old Testament prepared for the New; the New is built upon the Old. "Think not that I am come to destroy the law, or the prophets," said Jesus, "I am not come to destroy but to fulfil" (Matt. 5:17).
>
> The two testaments thus form the law by which humanity will be judged at the end of time and through which the saved may achieve eternal life in the Heavenly Jerusalem.[31]

Even the reduced size of the four evangelists may be interpreted as the symbolic dependency of the evangelists upon the teachings found in the Hebrew scriptures.[32] This interpretation depicts a realistic assessment of Christianity's relationship to and dependency upon Judaism for its self-perception.

Unfortunately, the depiction can also suggest the "supersessionist" theme that has predominated in Christian thought. Numerous Biblical passages were regularly cited to support this supersessionist theme. Pictorially, these lancet windows can depict the surpassing of the old way by the new, because Jesus has clearly stated the following:

> Neither is new wine put into old wineskins; otherwise, the skins burst, and the wine is spilled, and the skins are destroyed; but new wine is put into fresh wineskins, and so both are preserved (Mt 9:17, NRSV).

It might be suggested, therefore, that faithfulness to the text dictates that the new way has surpassed the old; that is, that Judaism constitutes the former (read surpassed, superseded, or abrogated) covenant, while Christianity represents the new (read present, continuing, fulfilled) covenant. This supersession theme is assuredly the view that dominated the medieval church, both in its theological formulations and in popular expression. As a teaching tool, iconography such as these

Chartres Cathedral (13th century). St. Matthew astride the
shoulders of the prophet Isaiah.

lancet windows, along with numerous similar representations, bespoke the birth and ascendancy of Christianity and the anticipated death and descent of Judaism.

Supersessionist theology is clearly depicted in a comparison of the parallel use of Biblical imagery in the Jewish and Christian scriptures. Isaiah 5:1–7 records the beautiful but haunting "Song of the Vineyard." Contextually this poem may have been a love song, a song associated with the harvest of the grapes, or simply an effective song of judgment against Judah delivered by the prophet. Critical issues are not so much the concern at this point, however, as is the recognition that, in spite of the pending judgment, there is absolutely no indication that Yahweh is rejecting his people and associating himself with another. This is a classical example of the suzerain God fulfilling his responsibility to render judgment upon his errant people to bring them into compliance with the covenant accepted at Sinai (see Exodus 24 for the covenant ratification ceremony). The crucial issue, however, is the fact that Israel continues to be Yahweh's covenant people, even if radical judgment be delivered upon them for their transgression of the covenant. It is indeed a beautiful if haunting poem filled with poignant imagery.

An irony of the Hebrew Bible is the way the writers so clearly portrayed the covenant people's waywardness and the resultant calls from God via the prophets that they repent or face judgment. In later Christian interpretation this honesty has been taken to mean that God has rejected his people and condemned them to judgment. This waywardness-judgment has created an alienation potentially resolved by the Christ event, but that event has not resulted in the rescue of the errant Jews (at least not yet! See Romans 9–11) but instead their replacement, and their covenant with God by a covenant that God has forged with a new people via the Christ event. It is remarkable that such Israelite honesty as regards their relationship with God should be turned on its head and used against them in this fashion.

The Synoptic Gospels (Mk 12:1–12; Mt 21:33–46; and Lk 20:9–19) record an allegorical parable that seems clearly to have in mind the Isaiah 5 poem. Again, our focus is not upon the intricacies of the Biblical critical understanding of the parable, such as differences existing between the various canonical recensions or the enlightenment offered by a less allegorical account in the Gospel of Thomas. It is the allegorical association, however, that should strike the reader when a comparison is made with Isaiah 5.

In the earliest canonical Gospel of Mark (written probably 64–69 C.E.), one is struck especially by the similarity in the preparation of the vineyards. But at that point a new element emerges, namely that the vineyard is leased to tenants rather than having definitive occupants.[33] Beyond that, the leaseholders are responsible for returning back to the owner his rightful share. They refused to do this on three different occasions, when the owner has sent as his messenger one of his slaves, returning to the owner the first two beaten and empty-handed, while killing the third. The owner then sent his "beloved son," thinking that surely the leaseholders would respond positively to him. Unfortunately, they also killed the "beloved son," and thus the vineyard owner determined to "destroy the tenants and give the vineyard to others" (12:9).

The Gospel depiction clearly falls into the supersessionist imagery noted above, the same type of thought expressed by the Matthean Gospel's assertion (Mt 9:17 NRSV) that "neither is new wine put into old wineskins; otherwise, the skins burst, and the wine is spilled, and the skins are destroyed; but new wine is put into fresh wineskins, and both are preserved." In different ways, the parable of the vineyard and the Matthew 9:17 statement are expressing the same thought—the way of Judaism has been surpassed by the way of Christianity! It is this Biblical imagery, initiated long before the iconography of Chartres Cathedral was developed, that is reflected in its lancet windows.

A third example of this "canonization" of antisemitism in the iconography of medieval churches and cathedrals of France is found in the twelfth-century *Church of La Madeleine* located at Vezelay. It is another example of the dichotomy, found in the iconography of the lancet windows at Chartres, between dependency and supersession.

Located in the south aisle of the nave is one of the better known of the capitals of Vezelay, namely the "mystic mill." The capital depicts a mill, Christ, into which the grain of the Hebrew scriptures is poured.[34] The individual who pours the grain into the mill is presumably Moses, who is dressed in high boots and a short garment. Standing on the other side of the mill and gathering the flour is the bare-footed apostle Paul, who is dressed in a long flowing garment and has a high forehead.

It is the symbolism of the mystic mill that is important. The traditional argument suggested that Torah and Prophets were indeed given

Basilique Sainte Madeleine, Vezelay, France (12th century).
Capital depicting the "mystic mill."

by God, but scripture was often difficult to understand, and furthermore, the old covenant restrictions could indeed enslave. It was necessary for the meaning of the old covenant to be made clear so that the
truth of salvation would not be hidden. According to this argument, it
was the work of the Christ to formulate the truths of the new covenant
that are captured in the teaching of the New Testament and that Paul
catches as it comes through the mill. It is now the special responsibility
of Paul to spread the truth of Jesus as the Christ, the message which is
open and unhidden, the truth that Torah held but that the new messianic
message now conveys with clarity. The proper proclamation of the
Hebrew scriptures will make manifest that the real reason for those
scriptures was to give prophecies of Jesus as the Christ. This assumes
that the Jewish scriptures are essentially valueless unless their relationship to Christianity can be established.

The person responsible for this capital is unknown, but the artistry
of the work is exquisite. The message conveyed, while admittedly open
to interpretation, is apparently a classic example of supersessionist theology. Such iconographic representations planted firmly within the popular psyche the antisemitism of the medieval era. As expressed by one
writer, the purpose of the iconographic forms was to prove "the superiority of the Christian faith...[and he notes further that]...this art
reflected the continuing polemic which all through the Middle Ages
Christian thinkers felt called on to conduct with Judaism and the Jews."[35]

The final example of iconographic canonization of antisemitism
is drawn from a stained-glass depiction at the thirteenth century *Le
Mans Cathedral*. Again, the interpretation of the iconography is subject
to differing perspectives, but one must rely upon the precedent view
characteristic of the period.

Three stained-glass panels tell the legend of a young Jewish boy
from Bourges who, apparently influenced by his Christian friends,
accepted Christianity. This is indicated in the first panel where the
young boy, along with his friends, participates in the eucharist. The
priest offers the wafer to the young Jewish boy with his right hand,
while in his left hand he holds the chalice. The radical anger and disil-
lusionment of the Jewish father, whose profession is that of a glazier, is
depicted in panel two, where he prepares to cast his son into the fiery
furnace rather than to accept the fact that the boy has rejected his Jewish heritage. In the background, behind the father, stands the mother,

Le Mans Cathedral (13th century). A Jewish boy who has converted to
Christianity receives the Eucharist.

Le Mans Cathedral (13th century). The father of the Jewish boy
throws him into a furnace.

who looks on compliantly as the father prepares to end his son's life. The boy's faith and acceptance of his plight is indicated by the lack of resistance in his body posture and the way that his hands are raised in the posture of prayer. Finally, in the third panel we see the faith of the boy rewarded when the Virgin Mary enters the furnace to protect him, gathering him unto herself and shielding him in her cloak.

On the one hand, this is a remarkable message to the faithful: that the Virgin will indeed be present to protect and preserve in times of difficulty and persecution. It was a message that a struggling church wanted to hear. On the other hand, given the antisemitic climate, the other side of this message was more likely the one that stood out, namely that of the obdurate Jew who refused to recognize the truth of the Christian message. Even the mother is portrayed negatively, for what type of mother could stand aside so compliantly as her child was about to be destroyed? In both the glazier and his wife, therefore, one sees the rebellious Jew who stands in opposition to and in rejection of all that Christianity embodies, who chooses death rather than life. Does not such obduracy, such flagrant rejection, deserve to be controlled if not eliminated? While quite different at one level, the message is similar to that of the synagogue image discussed earlier, namely that the Jew, while an individual possessed of every privilege of relationship with God, unfortunately rejected that privilege and is thus blinded by his own stubbornness. Thus we see how church iconography served to undergird and enforce the antisemitism which had embedded itself in the life of Christendom.[36]

CONCLUSION

Historical analysis indicates that the medieval era rarely encouraged constructive Jewish-Christian relationships and often actively worked to preclude them. The Jews were treated as obdurate beings who must be either converted or subjugated. The following passage, while focused on the cathedrals, addresses well the larger issues:

> The theologians and master-builders who conceived and constructed Chartres (and her sister cathedrals) were inspired by various Biblical sources, which include the descriptions of Noah's ark and the temple of Solomon, both symbols for Christ's Church—the ark as a means of salvation, the temple because it was built by

Le Mans Cathedral (13 century). The boy is protected by the Virgin Mary.

Solomon who prefigured Christ in his wisdom and as judge. The principal inspiration, however, came from the Book of the Revelation, in which the author describes his vision of the City of God, the Heavenly Jerusalem, for which the church is, in its turn, an earthly symbol. The porches with their hundreds of sculptures outside were richly painted and gilded and symbolize the gates of Heaven, through which we pass awesomely into the Celestial City, to perceive the inner walls set as with a myriad of glittering jewels, "garnished with all manner of precious stones" (Rv 21:19).[37]

The medieval church was a (the?) major player in the propagation of antisemitism during this period of history. What has been presented makes no claim to being exhaustive. Indeed, that is neither the point nor the purpose.

Contemporary Christians uphold the numerous positive aspects of the study of church history. They are often ignorant, or perhaps in a state of conscious or unconscious denial, about what that history records relative to the church's role in past antisemitism. Confronted with these relatively few examples drawn from church councils, art, and the general iconography of the period, it should be more difficult to live in ignorance of the facts or to remain comfortably in an attitude of denial. Now it is up to us individually as Christians and corporately as the body of the church to make purposeful exploration into this sordid side of our history, to recognize that what we do not understand looms just beyond the door threatening to ensnare us yet again. Understanding can lead to emancipation, but blindness leads only to the inevitable results learned from the Middle Ages. Either we study, understand, and excise or we fall victim again to being the principal agent of antisemitism within society. While this latter possibility sounds horrendous and to some impossible, history reminds us how easily the seemingly improbable becomes embraced as the accepted mode of action.[38]

The horrors of the Holocaust should constitute the clearest warning to Christians to deal with the reality of antisemitism. So much of what happened during the Holocaust was prefigured in events and actions supported by the church during those centuries leading up to the twentieth century. It is conceivable that, apart from this background, the Holocaust could not have occurred. Does this mean that the church is solely the responsible agent? Of course not! Could the event have occurred apart from this sickness that so pervaded and diminished the church? One must reluctantly but realistically respond, probably not.

Suggested Questions

1. Why should the medieval book burnings cause second thoughts about modern attempts to ban certain books from libraries and book stores?

2. Martin Luther's zeal for his cause turned into vitriolic bitterness against the Jews. Are there guidelines to help us know when we cross the bridge from zeal to unbridled fanaticism?

3. What manifestations of "polite" antisemitism have you observed or perhaps been an unwitting or purposeful participant in?

4. How does one effectively separate oneself from cultural acceptability to preclude being a participant in "polite" antisemitism?

5. Artistic expression may mirror a society's cultural values or it may seek to influence these values. Can you think of examples of artistic expression that exemplify each of these categories?

IV. The United States Experience and Antisemitism: From the Colonies to the Early Federal Period

INTRODUCTION

The Jew has traditionally been psychologically bound to the community which has nurtured his Jewishness, providing that critical mass of compatriots necessary to make life within community a realistic possibility. One departs this sheltering existence usually only as a result of dire circumstances, such as radical religious persecution or severe political or economic restrictions. In general, this usually involves a process of dehumanization that not only encourages emigration but indeed makes unthinkable the prospect of status quo.

THE COLONIAL INTEGRATION

The Jewish migration to the New World, whether to South America or North America, and whether it was during the colonial or the post-colonial era, certainly correlates with this traditional perception. Whether those settlers were from the Hispanic countries, England, the European countries, or Eastern Europe, relatively few of these immigrants departed their homes of their own volition. Given the communal nature of Jewish culture, it follows that relatively few Jewish immigrants to the New World were fortune hunters. The New World was a place of destiny, sometimes sought, oftentimes not. For some it became a marvelously receptive haven, while for others the separation from homeland and family became a living hell.

The earliest emigration of Jews to the New World was precipitated by the constant persecution experienced in Spain and Portugal. Many fled to Spanish and Portuguese dominions in South America, Mexico, and the West Indies. Only *marranos*¹ could settle, however, for professing Jews were excluded from all Spanish soil after 1492 and from Portuguese soil after 1508. The *marranos* were forced to keep their Judaism concealed, for even in the New World the reach of the Inquisition was felt. Finally, in 1631, the Dutch seized Brazil, at which point many *marranos* were attracted to Brazil's leading city, Recife, where the *marrano* cover was jettisoned. This respite was short-lived, however, for in 1654 the Portuguese recovered Brazil from the Dutch. The dangers for the earlier *marrano* Jews were now clear. It was against this background that the first Jews, twenty-three in number, seeking admission to the American colonies arrived aboard the *Ste. Catherine* at New Amsterdam in 1654, having sailed originally from Recife. The Jewish population was once again being forced to scatter and to seek new havens for security against persecution.²

The basis for the Jewish ghetto existence is rooted in the Third Lateran Council of 1179, which decreed that Christians were not to dwell among the infidel. The insidious intent of this decree reached fulfillment in 1516 in Venice when the Jews were restricted to an area known as the *Ghetto Nuovo* (New Foundry). Once instigated in Venice the ghetto existence for the Jews spread rapidly throughout Europe and termination began only with the French Revolution of 1789. It is no wonder, then, that as Stuart Rosenberg suggests: "Those who came to settle in America came to forget, not to remember."³

Chapter 3 has developed some of the medieval manifestations of antisemitism, and emphasis has been placed upon the added element of theological antisemitism that emerged with the early development of the church. By the time the refugees landed at New Amsterdam, this theological antisemitism was firmly entrenched wherever Jews were settled. Even though Jews who arrived in New Amsterdam in September 1654 had probably not originally intended coming there, as a Dutch-operated colony they could expect it to be better for them than Brazil. They were determined to find in this new land a settlement more favorable than what they had earlier experienced.

Antisemitism was not generally a strong phenomenon in the American colonies. There are numerous reasons why this was the case, but among these may be suggested the following.

First, there were very few Jews who settled there. As a general rule of thumb, it is generally accepted that the number of Jews living in the colonies at the time of the Revolution was somewhere between 1500 and 3000, with the figure more likely in the lower range. For a total population of approximately four million, this was statistically an insignificant number of Jews.

Second, this relative scarcity of Jews made it difficult for anyone to see them as a threat. Certainly the Jewish presence was not a threat economically, and it would have been ludicrous to suggest that it was a political one.

Third, the scant number of settlers made valuable every human resource. It was not possible to overlook contributions that came from any quarter, regardless of whether the contributor be Jewish or Christian. Anyone having a skill to contribute to the general welfare could not be ignored.

Fourth, while not true in every case, as, for example in the Puritanism of Massachusetts or the Anglicanism of Virginia, the colonies generally did not mandate adherence to a particular religious practice. One might argue that there was a concern that the individual be "religious," but there was not an abiding interest as to which of the faith options one might choose. For the Jew migrating from the Old World, with its carefully orchestrated religious structure, this was a welcome relief. The Jew was apparently free to be a Jew, an option rarely available.

Fifth, the colonial setting offered tremendous mobility for all the colonists, the Jews included. Should Jews discover themselves in a situation where they encountered Christian pressures for conversion, they had the luxury of moving to another colony, where such pressures were minimal or nonexistent.

Thus, the situation in the American colonies was unique for Jews, unlike any they had experienced throughout the long history of the Diaspora. Nonetheless, there are indications that antisemitism was present in this environment. Three examples taken from the colonial period will illustrate this fact, each pregnant with negative potential for the Jews settling into the colonies. Fortunately, that potential did not materialize, but this does not negate the fact that the potential for harm, indeed for the establishment of formal antisemitism, assuredly existed.

The first example is drawn from the earliest Jewish settlement in the colonies, with the arrival of twenty-three Jews aboard the *Ste. Catherine* at the port of New Amsterdam in 1654. These four men, six women, and thirteen young people were ill received by Governor Peter Stuyvesant, who had done everything he could to strengthen the Dutch Reformed Church after he was appointed governor of the colony in 1647. Two aspects of this rather well known saga claim our attention.

First, the correspondence that crossed between Stuyvesant and the directors of the Dutch West India Company indicate that he was determined to maintain the colony as a Dutch Calvinist colony. He did not wish to admit the Jews "with their customary usury and deceitful trading with the Christians."[4] As a result of his oppressive response, the Jews encountered in New Amsterdam the nearest analogy to the Old World medieval restrictions that they were to experience in the colonies. Doubtless the Jews who came to New Amsterdam from Recife had hoped to find a pleasant reception and relief from inquisitional policies. While it is readily acknowledged that the disabilities imposed upon them came directly from Stuyvesant and were not supported by the Directors of the Dutch West India Company, nonetheless disabilities were experienced, including the following:

> At first they were forbidden to purchase homes, to practice a craft, to sell at retail, or to trade with the outlying settlements and the Indians. The newcomers were not to stand guard with the militiamen, and were not to hold public religious services; they were not to vote, and not to hold office.[5]

As governor, Stuyvesant petitioned the directors of the Dutch West India Company to expel the Brazilian Jews. Perhaps he was aware of the issue of religious liberty, for his petition of October, 1655, stated: "Giving them liberty, we cannot refuse the Lutherans and the Papists."[6] Fortunately, the Jews in New Amsterdam did have some Jewish brethren in Amsterdam to intercede for them, a few of whom in fact were also directors of the Dutch West India Company. As a result, and this an all too cursory summary of the correspondence involved, the directors rejected the request of Stuyvesant and supported conditionally the settlement of the Jews in New Amsterdam "provided the poor

among them shall not become a burden to the company or to the community, but be supported by their own nation."[7] This same ruling precluded the Jews engaging in public worship in New Amsterdam,
although it should be acknowledged that this restriction derived pointedly from Dutch Calvinist concerns (Lutherans also were precluded
from holding public worship services in New Amsterdam). Nonetheless, according to an order from the directors dated 15 February 1655
and in response to Stuyvesant's comment about religious liberty, the
Jews were to be allowed "to travel to, live in, and trade to and in the
new colony."[8] Furthermore, when the governor did not fully comply
with the directives of the Dutch West India Company, such as maintaining the right of the Jews to participate in the fur trade, more correspondence passed and Stuyvesant was cautioned to execute the Company's
orders "punctually and with more respect."[9] There is thus no doubt that
Governor Stuyvesant, as a rigid Dutch Calvinist, opposed the Jews both
on religious and social grounds.[10]

A second part of the Stuyvesant encounter and the correspondence between the governor and the directors of the Dutch West India
Company deserves special mention. At one point the directors suggested to Stuyvesant that he should encourage the Jews to live in close
proximity to each other. The implications of this suggestion are not
clear, but clearly the suggestion leaves itself open to at least two interpretations. On the one hand, it is quite possible that the directors, aware
of the *sometimes rather noisy nature* of Jewish worship, made the judgment that the Jews would be better accepted if their worship were done
where the "noise" would not likely be disturbing to others. Recall that
in this earliest setting Jewish worship was conducted in the home of
one of the Jewish settlers. Thus, the suggestion may be only a prag-
matic approach to keeping the greatest degree of harmony possible
within the colony. On the other hand, it is possible to read the suggestion as a type of consent to quarter the Jews together, in other words to
create either a full-fledged or at least something approximating a ghetto
setting for the Jews. Even if the latter interpretation is correct,
Stuyvesant did not pursue this option, and it is a fact that neither in New
Amsterdam nor in any other American colony was the Jew ever
sequestered in a ghetto. This is all the more remarkable when it is seen
against the fact that ghettoization of the Jews still existed in Europe

during this time[11] and only began to break down with the start of the French Revolution in 1789.

With the passing of a decade and New Amsterdam's having become the property of James, Duke of York on 7 September 1664, thereafter to be designated as New York, the Jews had been "granted the rights to purchase real estate, to open retail stores, to be mechanics, to do military duty, to worship (although not publicly) and to have a burial ground."[12] While it would be approximately thirty years before they would establish a cemetery and three-quarters of a century (1728) following their entrance before they were able to build a synagogue,[13] the Jews were clearly involved in the common struggle for survival in the New World. However, they also wrestled uniquely with the difficulties of surviving as Jews. Salo Baron stated: "In this battle for their own religious freedom, in which they were aided at the beginning by their influential coreligionists in Amsterdam, the Jews helped blaze the path for the ultimate adoption of the principles of liberty of conscience and freedom of association."[14]

The second example of colonial antisemitism was one that occurred in the Maryland colony and involved Jacob Lumbrozo. Maryland was second only to North Carolina in having the fewest Jewish inhabitants of any southern colony during the eighteenth century.[15] This was to be expected, for according to the Maryland Constitution of 1776 Jews were barred from holding public office, a disability that was not removed until 1826.[16] According to Maryland's Toleration Act of 1649, it was

> ordered and enacted...that no person or persons whatever within this province...professing to believe in Jesus Christ, shall from henceforth be any ways troubled, molested, or discountenanced for, or in respect to, his or her religion, nor in the free exercise thereof within this province....[17]

This was toleration, but it was restricted to those "professing to believe in Jesus Christ...." To make the point more emphatically, "the act also ordained the death penalty for blasphemy and denial of the Trinity, and a fine of five pounds for speaking 'reproachful words of the Virgin Mary, the Apostles, or evangelists.'"[18] As suggested by Stanley Chyet, "It was only with the onset of the Revolution that the Jew could begin to hope for political equality in America."[19]

It was against this background that Jacob Lumbrozo, a Portuguese

Jew and physician, lived and worked in Maryland. During the summer of 1658 he was denounced by pious Puritans and Quakers "for uttering words of blasphemy against our Blessed Saviour Jesus Christ."[20] Lumbrozo "was charged under the law, but the court seemed unwilling to prosecute; he was never convicted or punished."[21] The records are unclear and from this distance it is impossible to unravel the circumstances surrounding his mysterious release. It may be that he benefited from the terms of an amnesty that was proclaimed in Maryland in March 1659 to celebrate Richard Cromwell's assumption of the Lord Protectorate after the death of his father, Oliver. On the other hand, it is possible that Lumbrozo submitted to baptism. It is known that he referred to himself as John Lumbrozo on 10 September 1663. It is also a matter of record that in 1664 he served as a juryman, a privilege reserved only for Christians. There is "soft" evidence, therefore, that in the person of Jacob/John Lumbrozo we see indication of an early *marrano* in the Maryland colony! Regardless, Stanley Feldstein can conclude in *The Land That I Show You:* "With the exception of the infamous Lumbrozo blasphemy case, no Jew was ever arrested, imprisoned, or harmed because he was a Jew."[22]

The third example from the colonial period raises the possibility of a colonial *marrano* even more clearly than the case of Jacob Lumbrozo. Rabbi Judah Monis of Massachusetts was born in 1683 and died in 1764. At the outset it should be acknowledged that reactions to Monis varied, ranging from the suggestion that he was an example of a colonial *marrano* to the denial that he should even be called a Jew!

Judah Monis is an enigmatic character whose career, while interesting, raises more questions than it answers.[23] Born either in Algiers or in Italy to Portuguese *marrano* parents on 4 February 1683, he apparently received some rabbinical training at the academies located in Leghorn and Amsterdam. Coming to New York about 1715 via Jamaica, where he probably served as a rabbi, he seemingly served in a rabbinical role in New York as well. When admitted as a freeman to New York, however, he was listed on the court's record as a merchant.

On 29 June 1720, Monis sent a letter to the Harvard corporation requesting assistance to publish a Hebrew grammar. The precise factors involved next are not clear, but at the graduation exercises one week hence Monis was awarded a Master of Arts degree, the first Jew to be so honored in the New World by Harvard or any other college and the only

Jew destined to receive a Harvard degree before 1800.[24] Less than two years later, Monis was baptized on 27 March 1722 in the College Hall in quite a public display. Monis was apparently the first Jew publicly baptized in the Colonies. The very next month he was appointed instructor of Hebrew at Harvard, the first instructor appointed exclusively to teach Hebrew, a position that would continue from 1722 until his resignation in 1760, soon after his wife's death.

One of the earliest endowed professorships at Harvard was the Hancock Professorship in Hebrew.[25] This is as should be expected since the school was named after John Harvard, a minister who left to the college his library and four hundred pounds. The earliest function of the college was to train ministers.

Recall also that Harvard College was located in Cambridge, Massachusetts, locus of Puritan thought. In their zeal for matters Hebraic, the Puritans placed significant emphasis upon the study of the sacred tongue. To be an effective minister, an individual needed to be able to read the Bible from the sacred text. Prior to Monis's appointment, however, the teaching of Hebrew had been handled by the president of the college and by tutors. Using the Bible as the principal text, "Harvard students were required to spend one day each week for three years on Hebrew and allied tongues."[26]

During this period from 1722 until 1760, Monis taught Hebrew; indications are that he was neither a popular nor an effective instructor. On 18 January 1724 he married a widow, Mrs. Abigail Marret, a lady of Puritan stock and the sister of a minister (the Reverend John Martyn). With corporation support, he published in 1735 the first Hebrew grammar published in this country (using Hebrew type imported from England). Throughout his teaching career he continued to supplement his salary by operating a shop in Cambridge, selling among other items hardware and tobacco. Nonetheless, questions or speculations about Monis are inevitable:

1. When the students hand copied his grammar prior to the 1735 publication, it was copied as "Composed by Rabbi Judah Monis."[27]

2. Even after his conversion to Christianity, Monis continued to observe the Sabbath.

3. Monis died 25 April 1764, and the initial portion of the epitaph inscribed on his tombstone is as follows:

> Here lies the remains of
> Rabbi Judah Monis, M.A.
> Late Hebrew Instructor
> at Harvard College in Cambridge....[28]

4. Perhaps the most basic issue is whether he would have been appointed to his post as instructor of Hebrew at Harvard had he not embraced Christianity.

Given the fact that Monis was apparently of *marrano* stock and that there was considerable question about the authenticity of his conversion at the time,[29] one must raise the possibility that, rather than the first authentic example of a Jew's public conversion to Christianity in the colonial period, we have in Monis an example of imposed (or self-imposed?) *marrano* existence carried over in the New World!

As is so often the case, we have only the printed page to convey to us the reactions of the Reverend Benjamin Colman, a Boston clergyman, who preached the sermon at the occasion of Monis's baptism, a sermon based on John 5:46: "If you believed Moses, you would believe me, for he wrote about me" (NRSV). As noted above, had we something other than the printed page, we would also better understand the reaction of the Reverend Increase Mather, who wrote the Preface to Monis's discourse, "The Truth," which Monis delivered following Colman's sermon.[30] Given the realities of history, it is understandable that Colman might have had some personal doubt regarding the authenticity of Monis's conversion:

> ...Be sure that you have no By-ends, no sinister and corrupt Views, no worldly Advantages, in what you do this day. God forbid, that these should act you.

Increase Mather in his Preface pointedly identified some Jews in Europe who had converted from Judaism to Christianity or "perverted to Popery...." (p. iii) and then later returned to Judaism. He stated:

> There is no cause to fear that Mr. Monis will renounce his Christianity, since he did embrace it voluntarily and gradually, and with much consideration, and from scriptures in the Old Testament.
> God grant that he (who is the first Jew that ever I knew converted in New England) may prove a blessing unto many and especially

to some of his own nation. Which is the Prayer and hearty desire of, Increase Mather. Boston, May 1, 1722 (pp. iii–iv).

Mather may have accepted the sincerity of Monis's actions, but one can certainly detect a possible skepticism in his comments.

And yet it must be acknowledged that if Monis's motive was monetary gain, he was not particularly successful. Although he was appointed an instructor at Harvard College, this was actually a position of lesser status than a tutor. Furthermore, he had a rather continuous correspondence with college officials about increasing or supplementing his income, and as noted above, he continued to function as a merchant even while serving as an instructor in the Hebrew language at the college.

The question of the authenticity of his conversion to Christianity will continue to be debated and probably cannot be resolved. Although his epitaph carries "Rabbi Judah Monis," it is interesting that in his varied correspondence, whether with President Wadsworth of Harvard or the college overseers or with others, he characteristically signed his correspondence either as "J. Monis" or "Judah Monis," while he was formally addressed in correspondence as "Mr." It might be suggested that, although the *marrano* question remains unanswered, these factors argue against a continued perception by others that Judah Monis was Jewish.

In these three examples derived from the colonial period—the actions and reactions of Governor Peter Stuyvesant to the twenty-three Jews from Recife who arrived at the port of New Amsterdam in 1654; the charging of Jacob/John Lumbrozo with blasphemy in 1658 in Maryland coupled with the colony's failure to prosecute him and the questions about why he was not prosecuted; and the case of Judah Monis, instructor in Hebrew at Harvard from 1722 until 1760, and the inevitable questions that surround his appointment at Harvard and his conversion to Christianity—we confirm the fact that, if one has to dig so deeply to uncover overt antisemitism during the colonial period, indeed there was little antisemitism to be found. On the other hand, these three examples do authentically represent either overt or incipient antisemitism. If it was possible for antisemitism to express itself during this period, even if in these muted forms, then once the value of the Jew to the society became lessened as more Christian immigrants arrived, and as the specter of xenophobia rose with massive Jewish immigration in the late nineteenth and early twentieth centuries, we observe history once again repeat itself in the typical European cycle: once the Jews were not so vital to the society, overt antisemitism again raised its ugly head.

THE REVOLUTIONARY SPIRIT

Occasionally a relatively brief era sandwiched between much longer periods is the determinative factor for understanding a people's history. Certainly this was the case for ancient Israel with the Babylonian Exile in the sixth century B.C.E. This brief span became the interpretive frame for subsequent Jewish history, with periods appropriately categorized as pre-exilic and post-exilic eras.

Such a crucial period also occurred in American Jewish history in the form of the American Revolution. This seems a strange statement in light of the fact that perhaps only 1,500 Jews lived in the colonies at the time of the American Revolution. How could the events determining the future of this portion of England's colonial holdings have such impact upon the Jews, particularly when so few were actually involved? Several items should be noted.

First, the Declaration of Independence, adopted on July 4, 1776 in Williamsburg, Virginia, serves as one of the essential cornerstones for religious liberty in the United States. This declaration made clear that people would no longer be expected to conform to one religious persuasion. A nation was emerging that would embrace the ideal of a pluralistic society, the optimal environment for Judaism to flourish. In this nation you could be Protestant, Catholic, or Jew, with the only concern being that you embraced one.

Second, Articles of Confederation were drawn in 1777, although they were not ratified until 1781. The course was determined, and, short of being defeated by the forces of Great Britain, there would be no backing away from the commitments expressed in the Declaration of Independence.

Third, economic, diplomatic, and political problems associated with the Articles of Confederation led to the convening of the Philadelphia Convention of 1787, resulting in the Constitution of the United States of America. By 1789 the necessary number of states ratified the Constitution, resulting in the inauguration of George Washington as the country's first President on 30 April 1789. Article VI, clause 3 of the

Constitution made it perfectly clear that "no religious test shall be required as a qualification to any office or public trust under the United States...." Here was a significant leap from theory to practice, and the seed for true religious freedom!

Fourth, when the Constitution was judged to be deficient in that it did not specify the protection of basic individual rights, the Bill of Rights was ratified in 1791 becoming part of the enabling legislation for this new Republic. In what emerged as the first amendment in the Bill of Rights, Article I, religious freedom was more explicitly protected:

> Congress shall make no law respecting an establishment of religion, or prohibiting the free exercise thereof; or abridging the freedom of speech, or of the press; or the right of the people peaceably to assemble, and to petition the Government for a redress of grievances.

Through Article VI of the Constitution and Article I of the Bill of Rights, "the United States of America thus became the first modern state to grant full equality of rights to its Jewish population."[31] It is no wonder that eventually Jewish immigrants flocked in great numbers to these shores. Constitutionally they had been granted rights their forefathers would have judged unthinkable. It is interesting to note that these Jewish immigrants felt a responsibility to preserve unblemished that gift and made a significant contribution to their adopted land.

It should be mentioned that before the Bill of Rights was approved, Thomas Jefferson had drafted The Statute of Virginia for Religious Freedom in 1777, which he sought without success to guide through the Virginia legislature. Later, while Jefferson was serving as Ambassador to France, James Madison reintroduced the statute into the Virginia legislature, and in 1786 it was signed into law. This Virginia Statute is so important because of its influence in drafting the religion clause for Article I of the Bill of Rights, and because the Supreme Court has often used the Virginia Statute as a guide for interpreting the intention of the religion clause in Article I.[32] The enabling wording of the Virginia Statute reads as follows:

> *Be it enacted by the General Assembly,* That no man shall be compelled to frequent or support any religious worship, place, or ministry whatsoever, nor shall be enforced, restrained, molested, or burthened in his body or goods, nor shall otherwise

suffer on account of his religious opinions or belief; but that all men shall be free to profess, and by argument to maintain, their opinion in matters of religion, and that the same shall in no wise diminish, enlarge, or affect their civil capacities.

Because of its more explicit language, it is understandable that the Supreme Court would seek to detect the intention of Article I of the Bill of Rights in the Virginia Statute. For the Jews, the passage of the statute was a milestone in their journey toward absolute religious freedom, for the language of the statute guaranteed *freedom* of expression rather than *toleration*. Freedom of religion cannot be offered and then withdrawn. Freedom is an indigenous right.

With the American Revolution, a new day had dawned for everyone who inhabited this new Republic, but especially for the Jews of the United States. Up to this point they had learned to live with the problems of inequality. Now they had to learn how to live with the possibility, indeed the promise of equality. The Jews had to accommodate to full acceptance rather than to the creative tension of toleration. This statute "gave Jews, among others, complete religious and political freedom by divorcing church and state."[33] It is no wonder that Jefferson judged this one of his three greatest accomplishments (along with writing the Declaration of Independence and founding the University of Virginia).

It would take many years before all of the ramifications of freedom of religion would become transparent. Equally, it would be many more years before the legal implications of freedom of religion would be fully implemented in the society. Understandably, many would argue that in the highly conservative and intensely Christian-oriented atmosphere which currently prevails, the full implications of freedom of religion for all people has still not been fully understood and implemented.

CONCLUSION

The relatively brief revolutionary period served to shape the focus of American Judaism. Although this period of revolutionary turmoil did not focus on the new nation's Jewish population, either positively or negatively, but ultimately the revolution impacted the religious elements in the minority even more than those in the majority. This influence was experienced in many ways, but certainly one of the most dramatic was in the nation's leaning toward a more secular society.

Henceforth we might permit a President to gain much power, but we would never permit the divine right of Kings. We may lapse into a type of civil religious activity, but we would never permit the establishment of a single religious perspective. The influence of the period of revolution was burned deeply into the fabric of the American psyche, and it had tremendous impact upon all of those who would live in this land. No people has profited more from the American experiment than the Jews, and in like fashion it could be argued that, relative to their numbers, no people has returned a greater positive contribution to this land than the Jews.

Suggested Questions

1.   The importance of enacting the past into the present is enjoined upon ancient Israel in Numbers 15:40: "So you shall remember and do all my commandments, and you shall be holy to your God" (NRSV). And yet, referring to Jews who early came to this country, Stuart Rosenberg stated that "Those who came to settle in America came to forget, not to remember" (see *The Search for Jewish Identity in America,* p. 3). What factors brought about such a change in perspective?

2.   When the Jews first settled into this land, and indeed until the French Revolution (1789) and its aftermath, the Jews lived in ghettos throughout most of Europe. What factors precluded the establishment of ghettos in the colonies?

3.   Relative to the practice of religion, there is considerable difference between "freedom" and "toleration" to practice ones religious belief. What is the basic difference in these two concepts? Into which camp does the United States Constitution fall?

4.   The type of elected government characteristic of the United States holds its elected officials responsible for their actions. Why is it not possible for a President of the United States, for example, to claim that the presidency is "above the law"? Why is this caveat important to the issue of Jewish and Christian relations?

5.   Investigate some sources and determine the role(s) of the Jews during the American Revolution. NOTE: Materials written by Jacob Rader Marcus would offer excellent resource data.

V. The United States Experience and Antisemitism: The Nineteenth and Twentieth Centuries

INTRODUCTION

Just as the colonies proved to be a haven for Jews displaced from the various European and Hispanic countries, so too has the United States continued to be a refuge for the downtrodden and dispossessed of the world. This is not to ignore the problems that have been experienced in the United States, for assuredly the litany of these problems would be lengthy. Nonetheless, opportunities have overshadowed problems, and hope has consistently been the victor over despair. Yet, antisemitism did finally rear its ugly head in the United States during the nineteenth and twentieth centuries.

GENERAL ULYSSES S. GRANT: GENERAL ORDER NUMBER 11

General Grant emerged as one of the Union heroes of the Civil War and later served as the eighteenth President of the United States, from 1869 until 1877. He was involved in a situation during the War, however, that had the potential of horrendous consequences for the country's future, especially since that future was so uncertain at that time. Until then the Jews had not sensed themselves to be a focused minority, even though they had understandings that differed from the majority and their speech and manner of dress often singled them out.

But after Grant's action, the Jews "found themselves viewed increasingly in the less acceptable image of outlanders."[1]

On December 17, 1862, General Grant issued General Order Number 11, which order expelled "Jews as a class" from the Department of the Tennessee, a portion of the area falling within his jurisdiction (the military district under his command included Mississippi, Kentucky, and Tennessee[2]), with the order to be implemented within twenty-four hours.[3] Grant was convinced that some Jews were involved in trading with the Confederacy, trading northern goods for southern cotton. The degree to which anything illegal was taking place has been debated, and indeed that issue is really moot. The critical issue is whether the power of the government could be used to expel the Jews as a group, or any other identifiable group of people, from any given area. Although rules are stretched during time of warfare, at the same time fulfillment of this order would have had the effect of reverting to 1290 C.E., when the Jews were expelled from England, the first of many such expulsions that would occur. Was the cycle of history to be repeated again?

It is fortunate that the Jews were not inclined to accept this order without question and that Abraham Lincoln was president of the United States. When the news of this order was brought to Lincoln's attention, he immediately rescinded it. Although the major tragedy of a Jewish expulsion was averted, considerable damage was done. In both the North and the South, this incident led to antisemitic responses to Jewish individuals and reinvigorated an ancient charge, namely the questioning of Jews' allegiance to the national entity within which they resided. General Order Number 11 was not implemented, but it nonetheless had serious ramifications. The fact that the Jews could be singled out in this fashion unfortunately portended even greater negativity that would follow, with an inevitable correspondence between numbers and antisemitism: the larger the number of Jews, the greater the likelihood of antisemitic acts within the society.

IMMIGRATION PATTERNS AND IMMIGRATION RESTRICTIONS

During the history of the United States, attitudes and conditions have generally reflected prevailing attitudes and conditions in Europe.

Just as it has been demonstrated anew in recent years that economic conditions tend to mirror global realities, the history of antisemitism has generally reflected European conditions. As Nathan Belth has pointed out, however, "rarely, in our over three centuries of American history, have anti-Semitic incidents attained the intensity—and never have they exacted the fearful price—of European bigotry."[4] This is the good news of post-revolution antisemitism, but there is also the bad news!

Where problems of antisemitism emerged in the United States, it was generally not ideological, like that in the Old World. Rather, the antisemitism that emerged was essentially attributable to the two intertwined factors of xenophobia and massive immigration. Thus, the antisemitism Jews experienced was similar to the reaction to Catholics, Italians, Japanese, and Blacks who happened to arrive in massive numbers and settled within a relatively small area.

The situation at the middle of the eighteenth century, which was essentially the same as that following the Revolution, has been ably described by the following statement:

> By the middle of the eighteenth century, a regime of freedom flourished so profusely that intermarriage was frequent and socially acceptable. Well-to-do Jews joined the same clubs and private libraries as their Christian peers, attended the same dancing assemblies and sent their children to the same schools. Jews contributed to Anglican and Catholic undertakings and, on at least one occasion, solicited the aid of Christians for a synagogue. Full political rights lagged somewhat behind social integration: In a few states, religious tests for holding public office lingered into the early nineteenth century. These tests, however, were not distinctively anti-Jewish, and in any case they survived only where the absence of an active Jewish community left them unchallenged and inconsequential.[5]

Even during this period of relative quiet, however, let us not be deluded into thinking that the phenomenon of antisemitism slept soundly. It was not until 1876 that New Hampshire formally removed all disabilities against the Jews, the final State to do so. While John Higham is correct that "the absence of an active Jewish community left [this unthinkable anachronism] unchallenged and inconsequential," one could seriously question the "inconsequential" evaluation. The presence of such a disability acts as a cancerous growth upon the social fabric of a nation's life. Eventually, a nation either excises the malignancy or that cancer will metastasize throughout the fabric of the nation.

Xenophobia coupled with massive immigration tends to result in social and economic discrimination. This was particularly acute for Jews during three periods when their numbers increased by massive proportions: the 1840s, the 1880s, and the 1920s.

At the beginning of the 1840s, there was a relatively secure Jewish population, predominately German, of perhaps 15,000 individuals in the United States. In the main these individuals had assimilated into the socioeconomic structure of the country rather effectively, and such positive integration was their desire. A good life was offered here. But, as a result of problems within Europe, particularly the aborted revolutions of 1848 that swept throughout the continent, there was massive immigration. By 1850 there were approximately 50,000 Jews in the country, and that number would increase to 100,000 by 1855, to 150,000 by 1860, and to 300,000 by 1880.

Such massive immigration cannot occur without repercussions, and in this case the unfortunate result was the active emergence of anti-semitism. In an area such as lower Manhattan, the streets were almost intolerably crowded with a massive number of Jewish peddlers. And let us not think only of the large eastern cities, for the Jews were making their way westward and southward as well. Second-hand shops became a staple in the Jewish economy, and the crowded living conditions were particularly insufferable. A social problem was being created for the society in general, but it especially posed a dilemma to those Jews already settled in the nation and effectively integrated as productive citizens. They did not need to have themselves marked as kinsmen to these immigrants. "Terribly poor and often not very clean, they looked unappealingly alien and untrustworthy to some."[6] Nonetheless, the "uptown" Jews sensed an abiding compulsion to assist their "downtown" compatriots, and thus was born the rich tradition of American Jewish philanthropy.

The xenophobic conditions of the 1880s and 1890s, which climaxed in the 1920s, focused primarily on the East European immigration. And yet it also had a spin-off effect on the earlier German immigrants. Many of the German Jews applied themselves and were remarkably successful in the society. But this economic rise was not generally accompanied by a social rise; more rarely was it matched by educational advancement. Thus, during the 1870s in particular, pressure built for these Jews to be accepted into clubs, educational institutions, and job opportunities, as well as to be admitted into various resorts. Such advances would signal the acceptance of Jews into U.S. society. The press of applicants confronting an establishment trying to preserve its own self identity and prestige led to the development of various mechanisms to prevent Jews from being admitted into private clubs, matriculating into educational institutions, being hired in a variety of jobs—especially professional positions—or registering in the typical "Christians only" resorts. As stated by Higham, "Social mobility was the essential mechanism of social assimilation in the United States; and Jewish immigrants, more than any others, were eager and able to pay for acceptance into prestige circles."[7] This problem, which emerged particularly in the 1870s, was exacerbated in all social institutions as the massive immigration of the 1880s began.

In 1870 there were approximately 250,000 Jews in the United States. But the truly massive immigrations from Eastern Europe were precipitated by the assassination of Alexander II of Russia in 1881,[8] so that by 1920 there were approximately 3,500,000 Jews in the United States.[9] The significance of this immigration is signaled by a statement of Henry Feingold: "While the general population increased 112 percent between 1881 and 1920, the Jewish population increased by 1,300 percent—eleven times as fast."[10]

Such runaway immigration figures had three primary results. A community that had earlier had a significant degree of homogeneity became excessively fragmented. This is indicated by the growth in the number of synagogues. In 1880 there were 270 synagogues in the United States, by 1890 there were 533, by 1906 there were 1,769, and by 1916 there were 1,901.[11] The import of this is even clearer when it is recalled that Philadelphia was the first United States city to have two synagogues, and this did not occur until 1802! At the time of the American Revolution, only five synagogues existed in the Colonies, all of them using Sephardic ritual. The rapid expansion of synagogues signaled the struggle between the Ashkenazim and the Sephardim and the Ashkenazic ascendancy. Increasing diversity among the Jews precipitated a focus not only upon religious issues, but also upon matters social, economic, and political.

The second and third results of the massive Jewish immigration during such a short period are really interwoven. One result was the development of immigration restrictions, a phenomenon that was particularly embodied in legislation extending from the Immigration Act of 1924 to the Immigration and Naturalization Act of 1965. The other result is the emergence of clear antisemitism. As the Jewish population began to break the boundaries of the established settlement areas, they encountered restrictive covenants that forbade sales of houses and rental restrictions that precluded their moving into certain neighborhoods. Fraternities at colleges were blackballing Jews in the 1880s (a practice that resulted in the founding in 1898 of the first Jewish fraternity in the United States), and around the turn of the century covert enrollment quotas surfaced in the various colleges where large numbers of Jews had been enrolled.[12]

The xenophobia that accompanied this massive immigration came to its logical conclusion with the passage of the Immigration Act of 1924 during the tenure of President Calvin Coolidge. Debate on the bill did not in general speak well for the lofty ideals of world citizenship espoused by our Congress. "The Act of 1924...adopted racist theory and substituted the goal of racial homogeneity for faith in America's democratic tradition...[and] set a quota of 150,000 for Europe based on the census of 1890...."[13] The Act of 1924 "gave overwhelming preference to immigrants from Northern and Western Europe...by setting the quota at 2 percent of the foreign stock living in the United States in 1890...."[14] There were various attempts to legislate away the restrictionist provisions of the Act of 1924, but it was not until 1965 during the presidency of Lyndon Johnson that the Immigration and Naturalization Act of 1965 was passed. Belth states:

> The new measure struck down the national origins quota and the Asia-Pacific Triangle provision, raised annual immigration to 350,000, and favored those with relatives in the country, the skilled, and the educated. At the same time, it preserved the tradition of asylum by providing a capability for emergency action in aid of the oppressed and the persecuted.[15]

President Johnson made provisions for the ceremonial signing of this bill into law at the base of the Statue of Liberty. For all immigrants and descendants of immigrants, Lady Liberty has special meaning. For Jews, the statue has special meaning because of the poem by Emma

Lazarus, herself a Jew, attached to its base. A portion of her poem, "The New Colossus," reads:

> ...Give me your tired, your poor,
> Your huddled masses yearning to breathe free.
> The Wretched refuse of your teeming shore.
> Send these, the homeless, tempest-tost to me.
> I lift my lamp beside the Golden Door![16]

Finally with Johnson's signing, after a period of slightly more than four decades, the country was coming back to the principles that had undergirded it from its founding.

Between World Wars I and II, antisemitism became sharpest in the area of employment. This was the period when second-generation Jews, now better educated than their East European immigrant parents, competed with non-Jews for white collar jobs. Higham states:

> The second-generation Jews' search for entry into middle class life made its greatest impact between the two World Wars. All types of social and economic discrimination reached a corresponding peak. Stringent quotas regulated admission to medical schools. Public schools and colleges commonly hired only Protestant teachers....Even the Jewish-owned *New York Times* accepted "help-wanted" advertisements specifying "Christians only"; other newspapers ran ads asking explicitly for Anglo-Saxons. The Depression made job discrimination more acute than ever.[17]

Thus, antisemitism clearly existed in the United States following the Revolution and continued on into the nineteenth and twentieth centuries. Much of what occurred and could be properly labeled as antisemitism was not essentially different, as noted above, from the type of xenophobic reactions that would be directed toward the Irish, the Italians, the Japanese, the Mexicans, or any other minority group that entered in massive numbers and was perceived as a threat, for whatever reasons, by a certain segment of the population. The land may have been perceived as a melting pot—although some would question the appropriateness of this concept today—but apparently it was felt that there was a maximum number capable of being absorbed productively within that melting pot during any given period. At what point do those who are different begin to influence us so that we become different ourselves?

Nonetheless, the story cannot end on so positive a note even as this, for, although, like the antisemitic reaction described above, most of the antisemitism in this country has been nonideological. This is not to say that such ideologically conditioned antisemitism has not existed. Again, as expressed by John Higham:

> ...ideological anti-Semitism condemns the Jews as incapable of assimilation and disloyal to the basic institutions of the country. In its more extreme forms, it portrays them as leagued together in a vast international conspiracy. The alleged plot usually centers on gaining control of the money supply and wrecking the financial system; sometimes it extends to polluting the nation's morals through control of communications and entertainment. The supposed eventual aim is to overthrow the government and establish a superstate. In America, anti-Semitism of this kind has not been so well organized or so productive of violence as other racial and religious phobias.[18]

TWENTIETH-CENTURY EXAMPLES OF ANTISEMITISM

Religious motifs have generally played a minor role in American antisemitism, but the phenomenon has not been entirely absent. During the difficult era of the teens through the thirties of the twentieth century, the religious issue was present. Let us focus briefly on four representative figures—Leo Frank, Gerald Winrod, Gerald L. K. Smith, and Father Charles E. Coughlin—to show how that question was present in U.S. antisemitism.

Leo Frank is in a totally different category than the three other individuals in our twentieth-century list. Those three figures were perpetrators of antisemitism, and their activities had far-reaching ramifications. Leo Frank was the unfortunate victim of blatant antisemitism, the only example of a Jew in the United States who lost his life to a lynch mob motivated exclusively by antisemitism. It is a horrendous story, but one that needs to be told to every generation, because of the depths of depravity to which humankind can slip.

The case has been covered extensively,[19] and thus we need to mention only the basic details. Without minimizing or diminishing the horror of what Frank experienced, our concern at this point is primarily with what this case relays to us about the American psyche relative to the relationship of Jews and Christians.

Frank, a Jew, was born in Paris, Texas, in 1884, but spent most of his youth in Brooklyn. He attended Cornell University, graduating with a degree in engineering, and eventually moved to Atlanta, Georgia, to manage the National Pencil Factory owned by his uncle. Working at the factory was a thirteen-year-old girl, Mary Phagan, whose murdered body was found in the basement of the pencil factory on April 27, 1913. Ignoring all other evidence, especially that associated with a black janitor named Jim Conley, and focusing exclusively on Frank, prosecutors brought Leo Frank to trial in what can only be termed a mockery of justice. He was accused of sexually violating and brutally murdering Mary Phagan. The trial was marked by blatant antisemitism and threats aimed at both the jurors and the judge. Frank was convicted, and the presiding judge sentenced him to hang. After all other avenues of redress had been exhausted, the governor, John Slaton, demonstrated himself to be a man of integrity more interested in justice than his own political future. Upon reviewing all of the available evidence, some of which had emerged following the trial, he commuted Frank's sentence to life imprisonment. An attempt was made by a fellow prisoner to murder Frank while in the prison farm, but he miraculously recovered. Then, on August 16, 1915, Frank was dragged from the hospital in the Milledgeville State Prison by a lynch mob of twenty-five men and driven to Marietta, Georgia, where he was hanged.

Ostensibly, one should say case closed. In 1982, however, Alonzo Mann, then eighty-five years old, came forward with the testimony that, as a young boy also working in the pencil factory, he had gone to the factory on Confederate Memorial Day (date of Mary Phagan's murder) and had seen Jim Conley carrying the body of Mary Phagan. Conley warned him that he would kill him if he said anything about what he had seen. After Mann reported the incident to his mother, she absolutely forbade his saying anything to anyone about it. Although he had tried unsuccessfully to clear his conscience of this issue, he finally came forward in 1982, before it was too late for him to do so. At first the Georgia Board of Pardons and Paroles denied a posthumous pardon for Leo Frank, indicating that no new evidence had come forward to prove conclusively that Frank was not guilty. Eventually, in 1986, the Georgia State Board of Pardons and Paroles posthumously pardoned Leo Frank.[20]

What understanding and guidance might be taken from this inexcusable series of events? It is important for citizens of the United States to recognize that it is not only elsewhere that the forces of ignorance and prejudice can combine to bring about a travesty of justice. Like the case of Captain Alfred Dreyfus in France and that of Menachem Beilis in Russia, these were situations marked by virulent xenophobia, social upheaval, and religious fanaticism, which combined to produce antisemitic outrages. Unfortunately, it must be emphasized that religious fundamentalism played an important role in all three of these cases—the right-wing Catholicism of France, the medievalism of the Russian Orthodox Church, and the Fundamentalist Protestantism of the South. Indeed, it is important for us to remember that ecclesiastical interests of all types have worked together with social, economic, and political factors to bring about the worst of these atrocities. There has been only one Leo Frank in United States history—his fate should encourage all persons of good will to resolve that ignorance and selfishness will never be permitted to become the dominant traits in interpersonal relationships.

Gerald B. Winrod of Wichita, Kansas, was the founder in 1925 of The Defenders of the Christian Faith "as a 'mailing list' fundamentalist organization opposed to modernism in religion...," and, in 1933, Winrod "discovered 'Jewish Bolshevism' at about the same time that [William Dudley] Pelley did."[21] Pelley was the founder of the Silver Shirt Legion, a paramilitary organization, who presented himself to the American public as the American Hitler. Belth describes Pelley as "the classical case of the frustrated personality who turned to the practice of anti-Semitism as a profession...a man of great ambitions and only modest talents, embittered because the world had not recognized his worth and left unrewarded his pursuit of fame and fortune."[22]

Born in 1885 as the son of an itinerant Methodist preacher, Winrod is described as a youth troubled by the religious fanaticism of his father.[23] "Pelley, who had been a newspaperman, a YMCA secretary, a Hollywood screenwriter, and a spiritualist—he claimed to have died but before returning to earth to have spoken with God—was described as an undersized man who 'sports a goatee and wears an oversized military hat.'"[24] As founder of the Christian party in 1934, he desired, among other objectives of the party, to smash "Jewish communism in the United States and...[to disenfranchise]...the Jew from further political and economic mischief...."[25] Working in this same vein, Winrod "built a gigantic publishing business, a magazine of large circulation, and became a prime distributor of anti-Semitic tracts, pamphlets, and books produced by others…he remained for decades in the lucrative business of disseminating hate materials,…[but he] never built a membership organization."[26] Winrod, in this fundamentalist era of the 1920s and 1930s, focused on the issue of theological antisemitism as a prime ingredient of what he disseminated.

Gerald L. K. Smith, inheritor of the Share-the-Wealth movement of Huey Long following Long's assassination in 1935, was essentially the Pied Piper for a rural constituency. Whereas Long had not displayed antisemitic tendencies, Smith became a persistent antisemite; one of his publications was an edition of *The Protocols of the Elders of Zion,* which was later heavily used by the Black Muslims in the early 1970s.[27] Smith's America First Party became a platform in rallies organized from St. Louis to Baltimore for warning "Jews to stop their anti-Nazi agitation."[28] Fortunately, because Smith's America First Party had advocated Charles A. Lindbergh as a presidential candidate against Franklin D. Roosevelt in the 1936 election, the America First Committee was irretrievably tarnished by a speech given by Lindbergh in Des Moines, Iowa:

> [Lindbergh]…charged Jews, along with the British and Roosevelt, as being one of the "most important groups…pressing this country toward war.…" Of the three, said Lindbergh, the Jews were "the most dangerous," because of "their large ownership plus influence on motion pictures, on press, on radio, and on government."[29]

The public reaction, especially from the press, repudiated Lindbergh's comments. The end result was the discrediting both of Lindbergh and of the America First Committee, and, while Smith's antisemitic activities continued, his image was badly tarnished and his influence diminished. The point to be emphasized here is that activities of Smith were focused largely around theological antisemitism.

Father Charles E. Coughlin was perhaps the best known of this antisemitic trio and the one most conditioned by the tenets of theological antisemitism. Smith and Winrod fit into the 1920s–1930s Fundamentalist movement that swept through Protestantism during the period, but as a Roman Catholic priest Father Coughlin obviously did not fit this mold. He indeed must be seen as correlating more closely to that traditional theological antisemitism that characterized the church through the medieval period.

Father Coughlin had been a Roosevelt New Dealer, but ultimately "he broke with Roosevelt, and ended up as the anti-Semitic leader of a profascist movement...though probably a closet anti-Semite all his life, he did not let his prejudice show overtly till 1938, near the apex of his public career."[30]

His followers were primarily Catholic and urban, most often blue collar workers with commensurate educational background. Such individuals were more easily manipulated as participants in the Coughlin phenomenon.[31]

Father Coughlin originally developed his radio program to help build up a local church, the Shrine of the Little Flower in Royal Oak, Michigan, and this program ultimately became his national platform. Enjoying the ardent support of his bishop, Michael J. Gallagher, the bishop of Detroit, and reaching an estimated audience of thirty million listeners each Sunday, Coughlin had amazing success. It has been suggested that "he was a man in the right place at the right time."[32] He began his radio program in 1926 when broadcasting was in its infancy. But beyond his ability to exploit a new medium, he also had an effective style. Brinkley states:

> Most important was the warm, inviting sound of his voice, a sound that could make even the tritest statements sound richer and more meaningful than they actually were. And there was, too, his ability to make his sermons accessible, interesting, and provocative to his audience.[33]

As a result of the 1936 Presidential election, Coughlin's antisemitism became overt. For two years he had been deeply involved in the struggle against a capitalism that he judged already doomed and unworthy of saving, and by 1935 he had broken totally with the New Deal.[34] In a sermon broadcast on November 11, 1934, he announced the formation of the National Union for Social Justice, which was ostensibly based on Sixteen Principles that he indicated should be indigenous to the national psyche, but clearly were intended to help Coughlin regain his Washington influence, which had eroded since his break with the New Deal.[35] In his sermon broadcast of January 27, 1935, he preached about "the Menace of the World Court," which helped to precipitate one of Roosevelt's significant losses, as the treaty fell short of approval by seven votes in the United States Senate.[36]

In the election of 1936, in conjunction with Gerald L. K Smith, he supported for President on the National Union party ticket William Lemke, a North Dakota congressman, and Thomas A. O'Brien of Massachusetts for Vice President. As the date of the election drew near, Coughlin was so confident that the Lemke-O'Brien ticket would amass 9,000,000 votes that he vowed to close down his radio program if that figure were not achieved. However, President Roosevelt carried all but two states (Maine and Vermont) and amassed 27,753,000 votes. The Lemke-O'Brien ticket received only 882,000 votes. Thus, on 7 November 1936, Father Coughlin informed his radio audience that he would go off the air waves.[37]

Unfortunately, on 24 January 1937, less than three months later, his program was reinstated over an expanded network. In March 1938 he proposed the establishing of a Corporate State of America, from which all non-Christians would be excluded. Now his antisemitism became even more transparent. Coupled with the journal, *Social Justice,* which he had begun publishing in March 1936 and which ultimately had a readership of approximately 200,000,[38] he now established in New York in August 1938[39] a supporting Nazi-type organization designated the Christian Front, "avowedly fascist and anti-Semitic, admittedly ready to take to the streets in bully-boy fashion."[40] As Alson J. Smith has indicated, this organization was "not only anti-Semitic, but also—in the best Nazi tradition—anti-labor, anti-liberal, anti-democratic."[41] Working through the traditional platoon system of 25 persons each, the Christian Front relied heavily upon distortion, terror tactics, and the power of the word. The advice of Hitler was followed: "Never tell a little lie, big lies are more easily believed."[42] Obviously, the Christian Front was Coughlin's equivalent of Hitler's Storm Troopers. At approximately this same time, the summer of 1938, *The Protocols of the Elders of Zion* was reprinted in *Social Justice.* Coughlin's tactics degenerated even further, and in the July 25, 1938 issue of *Social Justice,* he drew upon most of the traditional antisemitic charges, including deicide, the Shylock imagery, the money-lending and banking associations, charges that Jews were supporters of Communism, as well as others.[43]

Coughlin frequently used quotations out of context and sometimes blatantly altered them to meet his purpose (see Belth, *A Promise to Keep*, p. 136, for two examples involving a supposed United States Secret Service document and a fraudulent quotation from British Prime Minister Disraeli at a Rothschild family gathering), but not even public exposure of such fraudulent use slowed his antisemitic pace. Increasingly he relied on the development of cell groups in the Christian Front, which was developing an ever greater tendency toward violence.[44]

Ironically, the event that ultimately silenced Coughlin was *Kristallnacht* on 9–10 November, 1938. In a poll taken in the United States shortly thereafter, Americans by an 88 percent vote registered their disapproval of Germany's treatment of Jews. Misreading public sentiment, Coughlin used the *Kristallnacht* event to air his antisemitism. He finally was forced by the hierarchy of the Roman Catholic Church to give up his radio program in September 1940.[45] He was not silenced, however, before his brand of theologically supported antisemitic tactics and propaganda caused many American Jews to wonder how long it would be before the activities witnessed in Germany would also be a part of the American scene. Coughlin was eventually forced to sever his connections with *Social Justice* lest he face charges of sedition. This was the Spring of 1942. He remained at the Shrine of the Little Flower, however, until 1966, when he retired to "a comfortable home in a wealthy Detroit suburb."[46] He lived in retirement until his death in 1979.

AMERICAN JUDAISM LOOKS FORWARD

American Judaism is a unique phenomenon. It is in the United States that Jewish denominationalism came to full flower, with the development of Reform, Conservative, and Orthodox traditions.[47] The American scene has also contributed a movement that is uniquely born out of American soil, namely Jewish Reconstructionism. But, even with this division, there is nonetheless a common thread that holds all Jews together, namely the State of Israel, proclaimed May 14, 1948. Out of the ashes of the Holocaust Israel has been reborn, and American Jews, regardless of whether they have any desire to settle in Israel, have been beneficent in their support of the State.

American Jews number just short of six million individuals. In some ways they mirror the larger society in that approximately 50 percent of the Jews are affiliated with a synagogue, with the division being roughly one-third associated with each of the three major denominations. A comparison of Old World Judaism with American Judaism would indicate significant differences, especially in the sense that Old World Judaism was much more secluded from the external society, maintaining clear parameters around the Jewish community. In the American environment, Jews are generally much more integrated into the mainstream of the society, and Jews are treated much more like practitioners of a religion more akin either to Protestantism or Roman Catholicism than is actually the case. Judaism is more to be understood as a way of life which is all encompassing, a way of life that may but does not have to be associated with synagogal liturgical activities. It would be difficult to envision a Christian structure so defined.

As we discussed Jewish migration into the United States earlier in this chapter, it was stressed that Jews tended to settle in immigration waves dependent on events far separated from our shores. From the 1880s into the first quarter of the twentieth century, Jewish immigration was particularly heavy, and the immigrants were preponderately East European. This combination caused xenophobic responses that resulted in the Immigration Act of 1924, which greatly curtailed Jewish immigration. For American Judaism, this turned out to be a major turning point, because as a result of the curtailment of the steady and heavy stream of immigrants, the Jewish community became dependent upon internal growth. Even so, it was not until 1940 that the majority of Jews in the United States were native born rather than immigrants. Thus, it is roughly only within the last half century that Jews have had to contend with this significant factor in seeking to clarify self-identity. This added part of the equation comes during the same half-century when Jews have been trying to deal with other major events, such as the Holocaust and the rebirth of the State of Israel. Given both internal and external factors, should it be surprising if American Jews are somewhat confused as to their precise identity?

It was earlier noted that in 1840 there were approximately 15,000 Jews in the United States, while by 1850 there were roughly 50,000 Jews in the country. This more than tripling resulted from immigration precipitated by the aborted revolutions of 1848 throughout Europe. Such multiplication inevitably causes acceptance problems, and it is instructive that Jews in the United States did not greet passively whatever responses might be forthcoming. In 1843, B'nai B'rith ("Sons of the Covenant"), the world's largest Jewish organization, was founded in New York. Its primary purpose was to defend Jewish rights and to fight discrimination. The organization has since developed social, moral, educational, and philanthropic goals, and now has worldwide constituency. In its evolution, it has become a major organization seeking not just Jewish rights but human rights for all people. It has spawned numerous spin-off organizations that encourage education and inculcation of Jewish values and culture among Jewish youth, promote education at all levels, sponsor community programs that add value to the life of the wider community, and give assistance to elders in the form of quality housing and quality-of-life activities. The areas of outreach are too numerous to delineate briefly.

The existence of B'nai B'rith emphasizes that the Jewish community was determined to protect and preserve itself. The Anti-Defamation League (ADL) developed out of B'nai B'rith. It remains both affiliated with B'nai B'rith and one of American Judaism's most important organizations. The ADL developed in 1913, just four weeks after the death of Leo Frank.

That trial screamed out for an organization that would address inequities, antisemitic slurs, misstatements both accidental and intentional, as well as overt acts of antisemitism. As the Anti-Defamation League has developed, it has focused on issues of interfaith relations, antisemitism in its multiple manifestations, and civil rights and civil rights reforms necessary for true freedom and equality to exist within the society. Each year the ADL publishes an annual report. The following list of issues portrays the various types of concerns addressed by the ADL:

Fighting Anti-Semitism
Combating Hate & Bigotry
Protecting Religious Freedom
Hate Crimes Legislation
Combating Terrorism
Victim Support
Civil Rights Litigation
Anti-Prejudice Training
Interfaith Dialogue
Holocaust Education
Supporting Middle East Peace[48]

One of the tasks that the Anti-Defamation League has undertaken is the tracking of incidents of antisemitism on an annual basis through its *Audit of Anti-Semitic Incidents*. This publication has become an important barometer of the antisemitic climate in the United States, while at another level it has become an annual report card on the country's civility and humaneness. In the *1994 Annual Report,* p. 11, a graph is published which tracks the incidents both of "Vandalisms" and "Harassments, Threats and Assaults" from 1980 through 1994. Unfortunately, the combined incidents of "Vandalisms" and "Harassments, Threats and Assaults" in 1994 was the highest total in the sixteen-year history of keeping such statistical data. There were 869 "Vandalisms" and 1,197 "Harassments, Threats and Assaults," for a total of 2,066 incidents. This is to be contrasted with the lowest year on record, 1980, when there were 377 "Vandalisms" and 112 "Harassments, Threats and Assaults," for a total of 489 incidents.

It would be helpful to chart the graph found in the *1994 Annual Report* of the ADL (p. 11):

Year1	Vandalisms	Harassments, Threats and Assaults	Total
1980	377	112	489
1981	974	350	1,324
1982	829	593	1,422
1983	670	350	1,020
1984	715	363	1,078
1985	638	306	944
1986	594	312	906
1987	694	324	1,018
1988	823	458	1,281
1989	845	587	1,432
1990	927	758	1,685
1991	929	950	1,879
1992	856	874	1,730
1993	788	1,079	1,867
1994	869	1,197	2,066

Just viewing these numbers is frightening. Obviously, incident reporting in the 1980 survey was in its infancy and only a part of the data was recovered. 1981 showed a huge jump in the numbers, with 1982 being slightly larger. Then, with a slight aberration in 1984, years 1983 through 1986 indicate a decrease in incidents. Beginning with 1987, there is a consistent increase each year, with the exception of 1992, with the record highest number of incidents recorded in 1994. If indeed this annual *Audit of Anti-Semitic Incidents* is a measure of the nation's civility, of our humaneness, then our report card is abysmally weak.

It is obvious that this audit is not a condemnation of everyone in the country, nor is it an accusation that all persons are guilty of specific anti-semitic incidents. It should be a wake-up call to Christians, however, for if we as Christians were doing all that we could and should in the area of Jewish and Christian relations, our report card would look much better. The data uncovered by the annual *Audit of Anti-Semitic Incidents* is *not* a Jewish problem; it is primarily a Christian problem with which Jews have to contend.

CONCLUSION

Judaism has had to undergo many adjustments since the Jews first settled in the Colonies; their adaptation has been an issue primarily in the nineteenth and twentieth centuries. In recent years the rate of change has, if anything, been intensified. Certainly, one of the issues that Jews have to confront is that of acceptance itself. As long as you are the outsider, you experience your otherness as a force that brings you and your fellow outcasts together and keeps you focused. Dealing with acceptance is another issue totally, because when that external force pulls you outward rather than repelling you inward you suddenly realize that in the warp of assimilation you are losing your identity.[49] Feingold stated:

> For Jews, historically conditioned to apartness, this pressure toward ingathering presents both a prospect and a problem. They know all too well what they must do to survive in a hostile environment but hardly anything at all about how to cope with a benevolent one which seeks to absorb them.[50]

There is an imperative in all of this for Christians. Whatever problems Jews may experience with regard to issues of assimilation, we must set our sights to make certain that no issue confronted by Jews derives from Christian-based antisemitism. We need to remember that our antisemitism can be blatant or latent; it can be guilty of flagrant acts or hide (consciously or not) behind acts of "polite" antisemitism. We need through education and a more adequate understanding of Judaism to become individuals who monitor and seek to eliminate any manifestation of antisemitism encountered.

Suggested Questions

1. Let us attempt to pursue the road not taken. Let us assume that President Lincoln did not rescind General Order Number 11 issued by General Ulysses S. Grant on December 17, 1862. Had that order been implemented, what would have been the likely impact both upon the Jews in particular and upon Jewish-Christian relations in general?

2. In 1825 there were approximately 5,000 to 6,000 Jews living in the United States. That figure changed radically beginning in the 1840s, so that by 1860 there were 150,000 Jews living in the United States. These are significant demographic changes, but why should those demographic changes be accompanied by the eruption of active antisemitism in the United States?

3. Discuss the case of Leo Frank in Atlanta, who was accused and convicted of murdering Mary Phagan on April 27, 1913. What lessons should the Christian community derive from this horrendous miscarriage of justice?

4. Study the case of Father Charles E. Coughlin, priest at the Shrine of the Little Flower in Royal Oak, Michigan.What lessons should the church, Catholic or Protestant, derive from the activities of Father Coughlin? How can Christians assure that such demagoguery will not infest their ranks?

5. How can Christians and Jews work together to help the Christian community to recognize that theological antisemitism is a Christian rather than a Jewish problem?

VI. Recent Church Statements on the Relationship of Christianity to Judaism

INTRODUCTION: RESPONSES TO THE SHOAH

Since the conclusion of World War II and the full disclosure of what happened to the Jews during the Shoah (Holocaust), various Christian bodies have grappled with the role of Christians and Christianity during this horrendous period. As a result, some denominations have formulated statements addressing the relationship of Christians and Jews, statements that ultimately are responses to the Shoah. To understand better Christian reactions, we analyze and summarize several of them. Those ecclesiastical bodies used in the analysis are:

1. The Disciples of Christ
2. The Episcopal Church
3. The Evangelical Lutheran Church in America
4. The Roman Catholic Church
5. The United Church of Christ
6. The World Council of Churches (admittedly an umbrella organization rather than a denominational body but does function on occasion essentially as a denominational unit)
7. The Presbyterian Church (U.S.A.)

From the analysis, several general impressions initiate our discussion:

1. The statements endorsed by the various ecclesiastical bodies are not monolithic. It appears that *the greater the hierarchical, that is,*

authoritarian, structure, the more likely it is that the statement will deal with the difficult issues of the Jewish-Christian relationship. For example, pronouncements derived from the Roman Catholic Church, as *Nostra Aetate, 4* (1965) from Vatican II or the Statement on Catholic-Jewish Relations by the U.S. National Conference of Catholic Bishops in November 1975,[1] are likely to have a more significant impact because of ecclesiastical polity than a resolution passed by the Southern Baptist Convention in 1972 (following a similar action by the North Carolina State Baptist Convention in 1971). Southern Baptist Convention polity does not mandate any action of the annual convention upon the local, autonomous church. Verification of this is rendered by the fact that shortly after this, in July 1980, the Rev. Bailey Smith, pastor of the First Southern Baptist Church in Del City, Oklahoma, and also the popularly elected President (1980–82) of the Southern Baptist Convention, made the infamous statement:

> God Almighty does not hear the prayer of a Jew. For how in the world can God hear the prayer of a man who says that Jesus Christ is not the true Messiah? It is blasphemous.[2]

Granted many Southern Baptists disagreed violently with Smith's statement, but the fact that the sitting president of the Southern Baptist Convention could make such a statement indicates how little impact earlier convention actions have on later thought and action.

2. Given the assumption that there is strong, sensitive leadership in the structure, *the less democratic the denominational structure, the greater the potential for a really, strong statement emerging.* It is acknowledged, however, that this phenomenon can be a two-edged sword. On the one hand, the democratic process has a way of "watering down" the statement until it reaches the lowest common denominator. This makes the statement potentially ineffectual. On the other hand, strong, sensitive leadership can put aside or preclude certain popular ideas that, if included, might render the statement powerless or, even worse, a negative influence.[3]

3. *The growth of the religious right, so akin to and often joined with the political right, makes difficult a strong statement on Jewish-Christian relations because of presuppositions that precondition the outcome.* As an example, "The Willowbank Declaration on the

Christian Gospel and the Jewish People" "was developed and adopted on April 29, 1989 by all those present at the Consultation on the Gospel and the Jewish People after several days of intensive consultation, undergirded by prayer."[4] In the Preamble to the Declaration, it is stated:

> In making this Declaration we stand in a long and revered Christian tradition, which in 1980 was highlighted by a landmark statement, "Christian Witness to the Jewish People," issued by the Lausanne Committee for World Evangelization. Now, at this Willowbank Consultation on the Gospel and the Jewish People, sponsored by the World Evangelical Fellowship and supported by the Lausanne Committee, we reaffirm our commitment to the Jewish people and our desire to share the Gospel with them.[5]

Just a few quotations from the Declaration indicate the intention behind the evangelization:

> We deny that those without faith in Christ know the full reality of God's love and of the gift that he gave (Article 1.1).

> We deny that it is right to look for a Messiah who has not yet appeared in world history (Article 1.2).

> We deny that any person can enjoy God's favor apart from the mediation of Jesus Christ, the sin-bearer (Article l.5).

> We deny that the historical status of the Jews as God's people brings salvation to any Jew who does not accept the claims of Jesus Christ (Article 3.15).

> We deny that dialogue that explains the Christian faith without seeking to persuade the dialogue partners of its truth and claims is a sufficient expression of Christian love (Article 5.25).

Much more could be noted here, but suffice it to say that such evangelical fervor harkens back to the medieval disputation. The ingredients to encourage and promulgate antisemitism for future generations are evident. Let us acknowledge, however, that antisemitism was probably the least desired outcome by those developing and adopting the Willowbank Declaration.

4. *The reality of the Shoah has forced a deep introspective self-analysis on the part of the church.* This manifests itself in at least three distinct ways:

    A. *The first aspect of self-analysis has to do with the general relationship of Jews and Christians as people.* Any objective analysis recognizes the horrid behavior of the church through the centuries, the absolutely horrendous depersonalization of the Jew by the Christian. The Shoah may be the worst example of how this anti-Judaism manifested itself, but many horrible examples led up to this ultimate manifestation. The litany of horror includes the forced baptisms of Jews, the expulsions of Jews from numerous lands (beginning with England in 1290 C.E.), the imposition of the inquisitional torture machine to those *conversos,* or *marranos,* who continued as "secret Jews," and the establishment of the ghettos (beginning with Venice in 1516 C.E.). Behind such activities, and these are but a few that might be chronicled, we must acknowledge the individual, not just the collective body. This focus upon the individual is what our Biblical writers in the Torah have done with the trek of Father Abraham.[6]

    B. *The second aspect of self-analysis is closely tied to the first, namely the re-examination of scripture itself* to see whether in fact the New Testament, and for that matter certain readings from the *Tanak,* actually undergird and encourage the anti-Judaism that has so plagued the history of the church. More will be said about this later.

    C. *The third aspect involves the development of the literary genre of denominational statements regarding the relationship of Jews and Christians.* To that we now turn our attention.

SOURCES AND COLLECTIONS OF DENOMINATIONAL STATEMENTS

There are numerous affirmations that are shared by the various statements. Obviously, some affirmations are more clearly and/or forcefully stated than others, although one must acknowledge the bias of the evaluator when reaching such conclusions. I wrote to denominational officers requesting a copy of any officially approved statement which focused on Jewish and Christian relations. It was indicated that the material was being gathered for a study of Jewish and Christian relations, that the statements would form the discussion basis for a religion majors seminar where the statements would exemplify a positive approach to Jewish-Christian relations, and that my intention was to bring some of these statements to published form. Assurance was given, however, that specific permission would be sought prior to any publication. In response to my written requests, I received no response from some, indication that no official policy statement has been adopted by others (as the Friends United Meeting, The American Baptist Churches USA, the Southern Baptist Convention, and the Church of the Brethren), and concrete materials/statements were received from seven bodies (counting the National Council of Churches/World Council of Churches as such a body). Workable responses were received from the following bodies, with materials addressing each of the denominational statements as follows:

1. *The Disciples of Christ:*
   Clark M. Williamson, ed., *The Church and the Jewish People.* St. Louis: Christian Board of Publication, 1994.
2. *The Episcopal Church:*
   Guidelines for Christian-Jewish Relations, adopted by General Convention, 1988.
3. *The Evangelical Lutheran Church in America:*
   Harold H. Ditmanson, ed., *Stepping-Stones to Further Jewish-Lutheran Relationships.* Minneapolis: Augsburg, 1990. Also, crucially important for the ELCA is a statement adopted on April 18, 1994 entitled "The Declaration of the Evangelical Lutheran Church in America to the Jewish Community." NOTE: In a letter dated December 5, 1994, Daniel F. Martensen, Associate Director of the Division for Ecumenical Affairs, stated: "The 1974 statement by the American Lutheran Church is considered by the ELCA (which formed in 1988) to be operative" (see Ditmanson, pp. 67–74).
4. *The Presbyterian Church, U.S.A.:*
   A Theological Understanding of the Relationship Between Christians and Jews, passed by the 199th General Assembly (June, 1987) of the Presbyterian Church, U.S.A., meeting in Biloxi, Mississippi.
5. *The Roman Catholic Church:*
   "Nostra Aetate," 4 (October 1965), part of the Declaration on the Rela-

tionship of the Church to Non-Christian Religions from Vatican II (see Walter M. Abbott, S.J., ed., *The Documents of Vatican II.* New York: Corpus Books, 1966, esp. pp. 663–67). See also Helga Croner, compiler, *Stepping Stones to Further Jewish-Christian Relations.* New York: Stimulus Books, 1977, pp. 1–2; "Guidelines for Catholic-Jewish Relations," (1985 Revision of earlier approved and published 1967 statement), Secretariat for Catholic-Jewish Relations, The Bishops' Committee for Ecumenical and Interreligious Affairs (BCEIA) of the National Conference of Catholic Bishops (NCCB); "God's Mercy Endures Forever: Guidelines on the Presentation of Jews and Judaism in Catholic Preaching," (September, 1988), Bishops' Committee on the Liturgy, NCCB; "Criteria for the Evaluation of Dramatizations of the Passion," (1988), Secretariat for Catholic-Jewish Relations, BCEIA, NCCB; and "Notes on the Correct Way to Present the Jews and Judaism in Preaching and Catechesis of the Roman Catholic Church" (USCC Publication No. 970), June 24, 1985.

6. *The United Church of Christ:*
   "Social Policy Actions: General Synod 16, United Church of Christ," June 25–July 2, 1987, published by Office for Church in Society, United Church of Christ, New York, 1987, p. 37. See also Jewish-Christian Theological Panel, "A Message to the Churches," *New Conversations,* May 1990, pp. 5–8 (report of the Theological Panel on Jewish-Christian Relations appointed in 1987 to study and interpret the resolution of General Synod 16 on "The Relationship Between the United Church of Christ and the Jewish Community").

7. *The World Council of Churches:*
   "The Churches and the Jewish People: Towards a New Understanding," adopted at Sigtuna, Sweden by the Consultation on the Church and the Jewish People, World Council of Churches, November 4, 1988. For helpful explication, see Jay T. Rock, "Christian Understandings of Covenant and the Jewish People," *New Conversations,* Summer, 1990, pp. 44–49 (Jay Rock is Director of the Office on Christian/Jewish Relations for the National Council of Churches of Christ, and this paper was delivered before Congregation Oheb Shalom, South Orange, New Jersey, on May 5, 1990).

Several notable books have drawn together the various statements by the diverse Christian bodies. These include minimally the following (listed by date of publication rather than alpha by author or title):

Walter M. Abbott, S.J., ed., *The Documents of Vatican II.* New York: Corpus Books, 1966.

Helga Croner, compiler, *Stepping Stones to Further Jewish-Christian Relations.* New York: Stimulus Books, 1977 (Roman Catholic, beginning with *Nostra Aetate,* October 1965; Protestant documents both by the World Council of Churches and those adopted by various church groups; and a joint Protestant-Catholic statement developed in New York, 1973).

Helga Croner, compiler, *More Stepping Stones to Further Jewish-Christian Relations.* New York: Stimulus Books, 1985 (documents from 1975 to 1983, including Roman Catholic and Protestant documents—World Council of Churches, United States, and European church groups).

N.A., *The Theology of the Churches and the Jewish People: Statements by the World Council of Churches and Its Member Churches,* commentary by Allan Brockway, Paul van Buren, Rolf Rendtorff, and Simon Schoon. Geneva: WCC Publications, 1988.

Eugene J. Fisher and Leon Klenicki, *In Our Time: The Flowering of Jewish-Catholic Dialogue.* New York: A Stimulus Book, 1990.

Harold H. Ditmanson, ed., *Stepping-Stones to Further Jewish-Lutheran Relationships.* Minneapolis: Augsburg Press, 1990.

Clark M. Williamson, ed., *The Church and the Jewish People.* St. Louis: Christian Board of Publication, 1994.

Within the purview of these publications, apparently all of the denominational statements have been published with the exception of the following:

1. *The Presbyterian Church, U.S.A.,* statement entitled "A Theological Understanding of the Relationship Between Christians and Jews" was adopted by the 199th General Assembly of the Presbyterian Church, U.S.A., meeting in Biloxi, Mississippi, in June, 1987. It has been published with the 199th General Assembly proceedings, but it has not been disseminated for broader use.

2. *The United Church of Christ* resolution on "The Relationship Between the United Church of Christ and the Jewish Community," which was adopted by General Synod 16, convened June 25–July 2,

1987. It has been published in the General Synod l6 proceedings but not more broadly.

3. *The Episcopal Church* adopted "Guidelines for Christian-Jewish Relations" at its General Convention in 1988. It has been published in brochure form, but it has not been made available in a general publication form.

4. The Church Council of *The Evangelical Lutheran Church in America* adopted "The Declaration of the Evangelical Lutheran Church in America to the Jewish Community" on April 18, 1994. This is the only material on which official church action has been taken according to a letter dated December 5, 1994 from Daniel F. Martensen. This resolution has not been published and is therefore not widely available.

POINTS OF COMMONALITY ADDRESSED BY THE VARIOUS DENOMINATIONAL STATEMENTS

Our attention will now focus upon those affirmations made in the various denominational statements that are more or less shared by all. Since it is advantageous to have a common base for comparison, the seven theological affirmations that comprise the Presbyterian Church (U.S.A.) statement will be used as the point of comparison/contrast. This statement was adopted in 1987 at the 199th General Assembly and is entitled "A Theological Understanding of the Relationship Between Christians and Jews." Several reasons undergird my choice of the Presbyterian statement as the base for comparison. One reason is totally subjective, namely that the seven affirmations enunciated in the statement address more of the issues pivotal in this discussion. Succinctly stated, the seven affirmations deal with the following:

1. The one God.
2. Christian identity interwoven with Judaism.
3. The mystery of God's election of both Jews and Christians.
4. Jews continue in covenant relationship with God.
5. Christians must end "the teaching of contempt."
6. The issue of Israel's "land" and Christian theology.
7. Jews and Christians work together for the peaceable kingdom.

Secondly, the Presbyterian statement is especially well organized. The affirmations are clearly stated, and then exposition follows that includes both historical background and theological clarifications. Finally, I have personally found that the affirmations as stated in the Presbyterian statement invite individual reflection and communal discussion. This, after all, should be the primary intent, for neither individual nor communal self-flagellation profit the cause at all, but individual reflection and communal discussion may indeed move us toward the goal of productive Jewish and Christian relationships.

First Affirmation

We affirm that the living God whom Christians worship is the same God who is worshiped and served by Jews. We bear witness that the God revealed in Jesus, a Jew, to be the Triune Lord of all, is the same one disclosed in the life and worship of Israel.[7]

Each of the statements addresses this first affirmation, perhaps only because equally in Judaism and Christianity an affirmation of God is assumed. While expressing common understanding at one level, greater attention to the nuance of the statement raises the inevitable problems of definition. Christians and Jews talk meaningfully of the "One God," but Christian identification of Jesus with that "One God," that is, the entire focus of incarnational theology, wedges a practically insurmountable obstacle to Jewish and Christian agreement on this pivotal first affirmation. Our understanding of God, while remarkably alike, is nonetheless dissimilar at pivotal points.

The question of how to conceptualize the reality that is God has troubled Christians from an early period. By the fourth century, Arius, a charismatic presbyter of Alexandria, gathered a large following because of his view of Christology (understanding of the person and nature of Jesus as the Christ). He did not deny the divinity of Jesus, but he argued that Jesus was not by nature divine. The debate around the issue became so encompassing that the Council of Nicaea was convened in 325, leading ultimately to the formulation of the Nicene Creed. This was an early attempt to answer the trinitarian question, although it was far from the final word. The affirmations of the Western Church and the Eastern Church were expressed differently, with the result that considerable confusion existed among the laity, and clearly the clergy were far from unanimous in their views.

Relative to the issue of Jewish-Christian relations and the first Presbyterian affirmation, however, this may be asserted boldly: however the affirmation of God is stated and whether it is in Eastern or

Western Christianity, Christianity is a monotheistic faith. Whenever Christians step over that monotheistic line so as to portray our triune faith as something more than monotheistic, at that point we are blasphemous. With Judaism we affirm that God is one![8]

Second Affirmation

We affirm that the church, elected in Jesus Christ, has been engrafted into the people of God established by the covenant with Abraham, Isaac, and Jacob. Therefore, Christians have not replaced Jews.[9]

Whereas each of our investigated statements asserts a parallel to the Presbyterian statement, semantic nuance again raises its divisive head. Jay Rock, in an article entitled "Christian Understanding of the Jewish People,"[10] has helpfully captured something of how this nuanced sense might be fleshed out, suggesting three approaches to the question, "How is Christian covenant related to Jewish covenant?"[11]

The first approach "is the idea that God has made a *number of covenants* with those whom God chose....None of these covenants precludes or replaces another, they are not viewed as a series."[12] As suggested by Rock, none of the "official" church documents takes this position, and, even though some Christians within individual ecclesiastical bodies may have been comfortable with this concept, an exclusivistic form of christological affirmation would preclude such an approach to covenant, and this latter view seems to be more the majority view in most denominational bodies.

A second approach is the view that *"God has made a single covenant."* Rock states:

> This covenant was made first with the Jewish people, and was then expanded to include Gentiles. The Jewish and Christian covenants are continuous.[13]

As Rock notes, the Presbyterian statement takes this position by stating that the Christian community as been "elected in Jesus Christ, has been *engrafted into* the people of God established by the covenant with Abraham, Isaac, and Jacob." In like fashion, the Episcopal statement states in more creedal fashion that "Christians believe themselves to have entered [God's covenant with God's people] by grace through Jesus Christ...[through] the God who first made covenant with the people Israel."[14] Rock also notes that the Roman Catholic "Nostra Aetate" (plus the *Guidelines* and *Notes*) correlates with this approach, although Rock helpfully refers to this as "a non-supplanting theology of fulfillment." He states: "Christ fulfills God's redemptive plan, but Christianity does not invalidate or supplant Judaism: in the end, the Church itself, with the Jewish people and all other peoples, will be totally transformed."[15]

"A third approach to how Christian and Jewish covenants are related is that *they are in fact dual covenants.*"[16] This approach affirms two distinct covenants for Jews and Christians, specific to and valid only for the particular body. As Rock notes, one may either see the two covenants as "discontinuous" with each other or one may assert a "continuity" between the two. As he indicates, the World Council of Churches statement, "The Churches and the Jewish People," emphasizes that Jesus is the one who both binds Jews and Christians together but who also divides the two bodies.

Clearly, it is one thing to affirm that the various statements endorse the idea of a continuing covenant existent between God and the Jews. It is a more difficult issue when seeking to define what this means for the relationship of Jews and Christians.

Third Affirmation
We affirm that both the church and the Jewish people are elected by God for witness to the world and that the relationship of the church to contemporary Jews is based on that gracious and irrevocable election of both.[17]

The discussion associated with the second affirmation above, namely the nuance of covenantal perception, is equally applicable to this third affirmation. The witness of the two communities is to the One affirmed in the *Shema'*. Interestingly, none of the statements directly addresses the "mission" role of the Jews. The one that comes the nearest to this is the statement of The World Council of Churches when it refers to "two communities of faith, each called into existence by God, each holding to its respective gifts from God, and each accountable to God."

Given the historical relationship between these two communities, the question on just how Christians and Jews are each called by God as his witnesses to the world still needs more study. There must be substantive dialogue, and as we celebrate our differences, each must strive to understand the perspective of the other.

Fourth Affirmation

We affirm that the reign of God is attested both by the continuing existence of the Jewish people and by the church's proclamation of the gospel of Jesus Christ. Hence, when speaking with Jews about matters of faith, we must always acknowledge that Jews are already in a covenantal relationship with God.[18]

The explicit affirmation in the Presbyterian statement that "we must always acknowledge that Jews are already in a covenantal relationship with God" is one that the other statements do not express as well. The others will affirm the continuing covenant relationship, but the Presbyterian statement more clearly leads toward dialogue and away from conversionist activity. It seems that one of the hardest parts of the tradition for many Christians to jettison is the belief that Jews are ultimately objects of conversion. I think it clear, however, that so long as we view Jews in this manner, we are precariously close to and inevitably moving toward anti-Judaism. In Buberian terms, we are treating the Jews as objects, an I-It relationship, rather than as meaningful beings equal to ourselves, the I-Thou relationship.

Fifth Affirmation

We acknowledge in repentance the church's long and deep complicity in the proliferation of anti-Jewish attitudes and actions through its "teaching of contempt" for the Jews. Such teaching we now repudiate, together with the acts and attitudes which it generates.[19]

Fortunately, each of the statements investigated addressed the "teaching of contempt" issue. While exact wording is not always used, there is a clear acknowledgment of ecclesiastical culpability in that the church's teachings sparked various manifestations of antisemitism. There is a positive impact on Jewish-Christian relations deriving from the fact that all of the statements address this issue, even if some, such as the Roman Catholic "Nostra Aetate," do not reach far enough to be totally satisfactory. It should be noted, however, that later Roman Catholic documents do develop the statement further.

Sixth Affirmation

We affirm the continuity of God's promise of land along with the obligations of that promise to the people Israel.[20]

The sixth affirmation in the Presbyterian statement is one of the most difficult for Christian communions to address. There are so many issues involved. There is the question of the promise to Abraham/Israel and how one translates that promise today. There is the issue of peace and justice, and the inequities, more than ample, on both sides as the Jewish state was/is being established. To what extent, however, does the concept of covenant necessarily correlate with land possession? To what extent is the continuance of the land a test of God's faithfulness? If we affirm with Paul (Rom 11:29) that "the gifts and the call of God are irrevocable..." what special ingredient does this place in the equation? It is practically impossible for Christian denominational groups to develop consensus statements regarding the land. Nonetheless, this is an area which must be addressed. It is more important that a meaningful conversation take place than that consensus be reached.

Seventh Affirmation
We affirm that Jews and Christians are partners in waiting. Christians see in Christ the redemption not yet fully visible in the world, and Jews await the messianic redemption. Christians and Jews together await the final manifestation of God's promise of the peaceable kingdom.[21]

It is interesting that, in surveying the seven affirmations of the Presbyterian statement, it is with this seventh affirmation that the least parallel is found with the other statements. Maybe this should be expected, because the idea that Jews and Christians are "partners in waiting," the understanding that both communities of faith have a self-validating eschatological expectation, and the conviction that both shall share in the "final manifestation of God's promise of the peaceable kingdom" is to acknowledge absolute parity between Judaism and Christianity. It is to affirm that these two faith structures are equally valid paths to the center, and this is a step that clearly many Christians find difficult. Such parity may seem to some to result in the rejection of Christian affirmation. The few parallels that could be found in the six statements being compared with the Presbyterian statement attest to the problems associated with this seventh affirmation on the part of most Christian bodies.

CONCLUSION

The seven affirmations of the Presbyterian statement have been reviewed by way of a comparison/contrast perspective with statements developed by The Church of Christ, The Episcopal Church, The Evangelical Lutheran Church in America, The Roman Catholic Church, The United Church of Christ, and The World Council of Churches. What is not included in these statements that should/must be included if positive and constructive Jewish and Christian relations are to be experienced?

The issue that none of these statements addresses is the nature and authority of scripture, including questions of the origin and transmission of scripture. This issue is studiously avoided because Christian bodies have difficulty dealing with the nature of scripture, and yet the Biblical text undergirds every affirmation investigated. In the 1974 statement developed by the American Lutheran Church, the following is asserted:

> Lutherans and Jews will differ, sometimes drastically, about questions of biblical interpretation, especially in regard to Christian claims about the fulfillment of the Old Testament. Such disagreements should not be the cause of either anger or despair, but rather should be seen as the doorway to a dialogue in which there can occur the discovery of both the real sources of the divergences and their appropriate degree of importance.[22]

In like fashion, in the 1975 "Guidelines and Suggestions for Implementing the Conciliar Declaration Nostra Aetate (n. 4)," the following is stated:

> An effort will be made to acquire a better understanding of whatever in the Old Testament retains its own perpetual value...since that has not been cancelled by the later interpretation of the New Testament. Rather, the New Testament brings out the full meaning of the Old, while both Old and New illumine and explain each other....[23]

Both of these quotations raise justified difficulties for a Jewish individual—"Christian claims about the *fulfillment* of the Old Testament," and "whatever in the Old Testament retains its own perpetual value...." Let it be acknowledged that authority is vested in documents by the community of faith, and thus Christians need to look quite seriously at the nature of that authority that has been vested in the Biblical text. Does this view deny the importance of the text or denigrate that text? Of course not! Nonetheless, it should be recognized that many views that undergird antisemitism derive out of a humanly constructed text that has been melded into a canonical body by human agents. This allows acknowledgment that the ancient Israelites whose text so denigrated the Canaanites operated under the aegis of human prejudice rather than divine imprimatur. In like fashion, when individuals expressed ideas suggesting an anti-Jewish bias in materials that ultimately became the New Testament, they too wrote under the aegis of human prejudice. This is not a call for rejection of the canon but for a reevaluation and deeper understanding of the text. It is the writer's assumption, however, that negative Jewish-Christian relations will exist as long as Christians in churches hear without explication statements akin to the following:

> "Then the people as a whole answered, 'His blood be on us and on our children!'" (Mt 25:25 NRSV).

> "I am the way, and the truth, and the life. *No one comes to the Father except through me"* (Jn 14:6 NRSV).

> In the context of Jesus' healing on the sabbath, it is stated that *"the Jews* started persecuting Jesus...." (John 5:16 NRSV) and "for this reasons *the Jews* were seeking all the more to kill him, because he was not only breaking the sabbath, but was also calling God his own Father, thereby making himself equal to God" (Jn 5:18 NRSV).

> "Do not think that I have come to abolish the law or the prophets; I have come not to abolish but to *fulfill"* (Mt 5:17 NRSV).

Let us acknowledge that already *we vest absolute authority to the text only selectively.* Who in this modern age accepts the cosmological view expressed in the Tanak that we inhabit a three-tiered cosmos (such as described in Genesis, Job, and certain Psalms)? This is really not an issue for modern readers; the ancient mythology undergirding the text is acknowledged and the *significance* of the text is sought. Recognizing that so much of the New Testament is a type of midrashic development upon the Tanak, the interpreter must search for the *significance* of what the text conveys, while recognizing that contemporary significance is dependent upon maintaining the integrity of the text upon which the midrashic commentary is developed.

Until Christians are prepared to deal seriously with the nature and authority of scripture, to acknowledge that the text may be used to encourage and undergird antisemitism, to jettison consciously any hints of exclusivistic, supersessionist, or triumphalistic theological views, the specter of antisemitism will continue to haunt us. Whether antisemitism continues is up to us! Whether the Shoah will have a positive impact upon Jewish-Christian relations is uniquely our opportunity and our responsibility.

Suggested Questions

1. It is irresponsible to suggest that the church is responsible for the Shoah. On the other hand, how would you express the culpability of the church as regards the Shoah?

2. Why does the "religious right" frequently stand as an obstacle to Jewish and Christian relations? Try to be specific about those elements in their programs and beliefs that feed antisemitism.

3. Why is it necessary for Christians to address the traditional understandings of scripture if the issue of antisemitism is to be evaluated honestly and openly?

4. Is it possible for Jews and Christians to view one another as equally elected by God without disparaging one another at all? Which community, Judaism or Christianity, has to make the greatest move to accept such a thought possibility?

5. If you were responsible for writing a statement about Jewish and Christian relations for endorsement by your particular Christian denomination, what affirmation not included in the statement adopted by the Presbyterian Church, U.S.A., would you definitely want included?

VII. Conclusion: Improving Jewish-Christian Relations

INTRODUCTION

What Price Prejudice? This book has emphasized both the bases for and manifestations of antisemitism since Christianity's emergence. Unfortunately, theological antisemitism emerged early in the life of the church. Although it is possible that a preconceived and pervasive antisemitism influenced the formulation of the New Testament materials, that is an unlikely scenario, since most of the New Testament was written by Jews. It is more probable that the New Testament once formulated was victimized by an emerging antisemitic Christianity, encouraging the development of antisemitism in the church. What is unfortunately clear is that antisemitism did exist from an early period. Furthermore, the New Testament writings were generally interpreted to encourage antisemitism rather than serving to abate the vitriolic venom of antisemitism's prejudice and hatred. Thus, we do not debate the fact of the disease; rather, we concern ourselves with the precipitating causes and with understanding what should be labeled an antisemitic act.

THE PRICE OF PREJUDICE

Prejudice debases the actor more than the vilified recipient. Prejudice is the formulation of adverse, preconceived ideas about an individual, an idea, or a movement apart from a reasoned investigation of the facts.[1] Usually one bound by prejudice cannot rationally approach the "facts" surrounding the prejudice since a "blind spot" prevents open investigation. "So he *is* a hard worker; he is only trying to gather sufficient wealth to control the business!" Whatever positive is expressed is immediately refuted by some preconceived negative judgment.

Melvin M. Tumin, in a book entitled *Antisemitism in the United States,* has addressed clearly and concisely the major ingredients of antisemitism as well as the ludicrous nature of stereotypes. Tumin's definition of antisemitism was quoted in Chapter I but is deserving of repetition at this point:

> ...this belief in the identifiability of Jews need not concern us. But, if and when this belief is accompanied by some kind of fear of Jews—a feeling that they ought to be kept at a distance, and a desire to deny them certain rights enjoyed by others—then we have the phenomenon called anti-Semitism.[2]

With this statement Tumin has concisely identified the nature of incipient antisemitism. In equally clear fashion, he has listed in four points the major ingredients of antisemitism:

1. A belief that Jews are different, that they can be identified and distinguished from non-Jews;
2. Some kind of fear of them;
3. A desire to keep them at a distance;
4. A willingness to discriminate against them—in schools, jobs, housing, social clubs, resorts, and other such places.[3]

Since Judaism is a social and religious designation and not a racial category, and since persons of all races can and do embrace Judaism, it is impossible to identify a Jew by physical characteristics. In a novel rare in its humorous moments, Bernard Malamud graphically portrayed one such moment in *The Fixer* when Yakov Bok was being interviewed once again by the Prosecuting Attorney, Grubeshov. Grubeshov stated:

> A Jew is a Jew, and that's all there is to it. Their history and character are unchangeable. Their nature is constant. This has been proved in scientific studies....[4]

The conversation continues, and to make his point Grubeshov pulled out a sketch book portraying differing types of "Jewish noses":

"Here, for instance, is yours." Grubeshov pointed to a thin high-bridged nose with slender nostrils.
"And this is yours," Yakov said hoarsely, pointing to a short, fleshy, broad-winged nose.[5]

Even in his dehumanized situation, Yakov was able to make a valid point—those characteristics usually associated with a specific population group may also be found in persons not so identified. No external characteristics serve to demark Jews from others *unless* they assume certain characteristics, as when the Orthodox Jew, in obedience to the Torah (Lv 19:27), does not shave his beard and permits the earlocks *(pe'ot)* to grow. Such characteristics are secondary, thus changeable, rather than primary, or unchangeable. What distinguishes the Jew and the Christian is the individual's faith affirmation, not physical characteristics.

Tumin also mentioned the "fear of the Jews" that accompanies antisemitism. This fear may include such concerns as religion (defilement of the Host; Christ killers; etc.); politics (an international Jewish conspiracy to rule the world); economics (the Jews are seeking to control all international banking and publications); and/or social issues (fear of living with or participating alongside a Jew in social clubs, etc.). It is this fear, however unseemly based, that encourages and sometimes precipitates antisemitism. As a result, one seeks to separate Jews from Christians, to punish Jews for perceived historical wrongs, or to deny them certain rights and privileges enjoyed by non-Jewish members of the community.

Tumin's point four is the crucial issue, the willingness to move beyond prejudice to discrimination. It is this overt action that creates the divisions within a society, engenders distrust among societal participants, and prevents a society from developing culturally because of the inability of citizens to work together toward meaningful, commonly held goals.

Finally, Tumin has brought together some of the more commonly held but antithetical stereotypes associated with the Jews:

Jews are too clannish—but they are always trying to mix in;
Jews are international financiers—and also international communists;
Jews are too materialistic—and also too spiritual and moral;

> Jews are too concerned with business—and at the same time too
> bookish and intellectual;
> Jews are aggressive and pushy—but they are also too withdrawn,
> too ascetic, too introverted.[6]

The irrational nature of these antithetical claims hardly needs comment. No individual could affirm such contradictory claims unless his or her reason were fettered by prejudice.

Thus, when we ask *What Price Prejudice?* relative to anti-semitism, one answer is the fullness of our own humanity. When we function without fully engaging our rational capacity, we do not operate at the highest level of our humanity. From a human perspective, dogs may react irrationally to cats, and we may suggest behavioral explanations in terms of conditioning experienced by the species over time. For one person to react to another fellow human in dog-cat fashion, however, is simply to affirm that rational capability has been sublimated so that conditioning, rather than reason, governs activity.

For the church, there is also a response to the *What Price Prejudice?* question. The church, as the body of believers affirming the reality of God's act in the resurrection of Jesus of Nazareth as the Christ of faith, is built upon the foundation of love. The church affirmed a particular type of love, *agape,* to be the basis for the church. *Agape* is the type of love that goes out to the other without concern for what comes back to the giver. It was this type of love that the church saw symbolized in God's gift of the Christ, and Christians are called to participate in making this *agape* known to the world.

In 1 Corinthians 13, the case is made that for the Christian the manifestation of love *(agape)* takes precedence over all else:

> If I speak in the tongues of mortals and of angels, but do not have love, I am a noisy gong or a clanging cymbal....
>
> Love is patient; love is kind; love is not envious or boastful or arrogant or rude. It does not insist on its own way; it is not irritable or resentful; it does not rejoice in wrongdoing, but rejoices in the truth. It bears all things, believes all things, hopes all things, endures all things.
>
> Love never ends.... And now faith, hope, and love abide, these three; and the greatest of these is love (1 Corinthians 13:1, 4–8a, 13, NRSV).

This is the theoretical posture of the believer within the church; this is the expectation, however exalted, of the one who would call him/herself Christian.

Within the New Testament, there was also an *agape* prescription that folded that mandate into the fabric of one's daily life:

> Beloved, let us love one another, because love is from God; everyone who loves is born of God and knows God. Whoever does not love does not know God, for God is love....
> ...We love because he first loved us. Those who say, "I love God," and hate their brothers or sisters, are liars; for those who do not love a brother or sister whom they have seen, cannot love God whom they have not seen (1 Jn 4:7–8, 19–20, NRSV).

What Price Prejudice? When Christians fail to exemplify love in their relationships with their fellow Jews, Christians, Muslims, or persons making some other or no faith affirmation, when the teaching of the church becomes foundational for antisemitism, then the church has essentially renounced its commission and is no longer worthy to be designated the church!

WHERE TO FROM HERE?

What suggestions are possible for helping churches combat antisemitism in our American communities? Simply put, it is fact that Christianity has been the aggressor in Jewish-Christian relations through the centuries. It is also true that Christianity is the majority faith structure in the United States, while Judaism is a bare minority.[7] If positive steps are to be taken for the improvement of Jewish-Christian relationships, it behooves Christians to take the first steps, to lead the way in expressing a desire for improved relationships. Concretely, what might we do?

First, we should begin with the foundation: *every postulant for the clergy should be introduced to issues relating to Jewish and Christian relations in their course of study in a seminary or divinity school.* Having traveled this route, I know that the course of study is already fairly burdensome, but I also would judge this area of inquiry to be more important than some areas of required study. Every individual who will have the responsibility for leading a Christian congregation should be prepared in at least the following four areas:

1.   One should gain a basic understanding of Judaism so that its faith and practice are understood. Contemporary Jewish worship and how today's Judaism is both similar to and different from first century Judaism should be studied.

2.   The history of antisemitism should be studied, with particular attention to the interaction of Judaism and Christianity since Christianity's beginning.

3.   The Bible should be investigated as a potential agent for endorsing antisemitism. Christians should study the Tanak (the Jewish Bible) as seen through Jewish eyes. Christians must develop a sense of the relationship of Jewish and Christian scriptures. It would be helpful to study some of the traditionally problematic passages (as Isaiah 7:14) in Jewish and Christian relations, seeking to set these passages in an authentic historical context.

4.   The phenomenon of American Judaism should be understood. The local rabbi(s) should be a valued colleague and resource person for the Christian minister. In order for this to be the case, clergy must better understand each other.

While not absolutely necessary, it would be helpful if Christian theological schools had rabbis on their faculties, either in full- or part-time association, to teach some of the above mentioned courses. This would add authenticity to the study, and importantly, it would set the pattern of Jews and Christians working together for mutual understanding.

Second, *a reasonable starting point is an informed mind.* In suggestion one, we focused on the clergy. Here the emphasis is really more upon laypersons. Following this chapter, a selected bibliography is appended that offers suggested readings for areas covered in this book. Crucial to improving Jewish and Christian relations are laypersons who are informed on the issues. As a matter of fact, informed laypersons can be the most effective prod to make certain that clergy deal honestly and forthrightly with the issues surrounding the Jewish-Christian relationship.

Third, *through your minister or perhaps a college or university religion instructor in your community, arrange to form a discussion group focused on Jewish-Christian relations and antisemitism.* The group should select some reading material that all will commit themselves to read. Try to develop an understanding of Judaism as though you espoused that faith, for nothing extinguishes negative reactions to Judaism quite so effectively as being able to stand where the Jew stands. In like fashion, the reading of material focused on antisemitism is not intended to precipitate self-flagellation, for this is not helpful to any of the parties concerned. It is amazingly helpful, however, to have a clearer picture of the sweep of history as seen through Jewish eyes.

In seeking an understanding of Judaism and antisemitism, films are often quite helpful. College and university libraries often have films that may be borrowed, as do local public libraries. Do not overlook the local office of the Anti-Defamation League of B'nai B'rith, for usually some extremely helpful films are available through this agency at little or no cost to the borrower.

Fourth, *initiate a dialogue with a local Jewish group.* Once the Christian component of the study group has spent sufficient time with the materials to have a basic understanding of Judaism and of the issues involved with antisemitism, you are ready to initiate some dialogue with a Jewish group. Your minister may be a helpful intermediary in setting up such a dialogue. This possibility is more likely with a Reform congregation, but oftentimes it can be arranged with a Conservative congregation. Ground rules need to be established, such as the number of meetings to be held, the places for the meetings (they are usually more productive in homes, but may be alternated between the synagogue and the church), the topics to be discussed, and a covenant that the goal on both sides is understanding rather than proselytization. Again, a facilitator who has a rather good understanding of both Judaism and Christianity is extremely helpful.

Fifth, *look for ways to bring your dialogue about relationship into a concrete, practical focus.* For example, you might discuss the comparisons between Hanukkah and Christmas, and to the extent possible engage both groups in the practices of the other. Quite meaningful also is the comparison of Passover and Easter, and many communities have found a shared Seder Meal to be a helpful experience for both Jews and Christians.[8] These Jewish and Christian commemorations have been specifically mentioned because they fall at roughly the same time within the calendar and have both similar and dissimilar motifs, but other festivals observed within either community could also be fruitfully studied.

Sixth, *churches must take a proactive role in addressing anti-semitism.* There is a pressing need for churches as collective bodies and individual Christians to recognize the historic role of the church in anti-semitism, the unique association of the church with theological anti-semitism, and the specific part that churches and individual Christians can play in addressing this horrible blight within contemporary western culture. We need desperately to become acquainted with the phenomenon from a historical perspective, to understand the role that the New Testament writings have played in encouraging antisemitic acts and thoughts, and to wrestle with the contemporary manifestations of anti-semitism within our society. The Anti-Defamation League of B'nai B'rith can be an important ally in supplying concrete information to acquaint us with the contemporary phenomenon and to suggest ways to address the issue. As would be clear from Chapter 1, the church must carefully and constantly evaluate its understanding of the Bible. The intensified emphasis within some Christian denominations on a radical conservatism, if not fundamentalism, in Biblical interpretation, leaves little avenue open for the improvement of Jewish and Christian relations. Somehow the church needs to focus on the humanity of that document in terms of its origin, development, and transmission.

Another area that only the church can address is the entire issue of Christology (the understanding of the person and nature of Jesus as the Christ). In recent years there has been a considered movement on the part of New Testament scholars to reaffirm the humanity of Jesus. Traditionally, Jesus the man has become so obscured by the divine Christ that we find it difficult to deal with Jesus the Jew, the man of Nazareth, who authentically was born, lived, and died as a Jewish man. No meaningful relationship can exist either with Judaism or the individual Jew until this Christological issue is seriously addressed.

Clearly, there are many other approaches which might be taken in addressing the issues surrounding Jewish-Christian relations. If only these suggestions could be successfully implemented, however, tremendous improvement would result.

It should also be acknowledged that all of the suggestions above are pointedly for the Christian community. This is true for two reasons.

First, I am a Christian, and thus I know better what to suggest for the Christian community than for the Jewish community. Does the Jewish community know all it needs to know about Christianity in order for the dialogue to be most productive? Of course not! At the appropriate point in the dialogue, however, that issue can be addressed.

Second, I take my lead from Hillel, that great Jewish teacher of the first century B.C.E. You will recall that, when Jesus was discussing ethical issues, he suggested what has come to be called "the golden rule": "Do to others as you would have them do to you" (Lk 6:31, NRSV). This is a positive approach to action, but Hillel taught earlier the following:

What is hateful to you, don't do to anyone else. That's the whole Torah. The rest is commentary; go and learn it.[9]

This more negative statement of the "rule" was explained by the rabbis from the perspective that we know better what does harm to us than we know what is helpful to the other individual. In that regard, I know better what does harm to me, namely prejudice resulting in overt discrimination, than I know for certain what is good for the Jew to do. It is my responsibility, therefore, to address this issue where I know it and where I can perhaps make a contribution, namely within the Christian context. My injunction is to treat the Jew as I, a Christian, would wish to be treated.

CONCLUSION

These are a few suggestions that might be pursued as we seek solutions to the problem of antisemitism. The phenomenon has been so prevalent for so many centuries that it has appeared to be practically endemic to Christianity. Given the nature of prejudice, however, we recognize that we are conditioned culturally rather than being genetically shackled to antisemitism. That being the case, where individuals of good will and reason are willing to pursue the goal, it is possible both to understand the antisemitism and to make significant strides toward its eradication. To that goal, with the ultimate aspiration of removing antisemitism completely, every Christian should clamor to make absolute commitment to enlightenment and positive action!

Quite appropriate as a closing statement to this chapter is a quotation from Arthur Hertzberg, taken from a lecture he delivered in 1973; it is as applicable today as when he originally said it:

In the next century, as East and West encounter each other, many unlike communities will have to live together in decent peace, or the world will be in the deepest trouble. Anti-Semitism is indeed now indicative of the basic, persisting *hubris* of the West. Jews can survive anti-Semitism, but can the West survive its persisting nature?

Jewish history has always been an interweaving of what we are and what we have learned from our environment, of what we have fought for and of the attacks that we have resisted. So it is today. The journey is not ended, for the Messiah has not yet come—but, like all of my ancestors, I hear his footsteps.[10]

Suggested Questions

1. Let us assume that you are a delegate to a major church council where the New Testament and antisemitism is the focus of the discussion. What arguments might be marshalled to support both sides of the issue: on one hand, that the New Testament is indigenously an antisemitic document and on the other that the New Testament is antisemitic only if that interpretive spin be placed upon the text?

2. Discuss the general use of stereotypes to characterize a grouping of people. In specific, develop at least five stereotypes used in association with Jews and indicate your awareness that stereotypes are always characterized by the fact that they can be turned on themselves, meaning that an exact opposite can be developed to any stereotypical statement.

3. If you wished to establish an optimally productive discussion group on Jewish and Christian relations, what steps would you take to establish your group? ...who would be included in your group? ...what ground rules would govern the group's discussions? ...what outcomes would you desire?

4. Plan a Seder Meal involving both Jewish and Christian individuals. Secure a copy of *The Passover Haggadah*[11] to direct your thinking. Be especially careful that you do not inadvertently "Christianize" the Seder. Christians sometimes observe a Seder in conjunction with Easter as a way of designating Christian ties with Judaism. Unfortunately, when we portray Jesus as the agent of deliverance, when we affirm that, just as the Hebrews passed through the sea to deliverance, so too we must follow Jesus through the waters of death, etc., we assert by our actions that the Jews do not know how to interpret their own scripture. We must recognize that the deliverance at the sea is a part of the tradition for both Jews *and* Christians. Christians do not need to alter the event as though it were an allegory waiting to be fulfilled with the

Jesus event. To encourage meaningful Jewish-Christian relations, we must deal honestly and openly with the traditions recorded in the Torah. If we as Christians observe a Seder, faithfulness to the tradition as transmitted must be a primary concern.

5. Whatever your age, develop for your group a reading program that would give a reasonable awareness of Judaism as a faith perspective and an acquaintance with the phenomenon of antisemitism, most especially of the church's role in antisemitism through the centuries.

Appendix A: "A Theological Understanding of the Relationship Between Christians and Jews"

The 199th General Assembly of the Presbyterian Church, U.S.A., meeting in Biloxi, Missippi, in June, 1987, adopted "A Theological Understanding of the Relationship between Christians and Jews." Copyright 1987 by the Office of the General Assembly, Presbyterian Church (U.S.A.).

A THEOLOGICAL UNDERSTANDING OF THE RELATIONSHIP BETWEEN CHRISTIANS AND JEWS

Introduction

Purpose

Christians and Jews live side by side in our pluralistic American society. We engage one another not only in personal and social ways but also at deeper levels where ultimate values are expressed and where a theological understanding of our relationship is required. The confessional documents of the Reformed tradition are largely silent on this matter. Hence this paper has been prepared by the church as a pastoral and teaching document to provide a basis for continuing discussion within the Presbyterian community in the United States and to offer guidance for the occasions in which Presbyterians and Jews converse, cooperate, and enter into dialogue. What is the relationship which God intends between Christians and Jews, between Christianity and

Judaism? A theological understanding of this relationship is the subject which this paper addresses.

Context

Theology is never done in a vacuum. It influences and is influenced by its context. We do our theological work today in an increasingly global and pluralistic context—one that is interpersonal and intercommunal as well. Moreover, as Presbyterians, we do our theological work on the basis of Scripture, in the context of our faith in the living presence of Jesus Christ through the Holy Spirit, and of the church's theological tradition. A few words about each of these dimensions of our context may be helpful in understanding this paper.

The context in which the church now witnesses is more and more global and pluralistic. Churches have been planted in every nation on earth, but in most places Christians exist as a minority. The age of "Christendom" has passed, and the age of an interdependent global society is fast emerging. Things said by Christians in North America about the relationships of Christians and Jews will be heard by Christians in the Middle East, where there are painful conflicts affecting the entire region. Moreover it is increasingly difficult to ignore the existence of other religious communities and nonreligious movements in the world, many of which challenge our truth claims. What we say on the subject before us will be considered by these as well. We must be sensitive as we speak of the truth we know, lest we add to the suffering of others or increase hostility and misunderstanding by what we say.

The context in which the church now witnesses is also interpersonal and intercommunal. The reality of which we speak consists of individual persons and of entire peoples who carry within themselves real fears, pains, and hopes. Whatever the Presbyterian Church (U.S.A.) says about the relationship of Christians and Jews must be appropriate to our North American setting and yet sensitive to the deep longings and fears of those who struggle with this issue in different settings, especially in the Middle East. Recent General Assemblies of the Presbyterian Church (U.S.A.) have maintained a clear and consistent position concerning the struggle in the Middle East as a matter of the church's social policy. The General Assembly regards the theological affirmations of the present study as consistent with the church's prior policy statements concerning the Middle East, which speak of the right of statehood in Palestine for Palestinians (cf. *Minutes,* 1986, Part I, page 62) and the right of the State of Israel to exist within secure borders established by the United Nations General Assembly resolutions. Therefore, the attention of the church is again called to the church's policy enunciated in 1974, reaffirmed in 1984 which reads in part:

> The right and power of Palestinian people to self-determination by political expression, based upon full civil liberties for all, should be recognized by the parties in the Middle East and by the international community....The Palestinian people should be full participants in negotiations...through representatives of their own choosing. The right and power of Jewish people to self-determination by political expression in the State of Israel, based upon full civil liberties for all, should be recognized by the parties in the Middle East and by the international community. (*Minutes,* UPCUSA, 1974, Part 1, page 584; cf. *Minutes,* 1984, Part 1, page 338; see also pages 82, 335–39, "Resolution on the Middle East.")

The context of the church's witness includes also the fact that our church is deeply bound to its own heritage of Scripture and theological tradition. In discussing the relationship of Christians and Jews, we cannot separate ourselves from the Word of God, given in covenant to the Jewish people, made flesh in Jesus Christ, and ever renewed in the work of the Holy Spirit among us. Acknowledging the guidance of the church's confessional tradition, we recognize our responsibility to interpret the Word for our situation today. What the Presbyterian Church (U.S.A.) says on this complex subject will ultimately be evaluated in terms of the theological contribution that it makes.

The context of the church's witness includes, finally and most basically, the real presence of the risen Lord. We make our declarations within the love of Jesus Christ who calls us to witness, serve, and believe in his name. Since our life is a part of what we say, we seek to testify by our deeds and words to the all-encompassing love of Christ through whom we "who were far off have been brought near" to the covenants of promise.

Background

This theological study is not unprecedented. Since World War II, statements and study documents dealing with Jewish-Christian relations have been issued by a number of churches and Christian bodies. Among these are the Vatican's Nostra Aetate (1965), the Report of the

Faith and Order Commission of the World Council of Churches (1968), the statement of the Synod of the Reformed Church of Holland (1970), the statement of the French Bishop's Committee for Relations with the Jews (1973), the report of the Lutheran World Federation (1975), the statement of the Synod of Rhineland Church in West Germany (1980), the report of the Christian/Jewish Consultation Group of the Church of Scotland (1985), and the study of the World Alliance of Reformed Churches (1986).

The present study has been six years in preparation. It is the product of a project begun in 1981 within the former Presbyterian Church, U.S., then redeveloped and greatly expanded in scope and participation in 1983 upon the reunion which brought into being the Presbyterian Church (U.S.A.). The study has been developed under the direction of the church's Council on Theology and Culture, through a process which involved many people reflecting diverse interests and backgrounds, both in the United States and the Middle East.

In the course of addressing this subject, our church has come to see many things in a new light. The study has helped us to feel the pain of our Jewish neighbors who remember that the Holocaust was carried out in the heart of "Christian Europe" by persons many of whom were baptized Christians. We have come to understand in a new way how our witness to the gospel can be perceived by Jews as an attempt to erode and ultimately to destroy their own communities. Similarly, we have been made sensitive to the difficult role of our Arab Christian brothers and sisters in the Middle East. We have listened to the anguish of the Palestinians, and we have heard their cry.

The paper which we here present to the church does not attempt to address every problem nor to say more than we believe that we are able truly to say. It consists of seven theological affirmations, with a brief explication of each. Together they seek to lay the foundation for a new and better relationship under God between Christians and Jews. They are:

(1) a reaffirmation that the God who addresses both Christians and Jews is the same—the living and true God;

(2) a new understanding by the church that its own identity is intimately related to the continuing identity of the Jewish people;

(3) a willingness to ponder with Jews the mystery of God's election of both Jews and Christians to be a light to the nations;

(4) an acknowledgment by Christians that Jews are in covenant relationship with God and the consideration of the implications of this reality for evangelism and witness;

(5) a determination by Christians to put an end to "the teaching of contempt" for the Jews;

(6) a willingness to investigate the continuing significance of the promise of "land," and its associated obligations and to explore the implications for Christian theology;

(7) a readiness to act on the hope which we share with the Jews in God's promise of the peaceable kingdom.

These seven theological affirmations with their explications are offered to the church not to end debate but to inform it and, thus to serve as a basis for an ever deepening understanding of the mystery of God's saving work in the world.

Definitions and Language

The defining of terms on this subject is complex but unavoidable. We understand "Judaism" to be the religion of the Jews. It is practiced by many today and extends back into the period of the Hebrew scriptures. Judaism of late antiquity gave rise to that form of Judaism which has been developing since the first century, known as "Rabbinic Judaism." It gave rise to early Christianity as well. Both Christianity and Judaism claim relationship with the ancient people of Israel; the use of the term "Israel" in this study is restricted to its ancient reference. When referring to the contemporary State of Israel this document will use "State of Israel."

We understand "Jews" to include those persons whose self-understanding is that they are descended from Abraham, Isaac, and Jacob, and Sarah, Rebekah, Rachel, and Leah, and those converted into the Jewish community. We recognize that Jews are varied in the observance of their religion, and that there are many Jews who do not practice Judaism at all.

The language of this paper is conformable to General Assembly guidelines for inclusiveness within the Presbyterian Church (U.S.A.). It avoids gender-specific references either to God or to the people of God, except in reference to the Trinity and the Kingdom of God and in direct quotation from Scripture. The word "Lord" is used only with reference to Jesus Christ. The paper acknowledges the role of both women and men in the church's tradition.

The following affirmations are offered to the church for our common edification and growth in obedience and faith. To God alone be the glory.

AFFIRMATIONS AND EXPLICATIONS

Affirmation
1. We affirm that the living God whom Christians worship is the same God who is worshiped and served by Jews. We bear witness that the God revealed in Jesus, a Jew, to be the Triune Lord of all, is the same one disclosed in the life and worship of Israel.

Explication
Christianity began in the context of Jewish faith and life. Jesus was a Jew, as were his earliest followers. Paul, the apostle of the Gentiles, referred to himself as a "Hebrew of the Hebrews." The life and liturgy of the Jews provided the language and thought forms through which the revelation in Jesus was first received and expressed. Jewish liturgical forms were decisive for the worship of the early church and are influential still, especially in churches of the Reformed tradition.

Yet the relationship of Christians to Jews is more than one of common history and ideas. The relationship is significant for our faith because Christians confess that the God of Abraham and Sarah and their descendants is the very One whom the apostles addressed as "the God and Father of our Lord Jesus Christ." The one God elected and entered into covenant with Israel to reveal the divine will and point to a future salvation in which all people will live in peace and righteousness. This expectation of the reign of God in a Messianic Age was described by the Hebrew prophets in different ways. The Scriptures speak of the expectation of a deliverer king anointed by God, of the appearing of a righteous teacher, of a suffering servant, or of a people enabled through God's grace to establish the Messianic Age. Early Christian preaching proclaimed that Jesus had become Messiah and Lord, God's anointed who has inaugurated the kingdom of peace and righteousness through his life, death, and resurrection. While some Jews accepted this message, the majority did not, choosing to adhere to the biblical revelation as interpreted by their teachers and continuing to await the fulfillment of the messianic promises given through the prophets, priests, and kings of Israel.

Thus the bond between the community of Jews and those who came to be called Christians was broken, and both have continued as vital but separate communities through the centuries. Nonetheless, there are ties which remain between Christians and Jews: the faith of both in the one God whose loving and just will is for the redemption of all humankind and the Jewishness of Jesus whom we confess to be the Christ of God.

In confessing Jesus as the Word of God incarnate, Christians are not rejecting the concrete existence of Jesus who lived by the faith of Israel. Rather, we are affirming the unique way in which Jesus, a Jew, is the being and power of God for the redemption of the world. In him, God is disclosed to be the Triune One who creates and reconciles all things. This is the way in which Christians affirm the reality of the one God who is sovereign over all.

Affirmation

2. We affirm that the church, elected in Jesus Christ, has been engrafted into the people of God established by the covenant with Abraham, Isaac, and Jacob. Therefore, Christians have not replaced Jews.

Explication

The church, especially in the Reformed tradition, understands itself to be in covenant with God through its election in Jesus Christ. Because the church affirms this covenant as fundamental to its existence, it has generally not sought nor felt any need to offer any positive interpretation of God's relationship with the Jews, lineal descendants of Abraham, Isaac, and Jacob, and Sarah, Rebekah, Rachel, and Leah, with whom God covenanted long ago. The emphasis has fallen on the new covenant established in Christ and the creation of the church.

Sometime during the second century of the Common Era, a view called "supersessionism," based on the reading of some biblical texts and nurtured in controversy, began to take shape. By the beginning of the third century, this teaching that the Christian church had superseded the Jews as God's chosen people became the orthodox understanding of God's relationship to the church. Such a view influenced the church's understanding of God's relationship with the Jews and allowed the church to regard Jews in an inferior light.

Supersessionism maintains that because the Jews refused to receive Jesus as Messiah, they were cursed by God, are no longer in covenant with God, and that the church alone is the "true Israel" or the "spiritual Israel." When Jews continue to assert, as they do, that they are the covenant people of God, they are looked upon by many Christians as impertinent intruders, claiming a right which is no longer theirs. The long and dolorous history of Christian imperialism, in which the church often justified anti-Jewish acts and attitudes in the name of Jesus, finds its theological base in this teaching.

We believe and testify that this theory of supersessionism or replacement is harmful and in need of reconsideration as the church seeks to proclaim God's saving activity with humankind. The scriptural and theological bases for this view are clear enough; but we are prompted to look again at our tradition by events in our own time and by an increasing number of theologians and biblical scholars who are calling for such a reappraisal. The pride and prejudice which have been justified by reference to this doctrine of replacement themselves seem reason enough for taking a hard look at this position.

For us, the teaching that the church has been engrafted by God's grace into the people of God finds as much support in Scripture as the view of supersessionism and is much more consistent with our Reformed understanding of the work of God in Jesus Christ. The emphasis is on the continuity and trustworthiness of God's commitments and God's grace. The issue for the early church concerned the inclusion of the Gentiles in God's saving work, not the exclusion of the Jews. Paul insists that God is God of both Jews and Gentiles and justifies God's redemption of both on the basis of faith (Romans 3:29–30). God's covenants are not broken. "God has not rejected his people whom he foreknew" (Romans 11:2). The church has not "replaced" the Jewish people. Quite the contrary! The church, being made up primarily of those who were once aliens and strangers to the covenants of promise, has been engrafted into the people of God by the covenant with Abraham (Romans 11:17–18).

The continued existence of the Jewish people and of the church as communities elected by God is, as the apostle Paul expressed it, a "mystery" (Romans 11:25). We do not claim to fathom this mystery but we cannot ignore it. At the same time we can never forget that we stand in a covenant established by Jesus Christ (Hebrews 8) and that faithfulness to that covenant requires us to call all women and men to faith in Jesus Christ. We ponder the work of God, including the wonder of Christ's atoning work for us.

Affirmation

3. We affirm that both the church and the Jewish people are elected by God for witness to the world and that the relationship of the church to contemporary Jews is based on that gracious and irrevocable election of both.

Explication

God chose a particular people, Israel, as a sign and foretaste of God's grace toward all people. It is for the sake of God's redemption of the world that Israel was elected. The promises of God, made to Abraham and Sarah and to their offspring after them, were given so that blessing might come upon "all families of the earth" (Genesis 12:1–3). God continues that purpose through Christians and Jews. The church, like the Jews, is called to be a light to the nations (Acts 13:47). God's purpose embraces the whole creation.

In the electing of peoples, God takes the initiative. Election does not manifest human achievement but divine grace. Neither Jews nor Christians can claim to deserve this favor. Election is the way in which God creates freedom through the Holy Spirit for a people to be for God and for others. God, who is ever faithful to the word which has been spoken, does not take back the divine election. Whenever either the Jews or the church have rejected God's ways, God has judged but not rejected them. This is a sign of God's redeeming faithfulness toward the world.

Both Christians and Jews are elected to service for the life of the world. Despite profound theological differences separating Christians and Jews, we believe that God has bound us together in a unique relationship for the sake of God's love for the world. We testify to this election, but we cannot explain it. It is part of the purpose of God for the whole creation. Thus there is much common ground where Christians and Jews can and should act together.

Affirmation

4. We affirm that the reign of God is attested both by the continuing existence of the Jewish people and by the church's proclamation of the gospel of Jesus Christ. Hence, when speaking with Jews about matters of faith, we must always acknowledge that Jews are already in a covenantal relationship with God.

Explication

God, who acts in human history by the Word and Spirit, is not left without visible witnesses on the earth. God's sovereign and saving reign in the world is signified both by the continuing existence of and faithfulness within the Jewish people who, by all human reckoning, might be expected to have long since passed from the stage of history and by the life and witness of the church.

As the cross of Jesus has always been a stumbling block to Jews, so also the continued existence and faithfulness of the Jews is often a stumbling block to Christians. Our persuasion of the truth of God in Jesus Christ has sometimes led Christians to conclude that Judaism should no longer exist, now that Christ has come, and that all Jews ought properly to become baptized members of the church. Over the centuries, many afflictions have been visited on the Jews by Christians holding this belief — not least in our own time. We believe that the time has come for Christians to stop and take a new look at the Jewish people and at the relationship which God wills between Christian and Jew.

Such reappraisal cannot avoid the issue of evangelism. For Jews, this is a very sensitive issue. Proselytism by Christians seeking to persuade, even convert, Jews often implies a negative judgment on Jewish faith. Jewish reluctance to accept Christian claims is all the more understandable when it is realized that conversion is often seen by them as a threat to Jewish survival. Many Jews who unite with the church sever their bonds with their people. On the other hand, Christians are commissioned to witness to the whole world about the good news of Christ's atoning work for both Jew and Gentile. Difficulty arises when we acknowledge that the same Scripture which proclaims that atonement and which Christians claim as God's word clearly states that Jews are already in a covenant relationship with God who makes and keeps covenants.

For Christians, there is no easy answer to this matter. Faithful interpretation of the biblical record indicates that there are elements of God's covenant with Abraham that are unilateral and unconditional.

However, there are also elements of the covenant which appear to predicate benefits upon faithfulness (see Gen.17:1ff.). Christians, historically, have proclaimed that true obedience is impossible for a sinful humanity and thus have been impelled to witness to the atoning work of Jesus of Nazareth, the promised Messiah, as the way to a right relationship with God. However, to the present day, many Jews have been unwilling to accept the Christian claim and have continued in their covenant tradition. In light of Scripture, which testifies to God's repeated offer of forgiveness to Israel, we do not presume to judge in God's place. Our commission is to witness to the saving work of Jesus Christ; to preach good news among all the "nations" *(ethne)*.

Dialogue is the appropriate form of faithful conversation between Christians and Jews. Dialogue is not a cover for proselytism. Rather, as trust is established, not only questions and concerns can be shared but faith and commitments as well. Christians have no reason to be reluctant in sharing the good news of their faith with anyone. However, a militancy that seeks to impose one's own point of view on another is not only inappropriate but also counterproductive. In dialogue, partners are able to define their faith in their own terms, avoiding caricatures of one another, and are thus better able to obey the commandment, "Thou shalt not bear false witness against thy neighbor." Dialogue, especially in light of our shared history, should be entered into with a spirit of humility and a commitment to reconciliation. Such dialogue can be a witness that seeks also to heal that which has been broken. It is out of a mutual willingness to listen and to learn that faith deepens and a new and better relationship between Christians and Jews is enabled to grow.

Affirmation

5. We acknowledge in repentance the church's long and deep complicity in the proliferation of anti-Jewish attitudes and actions through its "teaching of contempt" for the Jews. Such teaching we now repudiate, together with the acts and attitudes which it generates.

Explication

Anti-Jewish sentiment and action by Christians began in New Testament times. The struggle between Christians and Jews in the first century of the Christian movement was often bitter and marked by mutual violence. The depth of hostility left its mark on early Christian and Jewish literature, including portions of the New Testament.

In subsequent centuries, after the occasions for the original hostility had long since passed, the church misused portions of the New Testament as proof texts to justify a heightened animosity toward Jews. For many centuries, it was the church's teaching to label Jews as "Christ-killers" and a "deicide race." This is known as the "teaching of contempt." Persecution of Jews was at times officially sanctioned and at other times indirectly encouraged or at least tolerated. Holy Week became a time of terror for the Jews.

To this day, the church's worship, preaching, and teaching often lend themselves, at times unwittingly, to a perpetuation of the "teaching of contempt." For example, the public reading of Scripture without explicating potentially misleading passages concerning "the Jews," preaching which uses Judaism as a negative example in order to commend Christianity, public prayer which assumes that only the prayers of Christians are pleasing to God, teaching in the church school which reiterates stereotypes and non-historical ideas about the Pharisees and Jewish leadership — all of these contribute, however subtly, to a continuation of the church's "teaching of contempt."

It is painful to realize how the teaching of the church has led individuals and groups to behavior that has tragic consequences. It is agonizing to discover that the church's "teaching of contempt" was a major ingredient that made possible the monstrous policy of annihilation of Jews by Nazi Germany. It is disturbing to have to admit that the churches of the West did little to challenge the policies of their governments, even in the face of the growing certainty that the Holocaust was taking place. Though many Christians in Europe acted heroically to shelter Jews, the record reveals that most churches as well as governments the world over largely ignored the pleas for sanctuary for Jews.

As the very embodiment of anti-Jewish attitudes and actions, the Holocaust is a sober reminder that such horrors are actually possible in this world and that they begin with apparently small acts of disdain or expedience. Hence, we pledge to be alert for all such acts of denigration from now on, so that they may be resisted. We also pledge resistance to any such actions perpetrated by anyone, anywhere.

The church's attitudes must be reviewed and changed as necessary, so that they never again fuel the fires of hatred. We must be willing to admit our church's complicity in wrongdoing in the past, even as we try to establish a new basis of trust and communication with Jews. We pledge, God helping us, never again to participate in, to contribute to, or (insofar as we are able) to allow the persecution or denigration of Jews or the belittling of Judaism.

Affirmation

6. We affirm the continuity of God's promise of land along with the obligations of that promise to the people Israel.

Explication

As the Church of Scotland's (1985) report says:

> We are aware that in dealing with this matter we are entering a minefield of complexities across which is strung a barbed-wire entanglement of issues, theological, political and humanitarian.

However, a faithful explication of biblical material relating to the covenant with Abraham cannot avoid the reality of the promise of land. The question with which we must wrestle is how this promise is to be understood in the light of the existence of the modern political State of Israel which has taken its place among the nations of the world.

The Genesis record indicates that "the land of your sojournings" was promised to Abraham and his and Sarah's descendants. This promise, however, included the demand that "You shall keep my covenant...." (Genesis 17:7–8). The implication is that the blessings of the promise were dependent upon fulfillment of covenant relationships. Disobedience could bring the loss of land, even while God's promise was not revoked. God's promises are always kept, but in God's own way and time.

The establishment of the State of Israel in our day has been seen by many devout Jews as the fulfillment of God's divine promise. Other Jews are equally sure that it is not and regard the State of Israel as an unauthorized attempt to flee divinely imposed exile. Still other Jews interpret the State of Israel in purely secular terms. Christian opinion is equally diverse. As Reformed Christians, however, we believe that no government at any time can ever be the full expression of God's will. All, including the State of Israel, stand accountable to God. The State of Israel is a geopolitical entity and is not to be validated theologically.

God's promise of land bears with it obligation. Land is to be used as the focus of mission, the place where a people can live and be a light to the nations. Further, because land is God's to be given, it can never be fully possessed. The living out of God's covenant in the land brings with it not only opportunity but also temptation. The history of the people of Israel reveals the continual tension between sovereignty and stewardship, blessing and curse.

The Hebrew prophets made clear to the people of their own day as well, indeed, as any day, that those in possession of "land" have a responsibility and obligation to the disadvantaged, the oppressed, and the "strangers in their gates." God's justice, unlike ours, is consistently in favor of the powerless (Ps.103:6). Therefore we, whether Christian or Jew, who affirm the divine promise of land, however land is to be understood, dare not fail to uphold the divine right of the dispossessed. We have indeed been agents of the dispossession of others. In particular, we confess our complicity in the loss of land by Palestinians, and we join with those of our Jewish sisters and brothers who stand in solidarity with Palestinians as they cry for justice as the dispossessed.

We disavow any teaching which says that peace can be secured without justice through the exercise of violence and retribution. God's justice upholds those who cry out against the strong. God's peace comes to those who do justice and mercy on the earth. Hence we look with dismay at the violence and injustice occurring in the Middle East.

For three-thousand years the covenant promise of land has been an essential element of the self-understanding of Jewish people. Through centuries of dispersion and exile, Jews have continued to understand themselves as a people in relation to the God they have known through the promise of land. However, to understand that promise solely in terms of a specific geographical entity on the eastern shore of the Mediterranean is, in our view, inadequate.

"Land" is understood as more than place or property; "land" is a biblical metaphor for sustainable life, prosperity, peace, and security. We affirm the rights to these essentials for the Jewish people. At the same time, as bearers of the good news of the gospel of Jesus Christ, we affirm those same rights in the name of justice to all peoples. We are aware that those rights are not realized by all persons in our day. Thus we affirm our solidarity with all people to whom those rights of "land" are currently denied.

We disavow those views held by some dispensationalists and some Christian Zionists that see the formation of the State of Israel as a signal of the end time, which will bring the Last Judgment, a conflagration which only Christians will survive. These views ignore the word of Jesus against seeking to set the time or place of the consummation of world history.

We therefore call on all people of faith to engage in the work of reconciliation and peacemaking. We pray for and encourage those who would break the cycles of vengeance and violence, whether it be the violence of states or of resistance movements, of terror or of retaliation. We stand with those who work toward nonviolent solutions, including those who choose nonviolent resistance. We also urge nation states and other political institutions to seek negotiated settlements of conflicting claims.

The seeking of justice is a sign of our faith in the reign of God.

Affirmation

7. We affirm that Jews and Christians are partners in waiting. Christians see in Christ the redemption not yet fully visible in the world, and Jews await the messianic redemption. Christians and Jews together await the final manifestation of God's promise of the peaceable kingdom.

Explication

Christian hope is continuous with Israel's hope and is unintelligible apart from it. New Testament teaching concerning the Kingdom of God was shaped by the messianic and apocalyptic vision of Judaism. That prophetic vision was proclaimed by John the Baptist, and the preaching of Jesus contained the same vision. Both Jews and Christians affirm that God reigns over all human destiny and has not abandoned the world to chaos and that, despite many appearances to the contrary, God is acting within history to establish righteousness and peace.

Jews still await the kingdom which the prophets foretold. Some look for a Messianic Age in which God's heavenly reign will be ushered in upon the earth. Christians proclaim the good news that in Christ "the Kingdom of God is at hand," yet, we, too, wait in hope for the consummation of the redemption of all things in God. Though the waiting of Jews and Christians is significantly different on account of our differing perception of Jesus, nonetheless, we both wait with eager longing for the fulfillment of God's gracious reign upon the earth—the kingdom of righteousness and peace foretold by the prophets. We are in this sense partners in waiting.

Both Christians and Jews are called to wait and to hope in God. While we wait, Jews and Christians are called to the service of God in the world. However that service may differ, the vocation of each shares at least these elements: a striving to realize the word of the prophets, an attempt to remain sensitive to the dimension of the holy, an effort to encourage the life of the mind, and a ceaseless activity in the cause of justice and peace. These are far more than the ordinary requirements of our common humanity; they are elements of our common election by the God of Abraham, Isaac, and Jacob, and Sarah, Rebekah, Rachel, and Leah. Precisely because our election is not to privilege but to service, Christians and Jews are obligated to act together in these things. By so acting, we faithfully live out our partnership in waiting. By so doing, we believe that God is glorified.

Recommendations

The Council on Theology and Culture makes the following recommendations to the 199th General Assembly (1987):

1a. That the General Assembly adopt for study and reflection the paper, "A Theological Understanding of the Relationship between Christians and Jews," and distribute it to the church as a provisional understanding of the subject, along with a brief study guide including a bibliography and response questionnaire, the latter of which is to be returned to the appropriate ministry unit;

1b. That instruction be given to the appropriate ministry unit to appoint a work group composed of some members of the task force, some staff with responsibilities for work in the Middle East, and others to be chosen and to invite Christians living in the Middle East to participate with the work group; that a conference be held with the Middle East Council of Churches (MECC) and partner churches of the FC(USA) in the Middle East in the spring of 1988 to discuss and negotiate an acceptable understanding between the PC(USA) and the MECC and partner churches concerning its content, status, and function in our ongoing work together; this committee is to report to the appropriate ministry unit at the conclusion of the conference.

1c. That instruction be given the appropriate ministry unit to report on the results of its study and reflection process and bring any appropriate recommendations to the 201st General Assembly (1989).

2. That the Stated Clerk be directed to print the report and to distribute it to each minister, Christian educator, and session within the church, to ecumenical partner churches in mission, to churches with which the Presbyterian Church (U.S.A.) is in correspondence, and to the major Jewish organizations in the United States and partner churches of the PC(USA) in the Middle East.

3. That the General Assembly request pastors and Christian educators to initiate educational programs designed to foster understanding and better relationships between Christians and Jews;

4. That the General Assembly urge the expansion of instruction in Judaic studies in the theological seminaries of the church;

5. That we communicate our sensitivity to the issue of including a Holocaust Remembrance Day in the liturgical calendar of the PC(USA) and to refer this matter to the appropriate ministry unit.

6. That the General Assembly instruct the General Assembly Council to give increased encouragement to those working for reconciliation of all parties in the Middle East through exploring the feasibility of joining with others, in as broadly an ecumenical way as possible, in developing those instrumentalities acceptable to all participants, which enable and facilitate constructive dialogue and common efforts to improve relationships between Jews, Christians, and Muslims, especially but not only in the Middle East and the U.S.A.

7. That the General Assembly Council be directed to monitor the implementation of these actions of the General Assembly and to report thereon periodically to the General Assembly.

Appendix B: "Guidelines for Christian-Jewish Relations"

The Episcopal Church adopted "Guidelines for Christian-Jewish Relations" at the General Convention of The Episcopal Church in 1988.

INTRODUCTION

"All real living is meeting."

These words of the Jewish philosopher, Martin Buber, point to the essence of Jewish-Christian dialogue. The General Convention of the Episcopal Church meeting in Detroit in July, 1988, adopted these Guidelines for Christian-Jewish Relations. Parishes and church leaders are encouraged to use the guidelines as a means of sharing in conversation with their Jewish neighbors.

As Christians, we should view our encounter with the Jewish people not as a threat but an opportunity. Sharing our faith freely with Jews enables us to view our own religious conviction more clearly, and to gain a new perspective on the faith and practice of those who remain in God's covenant with Israel.

Various means are available to us in our pursuit of Jewish-Christian understanding. The guidelines give suggestions for common work on social and community issues, study of our common scriptures, and common worship.

Help and direction for the practice of Christian-Jewish dialogue is available through the Presiding Bishop's Committee on Christian-Jewish Relations. Contact the Ecumenical Office of the Episcopal Church.

The first step in dialogue is the most vital. With the help of your rector or the diocesan Ecumenical Committee, reach out to your Jewish neighbors or to the synagogue down the street to share the joy of living and meeting in dialogue with the Jewish people.

The Rev. Dr. William L. Weiler
Presiding Bishop's Committee
on Christian-Jewish Relations

GUIDELINES FOR
CHRISTIAN-JEWISH RELATIONS
(FOR USE IN THE EPISCOPAL CHURCH)

The Episcopal Church and Christian-Jewish Dialogue

Among Christian communities, the Episcopal Church has special gifts to bring to the Christian-Jewish dialogue (see General Convention Resolution on this, Convention Journal 1979, pp. C47–48). It has a tradition of respect for truth wherever found and a critical appreciation of Scripture and historical development. It is, therefore, in a position to make a significant contribution to Jewish-Christian relations.

Preface to the Guidelines

One of the functions of the Christian-Jewish dialogue is to allow participants to describe and witness to their faith in their own terms. This is of primary importance since self-serving descriptions of other people's faiths are among the roots of prejudice, stereotyping and condescension. Careful listening to each other's expression of faith enables Christians to obey better the commandment not to bear false witness against their neighbors. Partners in dialogue must recognize that any religion or ideology which claims universality will have its own interpretations of other religions and ideologies as part of its own self-understanding. Dialogue gives the opportunity for mutual questioning of those understandings. A reciprocal willingness to listen, learn and understand enables significant dialogue to grow.

I. Principles of Dialogue

The following principles are offered to aid and encourage the Episcopal Church to make an increasingly vital and substantive impact on the dialogue.

1. In all dialogue, recognition of marked cultural differences is important. The words employed in religious discussion are not innocent or neutral. Partners in dialogue may rightly question both the language and the definitions each uses in articulating religious matters.

2. In the case of Christian-Jewish dialogue, an historical and theological imbalance is obvious. While an understanding of Judaism in New Testament times is an indispensable part of any Christian theology, for Jews a "theological" understanding of Christianity is not of the same significance. Yet neither Judaism nor Christianity, at least in the Western world, has developed without interaction with the other.

3. The relations between Jews and Christians have unique characteristics, since Christianity historically emerged out of early Judaism. Christian understanding of that process constitutes a necessary part of the dialogue and gives urgency to the enterprise. As Christianity came to define its own identity in relation to Judaism, the Church developed interpretations, definitions and terms for those things it had inherited from Jewish traditions. It also developed its own understanding of the Scriptures common to Jews and Christians. In the process of defining itself, the Church produced its own definition of God's acts of salvation. It should not be surprising that Jews resent those scriptural and theological interpretations in which they are assigned negative roles. Tragically, such patterns of thought have led Christians to overt acts of condescension, prejudice and even violent acts of persecution. In the face of those acts, a profound sense of penitence is the necessary response.

4. Many Christians are convinced that they understand Judaism since they have the Hebrew Scriptures as part of their Bible. This attitude is often reinforced by a lack of knowledge about the history of Jewish life and thought through the 1900 years since Christianity and Judaism parted ways.

5. There is, therefore, a special urgency for Christians to listen, through study and dialogue, to ways in which Jews understand their own history, their Scriptures, their traditions, their faith and their practice. Furthermore, a mutual listening to the way each is perceived by the other can be a step toward understanding the hurts, overcoming the fears, and correcting the misunderstandings that have separated us throughout the centuries.

6. Both Judaism and Christianity contain a wide spectrum of opinions, theologies, and styles of life and service. Since generalizations

often produce stereotyping, Jewish-Christian dialogue must try to be as inclusive of the variety of views within the two communities as possible.

II. The Necessity for Christians to Understand Jews and Judaism

1. Through dialogue with Jews, many, though yet too few, Christians have come to appreciate the richness and vitality of Jewish faith and life in the Covenant and have been enriched in their own understandings of Jesus and the divine will for all creatures.

2. In dialogue with Jews, Christians have learned that the actual history of Jewish faith and experience does not match the images of Judaism that have dominated a long history of Christian teaching and writing, images that have been spread by Western culture and literature into other parts of the world.

3. Jesus was a Jew, born into the Jewish tradition. He was nurtured by the Hebrew Scriptures of his day, which he accepted as authoritative and interpreted both in terms of the Judaism of his time and in fresh and powerful ways in his life and teaching, announcing that the Kingdom of God was at hand. In their experience of his resurrection, his followers confessed him as both Lord and Messiah.

4. Christians should remember that some of the controversies reported in the New Testament between Jesus and the "scribes and Pharisees" found parallels within Pharisaism itself and its heir, Rabbinic Judaism. The controversies generally arose in a Jewish context, but when the words of Jesus came to be used by Christians who did not identify with the Jewish people as Jesus did, such sayings often became weapons in anti-Jewish polemics and thereby their original intention was tragically distorted. An internal Christian debate has been taking place for some years now about how to understand and explain passages in the New Testament that contain anti-Jewish references.

5. From the early days of the Church, many Christian interpreters saw the Church replacing Israel as God's people. The destruction of the Second Temple of Jerusalem was understood as a warrant for this claim. The Covenant of God with the people of Israel was seen only as a preparation for the coming of Jesus. As a consequence, the Covenant with Israel was considered to be abrogated.

6. This theological perspective has had fateful consequences. As Christians understood themselves to replace the Jews as God's people, they often denigrated the Judaism that survived as a fossilized religion of legalism. The Pharisees were thought to represent the

height of that legalism; Jews and Jewish groups were portrayed as negative models; and the truth and beauty of Christianity were thought to be enhanced by setting up Judaism as false and ugly. Unfortunately, many of the early Church fathers defamed the Jewish people.

7. Through a renewed study of Judaism and in dialogue with Jews, Christians have become aware that Judaism in the time of Jesus was in but an early stage of its long life. Under the leadership of the Pharisees, the Jewish people began a spiritual revival of remarkable power, which gave them the vitality capable of surviving the catastrophe of the loss of the Temple. It gave birth to Rabbinic Judaism, which produced the Talmud, and built the structures for a strong and creative life through the centuries.

8. Judaism is more than the religion of the Scriptures of Israel (called by Christians the Old Testament and by Jews the Hebrew Scriptures or the Hebrew Bible). The Talmud and other later writings provide interpretations that for much of Judaism are central and authoritative with the Torah.

9. For Christians, the Bible (that is, the two Testaments) is also followed by traditions for interpretation, from the Church Fathers to the present time. Thus, both Judaism and Christianity are nurtured by their Scriptures, scriptural commentaries and living and developing traditions.

10. Christians as well as Jews look to the Hebrew Bible as the record of God's election of and covenant with God's people. For Jews, it is their own story in historical continuity with the present. Christians, mostly of gentile background since early in the life of the Church, believe themselves to have entered this Covenant by grace through Jesus Christ. The relationship between the two communities, both worshipping the God of ancient Israel, is a given historical fact, but how it is to be understood and explained theologically is a matter of internal discussion among Christians and Jews in dialogue.

11. What Jews and Christians have in common needs to be examined as carefully as their differences. Finding in the Scriptures the faith sufficient for salvation, the Christian Church shares Israel's trust in the One God, whom the Church knows in the Spirit as the God and Father of the Lord Jesus Christ. For Christians, Jesus Christ is acknowledged as the only begotten of the Father, through whom millions have come to share in the love of, and to adore, the God who first made covenant with the people of Israel. Knowing the One God in Jesus

Christ through the Spirit, therefore, Christians worship One God with a trinitarian confession involving creation, incarnation, and pentecost. In so doing, the Church worships in a language that is strange to Jewish worship and sensitivities, yet full of meaning to Christians. Dialogue is a means to help clarify language and to lead to the grasp of what the participants are really saying.

12. Christians and Jews both believe that God has created men and women and has called them to be holy and to exercise stewardship over the creation in accountability to God. Jews and Christians are taught by their Scriptures and traditions to recognize their responsibility to their neighbors, especially the weak, the poor, and the oppressed. In various and distinct ways they look for the coming of the Kingdom of God. In dialogue with Jews, many Christians have come to a more profound appreciation of the Exodus hope of liberation, praying and working for the coming of justice and peace on earth.

13. Jews found ways of living in obedience to Torah both before and after the emergence of Christianity. They maintained and deepened their call to be a distinctive people in the midst of the nations. Jews historically were allowed to live with respect and acceptance in some of the cultures in which they resided. Here their life and values thrived and made a distinct contribution to their Christian and Muslim neighbors. It is a sad fact, however, that Jews living in Christian countries have not fared better than those in non-Christian countries.

14. The land of Israel and the city of Jerusalem have always been central to the Jewish people. "Next year in Jerusalem" is a constant theme of Jewish worship in the diaspora. The continued presence of Jews in that land and in Jerusalem is a focal point for Judaism and must be taken into account in dialogue.

15. Many Jews differ in their interpretations of the religious and secular meaning of the State of Israel. For almost all Jewish people, however, Israel is an integral part of their identity.

16. Jews, Christians and Muslims have all maintained a presence in that land for centuries. The land is holy to all three, though each may understand holiness in different ways.

17. The existence of the State of Israel is a fact of history (see General Convention Resolution affirming "the right of Israel to exist as a free state within secure borders," Convention Journal 1979, p. C–104). However, the quest for homeland status by Palestinians —

Christian and Muslim — is a part of their search for identity also, and must be addressed together with the need for a just and lasting solution to the conflict in the Middle East.

III. Hatred and Persecution of Jews—A Continuing Concern

1. Christians need to be aware that hatred and persecution of Jews have a long, persistent history. This is particularly true in countries where Jews have been a minority presence among Christians. The tragic history of the persecution of Jews includes massacres by the Crusaders, the Inquisition, pogroms and the Holocaust. The World Council of Churches Assembly at its first meeting in Amsterdam in 1948 declared: "We call upon the churches we represent to denounce antisemitism, no matter what its origin, as absolutely irreconcilable with the profession and practice of the Christian faith. Antisemitism is sin against God and human life." This appeal has been reiterated many times. Those who live where there is a history of prejudice and persecution of the Jews can serve the whole Church by revealing that danger whenever it is recognized.

2. Teachings of contempt for Jews and Judaism in certain traditions have proved a spawning ground for such evils as the Nazi Holocaust. It has, in this country, helped to spawn the extremist activities of the Ku Klux Klan and the defacement of synagogues, and stimulates the more socially acceptable but often more pernicious discriminatory practices seen in housing patterns and in private clubs. The Church must learn to proclaim the Gospel without generating contempt for Judaism or the Jewish people. A Christian response to the Holocaust is a resolve that it will never happen again.

3. Discrimination and persecution of the Jewish people have not only deep-rooted theological but also social, economic, and political aspects. Religious differences are magnified to justify ethnic hatred in support of vested interests. Similar manifestations are also evident in many interracial conflicts. Christians are called to oppose all religious prejudices through which Jews or any people are made scapegoats for the failures and problems of societies and political regimes.

IV. Authentic Christian Witness

1. Christians believe that God's self-revelation is given in history. In the Covenant with the Jewish people at Mt. Sinai, the sacred law became part of our religious heritage. Christians see that same

God embodied in the person of Jesus Christ, to whom The Church must bear witness by word and deed among all peoples. It would be false to its deepest commitment if the Church were to deny this mission. The Christian witness toward Jews, however, has been distorted by coercive proselytism, conscious and unconscious, overt and subtle. The Joint Working Group of the Roman Catholic Church and the World Council of Churches has stated: "Proselytism embraces whatever violates the right of the human person, Christian or non-Christian, to be free from external coercion in religious matters" (Ecumenical Review, 1/1971, p. 11).

2. Dialogue can rightly be described as a mutual witness, for witness is a sharing of one's faith conviction without the intention of proselytizing. Participants are invited to hear each other in order to understand their faiths, hopes, insights and concerns. The goal of dialogue is to communicate truth as the participants perceive it within their own traditions. The spirit of dialogue is to be present to each other in full openness and human vulnerability.

V. Practical Recommendations

1. It is recommended that the relationship between Christians and Jews be observed liturgically each year. A fitting occasion would be on or near the observance of Yom HaShoah, the Holocaust remembrance, since Jews and Christians would then have a common, or approximately common, day of observance. Another such occasion for an annual observance might be the Feast of St. James of Jerusalem on October 23, or a Sunday before or after that date.

2. It is recommended that in the services of the Church and in church school teaching, careful explanations be made of the New Testament texts which appear to place all Jews in an unfavorable light, particularly the expression "the Jews" in the English translations of the Gospel of John and in other references (see General Convention Resolution on "Deicide and the Jews," Journal 1964, pp. 279–80).

3. It is recommended that each diocese of the Church not already having a Committee on Christian-Jewish Relations establish one at the first opportunity in order to coordinate efforts and help to avoid haphazard and unrelated activities.

4. It is recommended that each parish situated in an area with a significant Jewish population organize with proper care and oversight an ongoing dialogue with Jews. If the dialogue is to be thorough and

productive, it must include basic local exchanges between Episcopal and Jewish congregations.

5. It is recommended that seminaries of the Church undertake programs for their students which promote a greater understanding and appreciation for our common heritage with the Jews as well as for living Judaism today, addressing in particular those matters which eliminate prejudice and the presuppositions that feed it.

6. It is recommended that cooperation with Jewish and interreligious organizations concerned with service and the common good, interreligious programs, cultural enrichment and social responsibility be continued and intensified.

APPENDICES
"CHRISTIAN-JEWISH DIALOGUE"
—A RESOLUTION OF THE 1979 GENERAL CONVENTION

Whereas, the Church is reminded in all parts of Holy Scripture of those spiritual ties which link the community of the New Testament to the seed of Abraham and is exhorted by St. Paul to recall that she is nourished by root and sap of that good and consecrated olive tree onto which the wild olive branches of the Gentiles have been grafted (Romans 11:17–24); and

Whereas, the Church cannot forget that she has received the revelation of the Old Testament from that people with whom God, in his infinite goodness and mercy, established and nourished those ancient covenants; and that St. Paul bears witness that the Jews remain precious to God for the sake of the patriarchs, since God does not withdraw the gifts he has bestowed or revoke the choices he has made (Romans 11:28–29); and

Whereas, our Lord Jesus Christ was born, circumcised, dedicated, and baptized into the community of Israel to whom belong the sonship, the glory, the covenants, the giving of the Torah, the worship and the patriarchs (Roman 9:4–5); and the first apostles and witnesses themselves were all of Jewish lineage; and

Whereas, all the faithful in Christ consider themselves to be the offspring of Abraham (Galatians 3:7) and included in his call, being also the inheritors of that redemption figured in the Exodus of God's chosen people from bondage to Pharaoh; and

Whereas, Christian and Jew share the common hope for that day in which our God will be King over the whole earth (Zechariah 14:9), and, receiving the kingdom, will be "all in all" (1 Corinthians 15:28), and are thus bound by that hope to a common divine service; and

Whereas, a denial of or an ignorance of their spiritual roots by Christians has, more often than not, provided fertile ground for the festering of antisemitism even among leaders of the Church of Jesus Christ—the Holocaust in Hitler's Germany being only the most recent and painful memory; therefore be it

Resolved, the House of Deputies concurring, That this 66th General Convention of the Episcopal Church call anew upon the leadership of the Episcopal Church, both clergy and lay, to deepen their commitment to Episcopal-Jewish dialogue and to interfaith cooperation in local communities; and, wherever appropriate, to seek exposure to ancient and contemporary Jewish scholarship so as to better comprehend the Scriptures on which, and the religious environment in which, our Lord Jesus Christ was nourished; and to appreciate more fully the religious worship and experiences of our neighbors in the Jewish community; and be it further

Resolved, That, to the end of encouraging and furthering mutual understanding between Episcopalians and Jews by way of biblical and theological enquiry and through friendly discussion, the Presiding Bishop's Advisory Committee on Episcopal–Jewish Relations initiate a study on the methodology for and substantive issues of Episcopal-Jewish dialogue in the next triennium; and be it further

Resolved, That the report of the said Presiding Bishop's Advisory Committee on Episcopal-Jewish Relations, together with recommendations for implementation of the dialogue, be made to the 67th General Convention of the Episcopal Church.

"Deicide and the Jews"
–A Resolution of the 1964 General Convention

Whereas, within the Church throughout the centuries, loveless attitudes, including the charge of deicide, have frequently resulted in persecution of the Jewish people and a concomitant revulsion on the part of the Jewish people towards the un-Christ-like witness thus made; and

Whereas, obedience to the Lord of the Church requires an honest and clear expression of love for our neighbor; and

Whereas, persecution of the Jews has been recently intensified in certain areas of the world; and

Whereas, lack of communication between Christians and Jews, and the resulting ignorance and suspicion of each other, have been a barrier to Christian obedience of the Law of Love; be it

Resolved, the House of Bishops concurring, That the General Convention of the Protestant Episcopal Church in the United States of America, meeting in St. Louis in October, 1964, reject the charge of deicide against the Jews and condemn anti-Semitism; and be it further

Resolved, That the General Convention condemn unchristian accusations against Jews; and that this Church seek positive dialogue with appropriate representative bodies of the Jewish Faith; and be it further

Resolved, That the substance of this resolution be referred to the Joint Commission on Ecumenical Relations for continuing study and suggested implementation.

From *The Blue Book: Reports of the Committees, Commissions, Boards, and Agencies of the General Convention of the Episcopal Church,* 1988, pages 454–60, with changes made by General Convention. Printed 1989 by Forward Movement Publications, 412 Sycamore Street, Cincinnati, Ohio 45202.

Appendix C: "The Declaration of the Evangelical Lutheran Church in America to the Jewish Community"

"The Declaration of the Evangelical Lutheran Church in America to the Jewish Community" was adopted by the Church Council of the Evangelical Lutheran Church in America on April 18, 1994.

In the long history of Christianity there exists no more tragic development than the treatment accorded the Jewish people on the part of Christian believers. Very few Christian communities of faith were able to escape the contagion of anti-Judaism and its modern successor, anti-Semitism. Lutherans belonging to the Lutheran World Federation and the Evangelical Lutheran Church in America feel a special burden in this regard because of certain elements in the legacy of the reformer Martin Luther and the catastrophes, including the Holocaust of the twentieth century, suffered by Jews in places where the Lutheran churches were strongly represented.

The Lutheran communion of faith is linked by name and heritage to the memory of Martin Luther, teacher and reformer. Honoring his name in our own, we recall his bold stand for truth, his earthy and sublime words of wisdom, and above all his witness to God's saving Word. Luther proclaimed a gospel for people as we really are, bidding us to trust a grace sufficient to reach our deepest shames and address the most tragic truths.

In the spirit of that truth-telling, we who bear his name and heritage must with pain acknowledge also Luther's anti-Judaic diatribes and violent recommendations of his later writings against the Jews. As did many of Luther's own companions in the sixteenth century, we reject this violent invective, and yet more do we express our deep and abiding sorrow over its tragic effects on subsequent generations. In concert with the Lutheran World Federation, we particularly deplore the appropriation of Luther's words by modern anti-Semites for the teaching of hatred toward Judaism or toward the Jewish people in our day.

Grieving the complicity of our own tradition within this history of hatred, moreover, we express our urgent desire to live out our faith in Jesus Christ with love and respect for the Jewish people. We recognize in anti-Semitism a contradiction and an affront to the Gospel, a violation of our hope and calling, and we pledge this church to oppose the deadly working of such bigotry, both within our own circles and in the society around us. Finally, we pray for the continued blessing of the Blessed One upon the increasing cooperation and understanding between Lutheran Christians and the Jewish community.

Notes

Introduction

1. Charles E. Silberman, *A Certain People: American Jews and their Lives Today* (New York: Summit Books, 1985), has argued that Jews in this country are effectively assimilated in such fashion that they no longer need fear extermination. That the Judaism of the present differs from that of several generations earlier is obvious, but Judaism has always been a changing, emerging phenomenon.

2. A distinction is not intended between a Jew born into the faith and a Christian choosing same. Many Christians are in essence born into their faith association, although some actively choose their affiliation. In like fashion a person not born Jewish may choose to embrace Judaism via the conversion process.

I. Searching for Roots

1. See Hannah Arendt, "Antisemitism" (Part One of *The Origins of Totalitarianism,* New York: Harcourt, Brace & World, Inc., 1968). See Arendt, pp. vii–xii, where she comments helpfully on the distinction between "religious Jew-hatred" and antisemitism.

2. Amos Elon, *Herzl* (New York: Holt, Rinehart and Winston, 1975), p. 127. See also Norman H. Finkelstein, *Theodor Herzl* (New York: Franklin Watts, 1987). Albert S. Lindermann, *The Jew Accused: Three Anti-Semitic Affairs (Dreyfus, Beilis, Frank), 1894–1915* (Cambridge: University Press, 1991), gives broader but relevant coverage for our topic.

3. Melvin M. Tumin, "What is Antisemitism?" in *Antisemitism in the United States,* ed. Leonard Dinnerstein (New York: Holt, Rinehart and Winston, 1971), pp. 10–11.

4. Ibid., p. 11.

5. C. U. Wolf, "Semite," *The Interpreter's Dictionary of the Bible,* ed. G.A. Buttrick (New York: Abingdon Press, 1962), vol. 4, 269. Gavin I. Langmuir, in *Toward A Definition of Antisemitism* (Los Angeles: University of California Press, 1990), states: "Actually, the term *anti-Semitism* is a misnomer when referring to hatred only of Jews, for the word *Semite* really refers to groups of people whose languages have similar roots—the Hebrews, Arabs, Assyrians, Phoenicians, and Babylonians" (pp. 13–14).

6. Langmuir, *Toward A Definition of Antisemitism,* p. 311. See Langmuir, pp. 311–52, for a lucid critique of the various methodologies for defining antisemitism, whether the original use of the word as contrasted with developed use, definitions as determined by social psychologists and sociologists, intergroup hostility, definitions of "prejudice," etc. He lumps these types into "realistic, xenophobic, and chimerical assertions…" (p. 340).

7. *Webster's Seventh New Collegiate Dictionary* (Springfield, Massachusetts: G.& C. Merriam Company, Publishers, 1967), p. 40.

8. See Lee J. Levinger, *Anti-Semitism in the United States* (Westport, Connecticut: Greenwood Press, Publishers, 1972). This is applicable especially to the United States but a good summary of antisemitism in Europe is given as well. See also *Anti-Semitism in American History,* ed. David A. Gerber (Chicago: University of Illinois Press, 1986).

9. James William Parkes, *The Jew and his Neighbour: A Study of Antisemitism,* 2nd ed. rev. (London: Student Christian Movement Press, 1938), pp. 79ff.

10. See Rudolph Maurice Loewenstein, *Christians and Jews,* trans. Vera Damman (New York: International Universities Press, 1951), who presents an interesting and helpful psychological study that is strongly Freudian. He gives considerable attention to Jewish traits and psychological/social/economic/ religious factors accounting for same. The volume is helpful in its illustrative use of case examples to enlighten psychoanalytic terminology.

11. Note that one of the significant differences between the decalogues as found in Exodus 20 and Deuteronomy 5 is the rationale for observing the Sabbath. According to Exodus 20:8–11, the Israelite was to observe the Sabbath as an emulation of God's activity in creation. According to Deuteronomy 5:12–15, however, the rationale for observing the Sabbath is more the humanitarian concern—remember that once "you were a servant in the land of Egypt...."

12. Ida L. Jacobs, "They Came Bearing Gifts," n.p., n.d. Microfilm filed in the American Jewish Archives of the Hebrew Union College-Jewish Institute of Religion, Cincinnati, Ohio, p. 8.

13. Rosemary Ruether, *Faith and Fratricide: The Theological Roots of Antisemitism* (New York: The Seabury Press, Inc., 1974), pp. 23–63. On page

29, Ruether discusses several areas of Christian antisemitism finding roots in pagan antisemitism: degenerate people, repulsion against circumcision, Sabbath as excuse for laziness, Jewish misfortune, ritual murder, etc. See also Bernard Lazare, *Antisemitism, Its History and Causes* (New York: The International Library Publishing Company, 1903), pp. 7–41, who also discusses quite helpfully the nature of pre-Christian antisemitism.

14. See Friedrich Heer, *God's First Love: Christians and Jews over Two Thousand Years,* trans. Geoffrey Skelton (New York: Weybright and Talley, 1970), pp. 15–18.

15. Ruether, *Faith and Fratricide*, p. 24. It is known that approximately one million Jews lived in Alexandria by the first Christian century. See J. A. Sanders, "Dispersion," *The Interpreter's Dictionary of the Bible,* ed. G. A. Buttrick (New York: Abingdon Press, 1962), I, 855.

16. See Heer, *God's First Love: Christians and Jews over Two Thousand Years,* pp. 18–19.

17. Ruether, *Faith and Fratricide*, p. 25.

18. Ibid., p. 28.

19. Jules Isaac, *Has Anti-Semitism Roots in Christianity?* trans. Dorothy and James Parkes (New York: National Conference of Christians and Jews, 1962), pp. 57–60.

20. Ibid., p. 64.

21. Charles Y. Glock and Rodney Stark, *Christian Beliefs and Anti-Semitism* (New York: Harper & Row, Publishers, 1966), p. 60.

22. Ibid., p. 54.

23. Grace Halsell has written a thoughtful book entitled *Prophecy and Politics: The Secret Alliance Between Israel and the U.S. Christian Right* (Chicago: Lawrence Hill Books, 1986), which book exposed the alliance between the militant Christian right and certain Israeli extremists, which alliance has precipitated a flow of arms to Israel and a disregard for Palestinian rights. The principal point behind such Christian dispensationalist thought, however, is that the encouragement of such Armageddon thought has no real concern for the Jew except as the Jew becomes a factor to bring about the second coming of the Christ.

24. See in Chapter 5 the section entitled "American Judaism Looks Forward."

25. The Book of Esther, one of the latest Biblical writings and thus mentioned earlier as a counterpoint to the exodus narrative, has not been developed further since the story is so tradition laden. The Esther story is not treated as a historical narrative within literary critical circles.

26. Ruether, *Faith and Fratricide,* p. 30.

27. James Daane, *The Anatomy of Anti-Semitism and Other Essays on*

Religion and Race, (Grand Rapids, Michigan: William B. Eerdmans Publishing Company, 1965).

28. Ibid., p. 21. See also numerous other places in the tract for similar statements.

29. Gregory Baum, *Is the New Testament Anti-Semitic?* Rev. ed. (Glen Rock, N.J.: Paulist Press, 1965).

30. See Parkes, *The Jew and his Neighbour,* p. 63.

31. John P. Meier's *A Marginal Jew: Rethinking the Historical Jesus,* 1 (New York: Doubleday, 1991) is an excellent example of an attempt to understand the Jesus of history apart from the trappings of confessional affirmation. He suggests as premise for the book that a Catholic, a Protestant, a Jew, and an agnostic be locked in the bowels of the Harvard Divinity School library with the understanding that they would not be released until they reached a consensus portrait of Jesus! The portrait must be free of all confessional bias and express only what can be known of the historical Jesus from the available sources. It is a book such as that written by Meier to which one should look to respond to the various questions listed. Meier's volume 1 has been published and covers the "Roots of the Problem" and the "Roots of the Person." Volume 1, therefore, only takes us through the birth of Jesus. Volume 2, published in 1994 (New York: Doubleday), covers John the Baptist (Mentor), the Message of Jesus, and the Miracles of Jesus. In volume 1 Meier states that he will address the public ministry of Jesus and "the momentous and tragic final days of Jesus' life, ending with his crucifixion and burial" (p. 13). As he notes, the Resurrection is omitted, not because he denies it "but simply because the restrictive definition of the historical Jesus I will be using does not allow us to proceed into matters that can be affirmed only by faith" (p. 13). Volume 3, not yet published, will take the reader through the last days of Jesus, his death and burial.

32. It should be recognized that Judaism acknowledged numerous perceptions of the "anointed one" (Messiah in Hebrew, Christ in Greek), including the Davidic warrior-king, the new Moses, Son of Man, Suffering Servant, etc. See James D. G. Dunn, *The Partings of the Ways: Between Christianity and Judaism and Their Significance for the Character of Christianity* (Philadelphia: Trinity Press International, 1991), Chapter 9 (pp. 163–82), who investigates Jesus' use of or resistence to Jewish categories, with the conclusion that "Jesus himself still stood well within the boundaries of second Temple Judaism at the point of Jewish monotheism" (p. 182).

33. See Vincent Martin, *A House Divided: The Parting of the Ways Between Synagogue and Church* (New York: Paulist Press, 1995), p. 28.

34. See Martin, *A House Divided,* pp. 26–37, for development of these ideas.

35. See Dunn, *The Partings of the Ways,* especially pp. 105–6, where he discusses "the role of conflict in group self-definition." He suggests that "in

order to form and maintain their identity, groups have to differentiate themselves from other groups," and "Where the groups are close or very similar, the conflict is likely to be more intense...." This insight from sociology and social anthropology gives added insight to the conflict between early Christians and Jews.

36. Only Luke is seriously questioned as to whether he was Jew or Gentile. Were he actually Gentile, it should be noted that perhaps the most inconsequential bases for anti-Judaism are found in the Lucan corpus (Luke-Acts).

37. See Craig A. Evans & Donald A. Hagner, eds., *Anti-Semitism and Early Christianity* (Minneapolis: Fortress Press, 1993), esp. pp. 1–17.

38. Ibid., p. 9.

39. Ibid., pp. 14–17, which in brief compass notes some of the recent writers who have argued both on the side that the New Testament must be recognized as an antisemitic document and those that conversely challenge such an interpretation. Indeed, the chapters of *Anti-Semitism and Early Christianity* are predicated on the assumption "that these writings, though at times highly critical of Jews and Gentiles who for various reasons rejected the Christian proclamation, are not anti-Semitic" (p. 17).

40. Arthur Roy Eckardt, *Elder and Younger Brothers* (New York: Charles Scribner's Sons, 1967), p.8. See also by the same author *Christianity and the Children of Israel* (New York: King's Crown Press, 1948) in which a clear statement against antisemitism is expressed from a neo-Orthodox perspective.

41. Ibid., p. 22, developed pp. 22–30.

42. See Dagobert David Runes, *The Jew and the Cross,* 2nd ed. (New York: Citadel Press, 1966), pp. 14–15, 19, 25, 27, 35, 43. *et al.*

43. Broader than just an interest in Judaism's relationship to Rome, Lazare's coverage of the antisemitism factor during the first seven centuries of the Christian era (pp. 42–91) is instructive in placing the primary emphasis upon the religious causes for antisemitism. (See Lazare, *Antisemitism, Its History and Causes.*)

44. Heer, *God's First Love*, p. 23.

45. Baum, *Is the New Testament Anti-Semitic?* rev. ed., p. 107, but see pp. 100–8.

46. Heer, *God's First Love,* p. 23.

47. See Robert Kysar, "Anti-Semitism and the Gospel of John," in *Anti-Semitism and Early Christianity,* ed. Craig A. Evans and Donald A. Hagner (Minneapolis: Fortress Press, 1993), pp. 113–27, who suggests that a reading of the Gospel of John (and indeed of other portions of the New Testament) which takes seriously the question of Christian self-identity potentially gives an approach to the Fourth Gospel which removes the blatant antisemitic tone

associated with simply a surface reading of the text (which he readily admits strikes strongly of an anti-Jewish tone, see for example, p. 117).

48. See note 31 and the reference to Meier's *A Marginal Jew*. The development of Meier's book underlines how foolhardy we are when we make excessive historical claims regarding the New Testament.

49. Ruether, *Faith and Fratricide,* p. 78. See the section on Paul in Chapter 2, most especially the discussion of Romans 9–11. The one certainty is the ambiguity of the Pauline position. Whereas salvation was ultimately to be found through faith in the Christ, Paul still had expectations, albeit differing ones, of both the Jew and the Gentile relative to observance of the 613 *mitzvoth.*

50. Hare suggests that the identification of the Pharisees as the sole Jewish protagonists against Jesus is an oversimplification. He discusses helpfully the extent of Christian hostility against the Jews in the Gospel of Matthew. See Douglas R. A. Hare, *The Theme of Jewish Persecution of Christians in the Gospel According to St. Matthew* (Cambridge: The University Press, 1967). See especially pages 1–18 for a general statement of the problem.

51. Ruether, *Faith and Fratricide,* p. 80.

II. The New Testament Bases

1. Heer, *God's First Love,* p. 30. See also Martin Buber, *Two Types of Faith,* trans. Norman P. Goldhawk (New York: Harper Torchbook, 1961); Buber draws an incisive comparison between Jesus (and Pharisaic Judaism) and Paul (and Diaspora Judaism).

2. Heer, *God's First Love*, pp. 30–31.

3. Dr. Michael J. Cook, Professor at the Hebrew Union College-Jewish Institute of Religion in Cincinnati, made this statement in a paper read in New York City on December 3, 1986. This was a session specially convened by Bishop Browning, the Presiding Bishop of the Protestant Episcopal Church, who brought together Jewish and Christian scholars to discuss reactions to and the influence of the Pauline contribution. Professor Cook read an excellent paper representing a Jewish perspective.

4. See Vincent Martin, *A House Divided: The Parting of the Ways Between Synagogue and Church* (New York: Paulist Press, 1995), pp. 96–97, who presents a more separatist view of Paul's thought relative to Judaism than is here presented. As he states, "Despite the feelings of his heart, in his mind Christianity was eschatological, Judaism was historical, and the twain didn't meet" (p. 97). He also suggests that Paul's universalism brought a natural fear to synagogue-related Jews in the Diaspora as well as to the "Church of the Circumcision" in Jerusalem (p. 96), a fear that ultimately brought division. See also James

D. G. Dunn, *The Partings of the Ways: Between Christianity and Judaism and their Significance for the Character of Christianity* (Philadelphia: Trinity Press International, 1991), pp. 138–39 (but see pp. 117–39), who suggests that Paul did not object to the Law but to its abuse. He agreed with Jesus' concern that the Law drew internal boundaries within Judaism but went further to reject the "*external* boundaries drawn round Judaism" (p. 138). He notes that "Paul's stand at Antioch and thereafter *made a parting of the ways inevitable....*" (p. 139).

5. The portrayal of Paul presented here is akin to that suggested by Rudolf Bultmann in *Theology of the New Testament,* trans. by Kendrick Grobel, I (New York: Charles Scribner's Sons, 1951), pp. 259ff. Bultmann indicated that the Torah was Judaism's special gift, that it may be seen in terms of ritual and ethical components, that Paul's emphasis was upon the latter, and that, while the Gentile was not obligated to follow Torah, the Gentile did have a type of moral obligation to obey its ethical aspects. The question of Paul's understanding of the relationship of the Gospel message to the Gentiles will continue to be debated. The discussion of Romans 9–11 is perhaps most noteworthy because of its absence of a definitive conclusion. A good article discussing the shades of meaning in that section, e.g. Paul's role as the missionary to the Gentiles, the role of the Jews relative to the salvation of the Gentiles, the curtailment of the possibility of salvation for the Gentiles once the Parousia occurs, etc., is Terence L. Donaldson's "'Riches for the Gentiles' (Rom 11:12): Israel's Rejection and Paul's Gentile Mission," *Journal of Biblical Literature,* 112 (1993), 81–98. See the bibliographic suggestions in Donaldson's article for differing views relative to the questions raised.

6. Martin, *A House Divided,* suggests that Paul became convinced that, even though the Gentiles could be saved by observing the Noahide commandments, they were in fact condemned by their "idolatry, lust and greed" (p. 88). Because of his experience of "the ministry of the risen Jesus" and his conviction that thereby "salvation was offered to all," he "was ready to answer God's call and go to the Gentiles as minister of reconciliation" (p. 88).

7. If this is a correct portrayal of Paul's position, it is obvious that a differing salvic principle applies to the Jew and the Gentile. For the Jew, one relies upon the traditions of the Fathers as expressed in the Torah and upon the messianic hopes as asserted especially by the prophets. Jesus as Messiah would be an actualization of an anticipation expressed through the traditions and teachings of Israel. For the Gentile, the salvic principle is faith in Jesus as the Christ and thus mediator with God—in Paul's view a return to the Abrahamic perspective which was pre-Torah and faith based. It is the distinction clarified by Martin Buber in *Two Types of Faith,* pp. 24–42, namely that the characterization of Judaism is found in the Hebrew word *Emunah* (trust in God on the basis of past deeds although you cannot prove the validity of such trust) while the characterization of Christianity is focused in the Greek word *Pistis* (faith in the veracity

of an event for one's personal situation even though one cannot prove the validity of such vested faith). In Judaism one's trust is placed in Yahweh as the power behind the Exodus event, the series of occurrences that both cumulatively brought Israel into being and prototypically depicted the way of Yahweh's relating to Israel throughout the people's history, while in Christianity one's faith is placed in the Resurrection event, that event always affirmed as God's act and proclaimed by the individual believer to be the harbinger of personal victory over the ultimate relational enemy, death.

8. Gregory Baum, *Is the New Testament Anti-Semitic?* pp. 275–348. A volume such as *The Jewish Question,* by Arno Clemens Gaebelein (New York: Publication Office "Our Hope," 1912), is characteristic of a "soft" anti-semitism. Gaebelein assumes that it is still necessary for Israel to be saved, implicitly asserting thereby the ineffectiveness of the Jewish faith. See also Hare, *The Theme of Jewish Persecution of Christians,* pp. 149ff.

9. Ruether, *Faith and Fratricide,* p. 106.

10. Gregory Baum, Ibid., p. 6.

11. Will Herberg, *Faith Enacted as History,* ed. with an Introduction by Bernhard W. Anderson (Philadelphia: The Westminster Press, 1976), p. 48. See also Norbert Lohfink, *The Covenant Never Revoked: Biblical Reflections on Christian-Jewish Dialogue,* trans. John J. Scullion, S.J. (Mahwah, N.J.: Paulist Press, 1991), esp. Chapters 8 and 9 which deal directly with Romans 9–11.

12. Herberg, *Faith Enacted as History,* p. 50. While beginning from radically different presuppositions, see also Walther Eichrodt, *Theology of the Old Testament,* vols. 1 and 2, trans. J. A. Baker (Philadelphia: The Westminster Press, 1961, 1967) for best exposition of the centrality of the covenant in Biblical faith.

13. C. H. Dodd, *The Epistle of Paul to the Romans* in *The Moffatt New Testament Commentary,* ed. James Moffatt (London: Hodder and Stoughton, Limited, 1932), p. 150.

14. Ruether, *Faith and Fratricide,* p. 103.

15. Ibid., p. 104.

16. Herberg, *Faith Enacted as History,* p. 57. See also Jacob B. Agus, "Franz Rosenzweig," in *Modern Philosophies of Judaism* (New York: Behrman's Jewish Book House, 1941), p. 194.

17. This superiority is such as to abolish the Levitical priesthood and sacrifices; see 7:11–19 and 10:9–10.

18. See also William Manson, *The Epistle to the Hebrews* (London: Hodder and Stoughton, Ltd., 1951), who does accept the idea that Christianity removed Judaism's reason for being (p. 24) but who judges the sin of the 'Hebrews' group to be "remaining as Christians under the covert of the Jewish religion, living too much in the Jewish part of their Christianity, and so missing the true horizon of the eschatological calling" (p. 24). He was specifically

concerned to link this letter "to the teaching of Stephen and the world-mission" (p. 86). See also William Neil, *The Epistle to the Hebrews,* "Torch Bible Commentaries," ed. John Marsh, et al. (London: SMC Press, Ltd., 1955); Hugh Montefiore, *A Commentary on the Epistle to the Hebrews,* "Harper's New Testament Commentaries," ed. Henry Chadwick (New York: Harper & Row, Publishers, 1964); J. H. Davies, *A Letter to Hebrews,* "Cambridge Bible Commentary on the New English Bible," ed. P. R. Ackroyd, et al. (Cambridge: Cambridge University Press, 1967); as well as earlier commentaries, among them the excellent volume by James Moffatt (1924).

19. The Gospels of Matthew (80–85 A.D.), Mark (64–69 A.D.), and Luke (80–85 A.D.) are referred to as the Synoptic Gospels because they are understood to view essentially alike the mission, ministry, and message of Jesus. The format of Matthew and Luke is derived from Mark, with each of them supplementing Mark's outline of a time in Galilee (chapters 1–9), the journey to Jerusalem (chapter 10), and the Jerusalem ministry culminating with the cross event (chapters 11–16). Not only is the basic format the same, but indeed there is considerable use of material, whether it be Matthew and Luke's use of Mark or Matthew and Luke's use of Quelle (or Q), the so-called "Sayings Source" probably compiled in Antioch about 50 A.D. Scholars generally recognize the considerable difference between the Synoptic Gospels and the Gospel of John.

20. Baum, *Is the New Testament Anti-Semitic?* pp. 100–8, discusses the importance of Matthew 27:25 for the understanding of blood-curse anti-Semitism:

"And all the people answered, 'His blood be on us and our children!'"

Because Baum has so thoroughly and helpfully treated the passage and because the passage is so often discussed, it will not be discussed further here. The passage does have obvious importance, however, as perusal of the commentaries on the verse indicates. This idea of blood-curse or blood-guilt voluntarily assumed has been a major factor in Christianity's sanction of antisemitism.

21. C. H. Dodd, *The Parables of the Kingdom,* rev. ed. (New York: Charles Scribner's Sons, 1961), pp. 96–102; J. Jeremias, *The Parables of Jesus,* trans. S. H. Hooke (London: SCM, 1954), pp. 55–60.

22. F. W. Beare, *The Earliest Records of Jesus* (New York: Abingdon Press, 1962), p. 209.

23. Ibid., p. 209.

24. Hare, *The Theme of Jewish Persecution of Christians,* p. 151.

25. Ibid. Hare, p. 80, notes that whereas Luke follows closely Mark, Matthew's Gospel has greatly expanded the denunciation of the Jews.

26. Ibid., p. 153. Martin, *A House Divided,* p. 125, suggests on a more

positive note that Matthew's use of quotations from the Hebrew scriptures was to point to the continuity of revelation in the life and teaching of Jesus.

27. Beare, *The Earliest Records of Jesus,* p. 197.

28. Ruether, *Faith and Fratricide,* p.78. It is debatable whether this dichotomy is that of developed Christianity, which formulated its thought at some remove from Judaism, or actually a characteristic of incipient Christian thought. Most would argue the former.

29. Ibid., p. 81.

30. Martin Buber, *Two Types of Faith,* trans. Norman P. Goldhawk (New York: Harper Torchbooks, 1961), pp. 100–101.

31. Beare, *The Earliest Records of Jesus,* p. 81.

32. J. C. Fenton, *The Gospel of St. Matthew,* "The Pelican Gospel Commentaries," ed. D. E. Nineham (Baltimore: Penguin Books, 1963), p. 157.

33. See similar position in Theodore H. Robinson, *The Gospel of Matthew,* "The Moffatt New Testament Commentary," ed. James Moffatt (New York: Harper and Brothers, Publishers, 1927), pp. 89, 135. See also Suzanne de Dietrich, *The Gospel According to Matthew,* trans. Donald G. Miller, "The Layman's Bible Commentary," ed. Balmer H. Kelly (Richmond: John Knox Press, 1961), pp. 60, 61, 90.

34. Ruether, *Faith and Fratricide,* p. 83. See pp. 82–84 for discussion.

35. John B. Gabel, Charles B. Wheeler, and Anthony D. York, *The Bible as Literature,* third edition (New York: Oxford University Press, 1996), pp. 8–9. Emphasis added. Dunn, *The Partings of the Ways,* pp. 73–74, notes that it should be recognized that the Stephen incident not only marks the opening of a split between Judaism and Christianity but *"also* a split within the new movement..." (p. 74). One of the ideas to be avoided is that all of the early Christian movement was monolithic. This was no more true for the early Christian movement than for Judaism. See also his further development regarding "sacred space," pp. 95–96.

36. Heer, *God's First Love,* p. 23, states: "The Fourth Gospel ...is the most pro-Roman and anti-Jewish of them all" (i.e., of the four Gospels).

37. Ruether, *Faith and Fratricide,* p. 111. Approaching the issues from a different perspective, Dunn, in *The Partings of the Ways,* pp. 228–29, suggests that the Fourth Evangelist went beyond the bounds of traditional Jewish monotheism in the portrayal of Jesus. Whereas the Fourth Evangelist may not have agreed, from the perspective of "emerging rabbinic Judaism," "the parting of the ways had already happened" (p. 229).

38. Martin, *A House Divided,* pp. 136–37, suggests that the Prologue to the Fourth Gospel was intended to emphasize the "humanization of God," but instead his "humanity became a transparent icon of his divinity or a practical instrument of his divine activity" (p. 136). Through this process, he was "no

longer a Jew, he was the rootless, universal and abstract humanity of God's Word" (p. 137).

39. Alan Richardson, *The Gospel According to St. John* (New York: Collier Books, 1962), pp. 100–101.

40. Martin, *A House Divided*, p. 35, appropriately noted: "The fact that the fourth Gospel, for whatever reason, named these religious authorities 'The Jews' turned out to be a tragedy in subsequent history, because it became a source of lasting anti-Judaism."

41. Dunn, *The Partings of the Ways*, pp. 244–47, discusses the Jesus phenomenon relative to traditional Jewish monotheism. He suggests that "The point of recognizing that Wisdom(-Logos) christology is the dominant category in John, however, is that *it shows how John's christology remained within the bounds of Jewish monotheism*" (p. 244). However one understands the various writings, he properly notes that "*monotheism is a non-negotiable starting point for Christian thought about Christ, and remains the axiomatic starting point within which any 'high' christology must continue to be expressed*" (p. 246).

42. It should be acknowledged that the negative perception of the other was reciprocal. Martin, in *A House Divided*, notes that two events around 90 C.E. depict a type of culmination of the "parting of the ways between the two siblings… " (p. 152). On the Christian side, he was referring to the publication of the Fourth Gospel "in which 'The Jews' were condemned as the enemies of Jesus…" (p. 153). On the Jewish side, "the addition to the Eighteen Benedictions of a curse against the MINIM … was aimed primarily but not exclusively at the Nazarenes" (p. 153).

43. Ruether, *Faith and Fratricide*, pp. 94–95.

44. Ibid., p. 94.

45. See Martin, *A House Divided*, pp. 180–81, for discussion of the division between Judaism and Christianity.

46. Dunn, in *The Partings of the Ways*, pp. 242–43, suggests that the second Jewish revolt of 132–35 C.E., when bar Kokhba was proclaimed as Messiah, constituted "*the first time within Judaism since Jesus [that] there was a widely accepted alternative to the Christian claim that Jesus was Messiah*" (p. 243). The obvious inability of Christians to support this claim confirmed once and for all "that they [Jewish Christians] could no longer be both Jews and Christians, but had to decide which of the now separated ways they should follow" (p. 243). He proceeds then to discuss how the Christian way ultimately violated/rejected the four pillars of rabbinic Judaism: (1) God is one (pp. 244–47), (2) the people of God (pp. 248–51), (3) the law of God (scripture and tradition) (pp. 251–54), and (4) priesthood and ministry (pp. 254–58).

47. It is acknowledged that the latter part of the second century is too late to be a factor in determining the writing of New Testament passages, but an idea that blossomed in the second century did not just spontaneously occur

without any precedent thought and expression. It is not outrageous, therefore, to acknowledge deicide as one of the factors important in understanding the development of Christian antisemitism. This is particularly true with respect to the thought expressed in the Fourth Gospel, the latest written of the canonical Gospels.

48. Clark M. Williamson, *Has God Rejected His People?* (Nashville: Abingdon Press, l982), p. 93.

49. Williston Walker, *A History of the Christian Church,* rev. ed. (New York: Charles Scribner's Sons, l959), p. l29, indicates his birth to be "about 345–47...."

50. Ibid., p. l30.

51. Ibid., p. l29.

52. See Kenneth Scott Latourette, *A History of Christianity* (New York: Harper & Brothers, 1953), pp. 150–51.

53. Walker, *A History of the Christian Church,* rev. ed., p. 130.

54. See Wayne A. Meeks and Robert L. Wilken, *Jews and Christians in Antioch in the First Four Centuries of the Common Era,* in Society of Biblical Literature Sources for Biblical Study, ed. Wayne A. Meeks (Missoula, Montana: Scholars Press, 1978), pp. 83–84.

55. Ibid., p. 31.

56. Ibid.

57. Ibid., p. 86.

58. Ibid., p. 87.

59. Ibid., p. 90.

60. Ibid., p. 92.

61. Ibid.

62. Ibid., p. 97.

III. The Medieval Church and Antisemitism

1. Several books on Jewish history that would be helpful are H. H. Ben-Sasson, ed., *A History of the Jewish People* (Cambridge, Massachusetts: Harvard University Press, 1976); Paul Johnson, *A History of the Jews* (New York: Harper & Row, Publishers, 1987); Abram Leon Sachar, *A History of the Jews,* 5th ed. rev. (New York: Alfred A. Knopf, 1967); Norman Cantor, *The Sacred Chain: The History of the Jews* (New York: Harper Collins Publishers, 1994); and Cecil Roth, *A History of The Jews: From Earliest Times Through The Six Day War,* rev. ed. (New York: Schocken Books, 1970).

2. In l858, an incident of similar nature occurred when a seven-year-old Jewish child, Edgardo Mortara, was kidnapped at Bologna under the pretext that the child had been baptized six years earlier by a Christian

servant-girl. In spite of protests, the child was not returned and was thus brought up in the Christian faith. See Roth, *A History of the Jews,* pp. 345–46.

3. Lazare, in *Antisemitism, Its History and Causes,* pp. 91–375, gives an excellent analysis of antisemitism and its multiple causes from the eighth century to the time of the book's publication (1903).

4. Heer, *God's First Love,* p. 65.

5. Salo Wittmayer Baron, *Steeled by Adversity,* ed. Jeannette Meisel Baron (Philadelphia: The Jewish Publication Society of America, 1971), p. 19.

6. See Roth, *A History of the Jews,* pp. 224–27.

7. Parkes, *The Jew and his Neighbour,* 2nd ed. rev., p. 16. Although there were assuredly Jews who authentically converted to Christianity, many if not most put on a Christian facade; to external observation, they appeared to be Christians, but internally and behind closed doors they continued to practice as Jews. See Cecil Roth, *History of the Marranos,* 4th ed. (New York: Hermon Press, 1974).

8. Roth, *A History of the Jews,* p. 224.

9. Ibid., pp. 157ff.; and Sachar, *A History of the Jews,* pp. 168ff.

10. Franklin Sherman, ed., *Luther's Works: The Christian in Society,* vol. 4, Helmut L. Lehmann, gen. ed. (Philadelphia: Fortress Press, 1971), vol. 47, p. 124. Used by permission of Augsburg Fortress.

11. Ibid., pp. 124–25.

12. See Aarne Siirala, "Luther and the Jews," *Lutheran World,* XI (1964), 337–57, for a good statement of the reasons why Luther turned against the Jews. See also Sherman, ed., *Luther's Works,* pp. 125–27, for discussion of the transformation in Luther's proclamation.

13. Sherman, ed., *Luther's Works,* p. 137.

14. Meaning his correspondent, a Christian, by the name of Count Schlick.

15. Sherman, ed., *Luther's Works,* p. 172.

16. Ibid., p. 217.

17. Ibid., p. 268.

18. Ibid., pp. 268–72.

19. Ibid., pp. 285–86.

20. Ibid., pp. 289–90.

21. Calvin had little to say about the Jews. See Parkes, *The Jew and his Neighbour,* p. 76.

22. de Corneille, *Christians and Jews,* pp. 34–35.

23. Ibid., p. 39.

24. Henry Kraus, *The Living Theatre of Medieval Art* (Bloomington: Indiana University Press, 1967), p. 149.

25. See Nicholas de Lange, *Atlas of the Jewish World* (New York: Facts on File Publications, 1984), p. 37. See also Charles De Tolnay, *Hieronymus*

Bosch (Baden-Baden, Germany: Holle Verlag GMBH, 1966), esp. pp. 26–27 and Plate pages 310–11.

26. The present figure, located on the south transept, is a copy of the thirteenth-century original. Following World War I, some of the badly damaged sculptures were housed in the Tau Museum, which is located adjacent to the cathedral and is the former palace of the archbishop. The originals were then replaced by copies of same. See Martin Hurlimann and Jean Bony, with descriptive notes by Peter Meyer, *French Cathedrals,* rev. ed. (New York: The Viking Press, 1967) for both general and more specific information regarding the French cathedrals.

27. For example, at Bourges the glaziers placed Christ crucified in the center of a window. To his right was the church, "crowned and holding a chalice in her hands with which she receives the mingled blood and water...." To his left stands the synagogue with bandaged eyes. It is noteworthy that here, as with many such depictions, the crown is depicted as falling from synagogue's head. See Sartell Prentice, *The Voices of the Cathedral: Tales in Stone and Legends in Glass* (New York: W. Morrow and Company, 1938), pp. 160–61. See also Frank E. Manuel, *The Broken Staff: Judaism Through Christian Eyes* (Cambridge, Massachusetts: Harvard University Press, 1992).

28. Examples of this phenomenon may also be found in the Musée de l'Oeuvre associated with the Strasbourg Cathedral; a twelfth-century relief from a baptismal font originally located in the Church of Saint Larme of Selincourt but now in the Amiens Museum (see Kraus, *The Living Theatre of Medieval Art,* p. 152, plate 101); and the Troyes Cathedral, as well as numerous other examples which might be cited.

29. See Kraus, *The Living Theatre of Medieval Art,* pp. 139–62 for a good discussion of "Anti-Semitism in Medieval Art."

30. See Painton Cowen, *Rose Windows* (San Francisco: Chronicle Books/A Prism Edition, 1979), pp. 14–15. According to Biblical criticism, Daniel should be associated with apocalypticism rather than prophetism. This misalignment was common during the medieval era and was reenforced by the rearrangement of certain Biblical books done by the Jewish translators of the Septuagint, translators who, although Jewish, apparently both spoke and thought in Hellenistic terms. When Daniel was moved from the Writings (*Kethuvim*) to the Prophets (*Nevi'im*), the stage was set for a major interpretive confusion, as a book written in and for a given context (Maccabean Revolt) was interpreted as having derived from another (Babylonian Exile). Moreover, the problems were exacerbated by the assumption that one set of interpretive principles was appropriate (i.e., prophetic), while actually the material cried out for a totally different set of interpretive understandings (i.e., apocalyptic).

31. Malcolm Miller, *Chartres Cathedral,* photographs by Sonia Halliday and Laura Lushington (London: Pitkin Pictorials Ltd., 1985), p. 94.

32. Lawrence Lee, George Seddon, and Francis Stephens. *Stained Glass* (New York: Crown Publishers, Inc., 1976), p. 77.

33. One is struck by the similarity of this expression to Paul's statement in Galatians 3:19ff. Whereas Paul is not referring to ad hoc residents, he treats Torah as an ad hoc mechanism for relating to God. While Abraham related to God through faith, humankind proved incapable of continuing the relationship in this fashion. Thus God provided a temporary guide, namely the Torah, which is likened to the *paidagogos,* who was responsible for teaching the child until the child moved beyond the capability of the *paidagogos.* It was then the role of the *paidagogos* to lead the child to someone who would guide the child through the next developmental stage. In Paul's thinking, the Torah was such a *paidagogos,* and it was time for the *paidagogos* to relinquish the child and permit the child to recover again the Abrahamic relational principle of faith, now made possible by and through Jesus as the Christ.

34. Both teachings of the Torah and the Prophets constitute the grain needed to be ground in the mill. It is the Torah that gives instruction for living and the Prophets who speak to issues of messianic expectation. See Kraus, *The Living Theatre of Medieval Art,* p. 145.

35. Kraus, *The Living Theatre of Medieval Art,* p. 159.

36. Ibid., pp. 159–61.

37. Malcolm Miller, *Chartres Cathedral,* photographs by Sonia Halliday and Laura Lushington (London: Pitkin Pictorials Ltd., 1985), p. 94.

38. Highly recommended is a reenactment video entitled *The Disputation,* which recounts a disputation between Pablo Christiani, himself a converted Jew, and Rabbi Moses ben Nahman. This disputation actually occurred in 1263, when King James of Aragon sponsored the disputation in which the Jewish spokesman more than upheld his position. Although the Jewish protagonist not only escaped death but was dismissed by the King with a gift, the film is a good way of portraying the way theological antisemitism kept alive this hideous phenomenon.

IV. U.S. Antisemitism: From the Colonies to the Early Federal Period

1. *Marrano* was the name given to a Jew who converted to Christianity, more often referred to as a *Converso* by Christians. *Marrano* is the designation for swine, and this was the evaluation by the Jew of the Jew who converted to Christianity. Many of these individuals converted only to retain their place of domicile or their livelihood, and for these individuals their Christianity was a facade. Some Jews who converted, however, experienced an authentic conversion and motivation should not be questioned. See Cecil Roth, *A History of the Marranos,* 4th ed. (New York: Hermon Press, 1974).

2. See Sachar, *A History of the Jews,* pp. 300–301; and Abraham J. Karp, "The Colonial Period," *The Jewish Experience in America,* ed. Abraham J. Karp (New York: KTAV Publishing House, Inc., 1969), vol. 1, p. xi.

3. Stuart Rosenberg, *The Search for Jewish Identity in America* (Garden City, New York: Doubleday & Company, Inc., 1965), p. 3.

4. Lee Max Friedman, *Jewish Pioneers and Patriots* (New York: The Macmillan Company, 1943), p. 134. See also Jacob Rader Marcus, *Early American Jewry,* vol. 1 (Philadelphia: The Jewish Publication Society of America, 1951), pp. 24–33, for a helpful presentation on the New Amsterdam situation from 1654 to 1664.

5. Jacob Rader Marcus, *Early American Jewry,* vol. 2 (Philadelphia: The Jewish Publication Society of America, 1953), p. 384.

6. Karp, "The Colonial Period," *The Jewish Experience in America,* vol. 1, xiii.

7. Friedman, *Jewish Pioneers and Patriots,* p. 136.

8. Samuel Oppenheim, "More About Jacob Barsimson, The First Jewish Settler in New York," *The Jewish Experience in America,* vol. 1, ed. Abraham J. Karp (New York: KTAV Publishing House, Inc., 1969), p. 38.

9. Henry L. Feingold, *Zion in America,* rev. ed. (New York: Hippocrene Books, 1981), p. 38.

10. See Howard M. Sachar, *A History of the Jews in America* (New York: Alfred A. Knopf, 1992), pp. 9–16, for a succinct but helpful discussion of this earliest Jewish settlement.

11. See Cecil Roth, *A History of the Jews,* rev. ed. (New York: Schocken Books, 1970), pp. 273–94.

12. Doris Groshen Daniels, "Colonial Jewry: Religious, Domestic and Social Relations," *American Jewish Historical Quarterly,* 66 (1977), 375.

13. Salo W. Baron, "American Jewish Communal Pioneering," *The Jewish Experience in America,* vol. 1, ed. Abraham J. Karp (New York: KTAV Publishing House, Inc., 1969), pp. 2–3.

14. Ibid., p. 3.

15. Leonard Dinnerstein and Mary Dale Palsson, eds., *Jews in the South* (Baton Rouge: Louisiana State University Press, 1973), p. 26.

16. Richard B. Morris, "Civil Liberties and the Jewish Tradition in Early America," *The Jewish Experience in America,* vol. 1, ed. Abraham J. Karp (New York: KTAV Publishing House, Inc., 1969), p. 417.

17. Stanley F. Chyet, "The Political Rights of the Jews in the United States: 1776–1840," *Critical Studies in American Jewish History,* Introduction by Jacob R. Marcus, vol. 2 (New York: KTAV Publishing House, Inc., 1971), p. 33.

18. Ibid.

19. Ibid.

20. Stanley Feldstein, *The Land That I Show You* (Garden City, New York: Anchor Press/Doubleday, 1979), p. 11.

21. Nathan C. Belth, *A Promise to Keep* (New York: Schocken Books, 1981), p. 6.

22. Feldstein, *The Land That I Show You*, p. 12.

23. See Abraham Vossen Goodman, *American Overture: Jewish Rights in Colonial Times* (Philadelphia: The Jewish Publication Society of America, 1947), pp. 21–23; George Foot Moore, "Judah Monis," *Proceedings of the Massachusetts Historical Society*, 70 (October, 1918–June, 1919), 285–315; Lee M. Friedman, "Judah Monis, First Instructor in Hebrew at Harvard University," *Publications of the American Jewish Historical Society*, 22 (1914), 1–24; Lee M. Friedman, "Some Further Notes on Judah Monis," *Publications of the American Jewish Historical Society*, 37 (1947), 121–34; Isidore S. Meyer, "Hebrew at Harvard (1636–1760), A Resume of the Information in Recent Publications," *Publications of the American Jewish Historical Society*, 35 (1939), 145–70; Louis Meyer, *The First Jewish Christian in North America—Judah Monis* (Hopkinton, Iowa, No Publisher: No Date), et al.

24. Goodman, *American Overture: Jewish Rights in Colonial Times,* p. 21. Goodman, p. 23, comments that a Jew was first awarded a degree at Oxford University in 1870! See also Tina Levitan, *Jews in American Life* (New York: Hebrew Publishing Company, 1969), p. 13.

25. Meyer, "Hebrew at Harvard (1636–1760), A Resume of the Information in Recent Publications," *PAJHS,* 35 (1939), 155, points out: "The third oldest chair at Harvard is that of the Hancock Professorship in Hebrew (1764)." He also indicates that, according to the enabling will of Thomas Hancock, the incumbent must be "of the protestant reform'd Religion" (p. 156).

26. Leviatan, *Jews in American Life,* p. 12.

27. Moore, "Judah Monis," *Proceedings of the Massachusetts Historical Society,* 70 (October, 1918–June 1919), 297.

28. Ibid., pp. 300–301.

29. One must admit that the tone of his three essays, "The Truth" (delivered at the time of his baptism), "The Whole Truth," and "Nothing But the Truth" has the ring of authenticity. See Meyer, *The First Jewish Christian in North America—Judah Monis,* pp. 7–8. See also Moore, "Judah Monis," *Proceedings of the Massachusetts Historical Society,* 70 (October, 1918–June, 1919), who calls attention to the obvious question regarding Monis's sincerity in the mind of Increase Mather, who wrote a preface to Monis's three essays. Moore also notes that Monis drew heavily on cabalistic literature in formulating his third essay, which sought to prove the doctrine of the Trinity (pp. 304, 306). Moore indicates specifically: "It is not difficult to find a trinity in the Cabala, and not a few Jews found their way to Christianity through it" (p. 306).

30. "The Truth" addressed nine arguments devised by the Jewish Rabbis to prove that the Messiah was yet to come, and the address was "Dedicated to the Jewish Nation." "Nothing But The Truth" summarizes the promise-fulfillment themes which he obviously embraced and which were broadly accepted in the eighteenth century. Throughout his addresses he draws heavily on both the promise-fulfillment theme as well as typology.

31. Raphael Mahler, *A History of Modern Jewry, 1780–1815* (New York: Schocken Books, 1971), p. 5.

32. See *James Madison on Religious Liberty,* ed. with introductions and interpretations by Robert S. Alley (Buffalo, New York: Prometheus Books, 1985), esp. pp. 53–62.

33. Jacob Rader Marcus, *Early American Jewry: The Jews of Pennsylvania and the South, 1655–1790,* vol. 2 (Philadelphia: The Jewish Publication Society of America, 1953), p. 180.

V. U.S. Antisemitism: The Nineteenth and Twentieth Centuries

1. Nathan C. Belth, *A Promise to Keep: A Narrative of the American Encounter with Anti-Semitism* (New York: Schocken Books, 1981), p. 21.

2. Hasia R. Diner, *A Time for Gathering: The Second Migration, 1820–1880,* in "The Jewish People in America," vol. 2, ed. Henry L. Feingold (Baltimore: The Johns Hopkins University Press, 1992), p. 159.

3. See Belth, *A Promise to Keep,* pp. 21–23; Leonard Dinnerstein, *Antisemitism in America* (New York: Oxford University Press, 1994), pp. 31–34; and Diner, *A Time for Gathering,* pp. 158–60.

4. Belth, *A Promise to Keep,* p. 1.

5. John Higham, "American Antisemitism Historically Reconsidered," in *Antisemitism in the United States,* ed. Leonard Dinnerstein (New York: Holt, Rinehart and Winston, 1971), p. 69.

6. Higham, "American Antisemitism Historically Reconsidered," in Dinnerstein, p. 69.

7. Ibid., p. 70.

8. Belth, *A Promise to Keep,* p. 26.

9. Statistics given by Belth, pp. 27–28: Between 1880 and 1910, 2,000,000 Jews entered the United States, with 500,000 more entering in the next decade. He suggests that about 300,000 Jews were already in the United States in 1880. The 2,000,000 Jewish immigrants were part of the approximately 24,000,000 immigrants who entered the country during this period. He notes further that the population of the United States in 1880 was about 50,000,000, while it was approximately 105,000,000 in 1920. This means that:

a. Immigration and native birth were roughly equal during the period.

b. Jews constituted slightly less than 10 percent of the immigration growth.

10. Henry L. Feingold, *Zion in America,* rev. ed. (New York: Hippocrene Books, Inc., 1981), p. 120.

11. Stuart E. Rosenberg, *The Search for Jewish Identity in America* (Garden City, New York: Doubleday & Company, 1965), p. 63.

12. Higham, "American Antisemitism Historically Reconsidered," in *Antisemitism in the United States,* ed. Dinnerstein, p. 70.

13. Belth, *A Promise to Keep,* pp. 93–94.

14. Priscilla Fishman, ed., *The Jews of the United States* (New York: Quadrangle/The New York Times Book Co., 1973), pp. 61–62.

15. Belth, *A Promise to Keep,* p. 173. See the broader coverage relative to Presidents Truman through Johnson, pp. 163–75.

16. See the poem in Geoffrey Wigoder, ed., "Lazarus, Emma," in *Dictionary of Jewish Biography* (New York: Simon & Schuster, 1991), p. 292. For data regarding Emma Lazarus, see Saul Friedman, "Lazarus, Emma," in *Jewish-American History and Culture: An Encyclopedia,* ed Jack Fischel and Sanford Pinsker (New York: Garland Publishing, Inc., 1992), pp. 347–48.

17. Higham, "American Antisemitism Historically Reconsidered," in *Antisemitism in the United States,* ed. Dinnerstein, p. 71.

18. Ibid.

19. See Leonard Dinnerstein, *The Leo Frank Case* (New York: Columbia University Press, 1968); Leonard Dinnerstein, "Atlanta in the Progressive Era," in *Jews in the South,* eds. Leonard Dinnerstein and Mary Dale Palsson (Baton Rouge: Louisiana State University Press, 1973), pp. 170–97; Francis X. Busch, *Guilty or Not Guilty?* (New York: The Bobbs-Merrill Company, Inc., 1952); Albert S. Linderman, *The Jew Accused: Three Anti-Semitic Affairs (Dreyfus, Beilis, Frank),* 1894–1915 (New York: Cambridge University Press, 1991), esp. pp. 235–72; Fay S. Joyce, "Pardon Denied for Leo Frank in 1913 Slaying," *The New York Times,* December 23, 1983, p. A10; Shirley Kolack, "The Leo Frank Case," *Midstream* 34 (No. 3), April 1988, pp. 33–35, et al. The case was covered broadly from 1913 onward in major law journals as well as in the nation's dominant newspapers. Note Linderman, p. 235, n. 2, a pardon was granted to Frank in March, 1986.

20. Kolack, "The Leo Frank Case," *Midstream* 34, (April, 1988), p. 33.

21. Belth, *A Promise to Keep,* p. 130.

22. Ibid., p. 167.

23. Ibid., p. 127.

24. Feldstein, *The Land That I Show You,* p. 404.

25. Belth, *A Promise to Keep,* p. 128.

26. Ibid., p. 130.

27. Ibid., pp. 117 and 229.

28. Feldstein, *The Land That I Show You,* p. 402.

29. Ibid.

30. Belth, *A Promise to Keep,* p. 117. Brinkley, *Voices of Protest,* p. 273, is correct when he states as follows:

Even before 1938, Coughlin could hardly be termed a warm friend of the Jew. At best, his message in the early and mid-1930s was neutral on the subject. At worst, his rhetoric—with its excoriation of 'international bankers' and its references to 'money changers' and the 'sin of usury'—may have worked in a diffuse way to evoke images and produce stereotypes that could be translated easily into hostility toward Jews. But Coughlin himself did little before 1938 to encourage such a translation. His rhetoric was not incompatible with some forms of anti-Semitism; and his excoriation of Jews after 1938 did not, therefore, emerge unnaturally from his earlier positions. Neither, however, did it emerge inevitably from them. Whatever Coughlin's private feelings about Jews, there is nothing to indicate that anti-Semitism played an appreciable role in building his early national popularity.

31. Belth, *A Promise to Keep,* p. 131.

32. Alan Brinkley, *Voices of Protest: Huey Long, Father Coughlin, and the Great Depression* (New York: Alfred A. Knopf, 1982), p. 97.

33. Ibid., p. 97.

34. Belth, *A Promise to Keep,* p. 131.

35. Brinkley, *Voices of Protest,* pp. 133–34, 287–88. Belth suggests that the National Union for Social Justice was to promote his "embryonic fascist program" (Belth, *A Promise to Keep,* p. 131).

36. Ibid., pp. 135–36.

37. Belth, *A Promise to Keep,* pp. 132–33.

38. Feldstein, *The Land That I Show You,* p. 406.

39. Alson J. Smith, *The "Christian" Front* (New York: American League for Peace and Democracy, 1939), p. 5.

40. Belth, *A Promise to Keep,* p. 134.

41. Smith, *The "Christian" Front,* p. 4. As Brinkley, *Voices of Protest,* p. 269, suggests: "There can be little doubt about Coughlin's open and strident anti-Semitism after 1938.... His retreat into bigotry and hysteria was largely an act of resentful desperation."

42. Taken from Smith, *The "Christian" Front,* p. 9. See the entire pamphlet, pp 3–22, for support of other strategies of the Christian Front.

43. David H. Bennett, *Demagogues in the Depression: American Radicals and the Union Party, 1936–1946* (New Brunswick, New Jersey: Rutgers University Press, 1969), p. 279, catalogs effectively the nature of Coughlin's antisemitism, which became pronounced as of November, 1938:

Coughlin attacked Jews for believing they were the chosen people, for having a double-standard toward non-Jews, for thinking of themselves as messiahs. He accused them of starting Freemasonry and the French Revolution, of destroying medieval Christian civilization and of threatening modern Christianity. Echoing an earlier theme, he played most heavily on the contradictory notion that Jews were both international bankers (decadent, evil capitalists) and international Communists. He warned that if Jews did not 'change their ways,' they would get no sympathy for conditions in Hitler's Germany. Indeed, he praised the 'social justice' dispensed by the Third Reich and his newspaper began to reprint speeches of Paul Josef Goebbels, distributed by the Nazi propaganda society, the World Press Service.

44. Belth, *A Promise to Keep,* pp. 137–38. Brinkley, *Voices of Protest,* p. 267, suggests that the Christian Front was always small in membership, perhaps no more than 1,200 individuals. It was effective, as is generally true of such groups, because it was a bully-type organization which trained young men to protect their streets, primarily against Jews and communists.

45. Belth, *A Promise to Keep,* p. 142.

46. Brinkley, *Voices of Protest,* p. 268.

47. This is not to deny that Jewish denominationalism had its birth in Germany, but the full flowering of Jewish denominationalism found its development in the unique climate of the United States.

48. Listing found on the cover of the *1994 Annual Report* of the ADL (copyright 1995, ADL, New York, N.Y.). Correspondence should be addressed to ADL, 823 United Nations Plaza, New York, N.Y. 10017.

49. This problem has been developed in several recent books, such as Stuart E. Rosenberg, *The New Jewish Identity in America* (New York: Hippocrene Books, 1985); Charles E. Silberman, *A Certain People: American Jews and Their Lives Today* (New York: Summit Books, 1985); Leonard Fein, *Where Are We? The Inner Life of America's Jews* (New York: Harper & Row, Publishers, 1988); Jack Wertheimer, *A People Divided: Judaism in Contemporary America* (New York: Basic Books/Harper Collins Publishers, 1993); and Seymour Martin Lipset and Earl Raab, *Jews and the New American Scene* (Cambridge, Massachusetts: Harvard University Press, 1995).

50. Feingold, *Zion in America,* p. xiii.

*VI. Recent Church Statements
on the Relationship of Christianity to Judaism*

1. See Walter M. Abbott, S.J., ed., *The Documents of Vatican II* (New York: Corpus Books, 1966), pp. 663–67. See also Helga Croner, compiler, *Stepping Stones to Further Jewish-Christian Relations* (New York: Stimulus Books, 1977), pp. 29–34. Note: the statement also makes reference to "Vatican

Guidelines of 1975 and the American Bishops' Guidelines for Catholic-Jewish Relations of 1967" (p. 34).

2. See "Tuning Out: Can God Hear a Jew's prayer?" *Time,* vol. 116, no. 13, September 29, 1980, p. 85. See also Kenneth L. Woodward with Joe Contreras, "The Battling Baptists," *Newsweek* vol. 97, no. 25, June 22, 1981, p. 81.

3. See the footnotes in Abbott, pp. 663–67.

4. Taken from page circulating the Declaration, statement found at the end of the Declaration.

5. Paragraph 3, Preamble, "The Willowbank Declaration on the Christian Gospel and the Jewish People."

6. Some evidence for this is seen in the fact that Terah, Abraham's father, initiated the journey from Ur. He died at Haran, at which point Abraham took part of the clan and moved into Canaan, whereas his brother, Nahor, stayed in the North Mesopotamian Valley. The two parts of the clan continued to have significant interchange.

7. *The Disciples of Christ* state explicitly: "We confess that the God who was present in Jesus Christ reconciling the world to God is none other than the God of Israel" (1, #1 under "Theological Foundations").

The Episcopal Church acknowledges that both communities worship "the God of ancient Israel...." (2, #10 under "Necessity for Christians..." and also: "Christians believe that God's self-revelation is given in history. In the Covenant with the Jewish people at Mt. Sinai, the sacred law became part of our religious heritage. *Christians see that same God embodied in the person of Jesus Christ....*" (2, #1 under "Authentic Christian Witness," emphasis added).

The Evangelical Lutheran Church in America acknowledges that Jews and Christians "worship the same God" (Ditmanson, p. 67) and "Judaism and Christianity both worship the one God" (Ditmanson, p. 69).

The Roman Catholic Church, in "Notes on the Correct Way to Present the Jews in Preaching and Catechesis of the Roman Catholic Church" (USCC Publication No 970), June 24, 1985 states: "Attentive to the same God who has spoken, hanging on the same word, we have to witness to one same memory and one common hope in Him who is the master of history" ("Notes," I, 11).

The United Church of Christ in its resolution entitled "The Relationship Between the United Church of Christ and the Jewish Community" affirms clearly that "the God we worship is the God of all creation...." (III).

The World Council of Churches affirmed in the 1988 "The Churches and the Jewish People" that "God is the God of all people...." (C.1.), but this affirmation immediately follows the statement: "We as Christians firmly hold to our confession of faith in Jesus Christ as Lord and God (Jn. 20:28)...." (C), a juxtaposition obviously acceptable to Christians but unacceptable to Jews.

8. See Karen Johnson, *A History of God: The 4000-Year Quest of*

Judaism, Christianity and Islam (New York: Alfred A. Knopf, 1993), especially pp. 107–31, where she discusses "Trinity: The Christian God."

9. *The Disciples of Christ* have several statements that address this issue: "God's presence in Jesus Christ for the redemption of the world is rooted in God's call and election of Israel.... We confess that both the church and the Jewish people are elected by God for witness to the world and that the relation of the church and the Jewish people to each other is grounded on God's gracious election of each" (#3 under "Theological Foundations"). "God is faithful to that covenant in the historical life of Israel...." (#4 under "Theological Foundations"). "We confess that the covenant established by God's grace with the Jewish people has not been abrogated but remains valid, precisely because 'the gifts and the call of God are irrevocable' (Rom. 11:29)" (#5 under "Theological Foundations").

The Episcopal Church does not assert specifically the continuation of the Jewish covenant, but in several statements (#5, 6, 7 under II. The Necessity for Christians ...) it rejects the supersessionist (my term) thought indicative of so much Christian thought in which "the Covenant with Israel was considered to be abrogated" (#5 under II. The Necessity for Christians ...).

The Evangelical Lutheran Church in America statement affirms: "We both view ourselves as communities covenanted to God" (Ditmanson, p. 69 [I]).

The Roman Catholic Church in "Nostra Aetate," 4, acknowledged: "The Church ... cannot forget that she received the revelation of the Old Testament through the people with whom God in his inexpressible mercy designed to establish the Ancient Covenant" (Abbott, p. 664) and acknowledges that "the Jews still remain most dear to God because of their fathers, for He does not repent of the gifts He makes nor of the calls He issues (cf. Rom. 11:28–29)" (Abbott, p. 664).

The United Church of Christ in "The Relationship Between the United Church of Christ and the Jewish Community" in the Resolution (III) states:

"WHEREAS, the Christian communities of recent times have come more and more to recognize that God's covenant with the Jewish people stands inviolate (Romans 9–11); and

"WHEREAS, the Christian Church also stands bound to the same God in covenant, the covenant affirmed and embodied in Jesus as the Christ ...," and

"THEREFORE, the Sixteenth General Synod of the United Church of Christ affirms its recognition that God's covenant with the Jewish people has not been rescinded or abrogated by God, but remains in full force...." (p. 37).

The World Council of Churches in its 1988 statement, "The Churches and the Jewish People," acknowledges "with the apostle Paul that the Jewish people have by no means been rejected by God (Rom. 11:1, 11)" (Affirmations, 7) and "We see not one covenant displacing another, but two communities of faith, each called into existence by God, each holding to its respective gifts from God, and each accountable to God" (Affirmations, 8).

    10. *New Conversations* (Summer, 1990), pp. 44–49.

    11. Ibid, p. 46.

    12. Ibid.

    13. Ibid.

    14. Ibid.

    15. Ibid., p. 47.

    16. Ibid., p. 47, emphasis added.

    17. *The Disciples of Christ* assuredly affirm the continuing election of Israel (Williamson, "Report," statements 3–5, and 11.c. under "Statement of Theological Foundations").

    The Episcopal Church "Guidelines" affirms in #5, 6, 7, and 10 (under II. Necessity for Christians ...) the continuing election and parallel role of the two communities.

    The Evangelical Lutheran Church in America statement (see Ditmanson, pp. 67–74) does not address the issue directly, but it clearly assumes the ongoing continuity of the Jewish community and its continuing role in its relationships with God. Both the "Preamble" and "Distinctive Ideas, Doctrines, Practices" sections are relevant.

    The Roman Catholic Church's "Nostra Aetate" clearly accepts the continuing covenant relationship of God and the Jews (based on Rom 11:28–29; see Abbott, *The Documents of Vatican II,* p. 664). In "Guidelines for Catholic-Jewish Relations," see under "General Principles" items 1, 4, and 6. The entire thrust of the "Guidelines and Suggestions for Implementing the Conciliar Declaration *Nostra Aetate* (n. 4)" by the Vatican Commission for Religious Relations with the Jews, January 1975 (see Croner, compiler, *Stepping Stones to Further Jewish-Christian Relations,* pp. 11–16) and the dialogue it encourages accords with the view of a continuing Jewish covenant with God and the parallel roles of Jews and Christians "for witness to the world...."

    The United Church of Christ accepts the covenant relationship of both Jews and Christians (see "Relationship," I and III). The statement does not deal explicitly, however, with the "mission" of the two communities.

    The World Council of Churches ("The Churches and the Jewish People," 1988) acknowledges "a special relationship between Jews and Christians because of our shared roots in biblical revelation" (see "Preamble"), that "the Jewish people have by no means been rejected by God (Rom. 11:1, 11)" (see C.7), and the affirmation of "two communities of faith, each called into existence by God, each holding to its respective gifts from God, and each accountable to God" (see C.8).

    18. *The Disciples of Christ* in the "Report from the Commission on

Theology" state: "We confess that both the church and the Jewish people are elected by God for witness to the world and that the revelation of the church and the Jewish people to each other is grounded on God's gracious election of each" ("Theological Foundations... ," #3) and Christians "cannot appropriately say that God's election of and covenant with Israel have been canceled" ("Theological Foundations ... ," #11.c.).

The Episcopal Church statement does not replicate the fourth Presbyterian statement precisely, but it does talk about the continuing covenant of God with the Jews and problems of denigration associated with a failure to understand this. It also notes how a "renewed study of Judaism" has brought about a clearer understanding of first-century Judaism and the developmental nature of Rabbinic Judaism (II, #5, 6, and 7). Item #1 (under "IV. Authentic Christian Witness") endorsed a statement derived from "The Joint Working Group of the Roman Catholic Church and the World Council of Churches" as follows: "Proselytism embraces whatever violates the right of the human person, Christian or non-Christian, to be free from external coercion in religious matters" (see *Ecumenical Review,* 1/1971, p. 11).

The Evangelical Lutheran Church in America, in operating on the 1974 statement of The American Lutheran Church, does not address directly the Presbyterian fourth statement. It does acknowledge: "We [Jews and Christians] are after all, brothers one to another" (Ditmanson, p. 69) and "We both view ourselves as communities covenanted to God" (Ditmanson, p. 69). "Our Common Humanity" and "Our Common Heritage" lead to "Our Spiritual Solidarity" (Ditmanson, pp. 68–69). In the 1994 statement, ELCA asserts that "... we express our urgent desire to live out our faith in Jesus Christ with love and respect for the Jewish people" (paragraph 4).

The Roman Catholic Church in "Nostra Aetate," 4, does single out for special consideration the Jews, and there is acknowledgement that the covenant with the Jews has not been abrogated (see Abbott, p. 664). Nonetheless, "Nostra Aetate" does explicitly assert that "the Church awaits that day, known to God alone, on which all peoples will address the Lord in a single voice and 'serve him with one accord' ..." (Abbott, p. 665). Nonetheless, the "Guidelines" do express strongly a promise-fulfillment relationship, stating, "We believe that those promises were fulfilled with the first coming of Christ" (as Croner, compiler, *Stepping Stones to Further Jewish-Christian Relations,* p. 13 [under "Liturgy"]. In "Within Context ...," it states: "In presenting the early Church's witness as a living reality pertinent to contemporary life, catechists do well to present also the living of the Jewish people to God's enduring fidelity to His covenant with them (*Notes,* VI)" (see *Within Context,* p. 5). It is noteworthy that on April 13, 1986, Pope John Paul II visited Rome's Grand Synagogue, the "first bishop of Rome to visit a synagogue since the time of Simon-Peter" (see Eugene J. Fisher, "Eighteen Months in Catholic-Jewish

Relations [April 13, 1986–September 11, 1987]," in *Overcoming Fear: Between Jews and Christians,* ed. James H. Charlesworth [New York: The American Interfaith Institute, The Crossroad Publishing Company, 1992], p. 140). This action says more than books can record about the Pope's attitude toward his Jewish brethren.

   The United Church of Christ statement acknowledges that "… the Christian Church has denied for too long the continuing validity of God's covenant with the Jewish people…" (III, 3d "Whereas") and implicitly by its recommendations acknowledges this unique relationship with the Jews (see recommendations 1, 2, 3, and 4).

   The World Council of Churches statement acknowledges "a special relationship between Jews and Christians because of our shared roots in biblical revelation (Paragraph 2 under "Preamble"). Under "Affirmations," #9, it states: "We affirm that the Jewish people today is in continuation with biblical Israel and are thankful for the vitality of Jewish faith and thought. We see Jews and Christians, together with all people of living faiths, as God's partners, working in mutual respect and cooperation for justice, peace, and reconciliation."

   19. *The Disciples of Christ,* in the "Report from the Commission on Theology," states: "We confess and repent of the church's long and deep collusion in the spread of anti-Jewish attitudes and actions through its 'teaching of contempt' for Jews and Judaism. We disclaim such teaching and the acts and attitudes which it reflects and reinforces" (see "Statement of Theological Foundations," #2).

   The Episcopal Church, in "Guidelines for Christian-Jewish Relations," part 3, #1, 2, and 3, addresses the issue of "Hatred and Persecution of Jews—A Continuing Concern." It states, for example, "The Church must learn to proclaim the Gospel without generating contempt for Judaism or the Jewish people" (#2). Also, "Christians are called to oppose all religious prejudices through which Jews or any people are made scapegoats for the failures and problems of societies and political regimes" (#3).

   The Evangelical Lutheran Church in America, accepting the 1974 statement of the American Lutheran Church, thus affirms: "It is undeniable that Christian people have both initiated and acquiesced in persecution. Whole generations of Christians have looked with contempt upon this people who were condemned to remain wanderers on the earth on the false charge of deicide" (Ditmanson, p. 67). The 1994 statement of the ELCA regarding Luther does not address the "teaching of contempt" directly, but certainly the tone of the document rejects such.

   The Roman Catholic Church states in "Nostra Aetate," 4, that "the Church repudiates all persecutions against any man. Moreover, mindful of her common patrimony with the Jews, and motivated by the gospel's spiritual love and by no political considerations, she deplores the hatred, persecutions, and displays of anti-Semitism directed against the Jews at any time and from any source" (Abbott, pp. 666–67). In a footnote to this statement, the enactments of the Fourth Lateran Council (1215 A.D.) are noted in terms of the way they dealt with the Jews. After listing several edicts, such as "Jews may not appear in public during Easter week ...," it is stated: "If there was anti-Semitism in these laws, it is here repudiated by the Second Vatican Council" [it is no wonder that many Jews found this "if" to be offensive and unacceptable]. In the "Guidelines and Suggestions" it is stated: "... the spiritual bonds and historical links binding the Church to Judaism condemn (as opposed to the very spirit of Christianity) all forms of anti-Semitism and discrimination, *which in any case the dignity of the human person alone would suffice to condemn*" (Croner, compiler, *Stepping Stones to Further Jewish-Christian Relations,* p. 11, emphasis added).

The United Church of Christ 1987 statement asserts: "The Church's frequent portrayal of the Jews as blind, recalcitrant, evil, and rejected by God has found expression in much Christian theology, liturgy, and education. Such a negative portrayal of the Jewish people and of Judaism has been a factor in the shaping of anti-Jewish attitudes of societies and the policies of governments" (see under "I. Historical Background and Theological Rationale," paragraph 2).

The World Council of Churches, in "The Churches and the Jewish People," affirms what "a number of member churches of the WCC and/or church conferences to which they belong" have affirmed, including "that antisemitism and all forms of the teaching of contempt for Judaism are to be repudiated" (see "B. Historical Note," #2). It also states: "We deeply regret that, contrary to the spirit of Christ, many Christians have used the claims of faith as weapons against the Jewish people, culminating in the Shoah, and we confess sins of word and deed against Jews through the centuries" (see "C. Affirmations," #6).

20. *The Disciples of Christ* statement: "In acknowledging God's covenant with Israel, Christians today must take seriously the meaning of land to Jewish people and the relation of land to the contemporary state of Israel" (see "Statement of Theological Foundations," #11.e.). Attention is drawn to Walter Harrelson, "The State of Israel and Jewish/Christian Relations" (Chapter 8), in Clark M. Williamson, *The Church and the Jewish People,* pp. 59–63.

The Episcopal Church, in "Guidelines," addresses this issue under "II. The Necessity for Christians to Understand Jews and Judaism," especially #14–17. These statements acknowledge the Biblical importance of the land (#14–15) but do recognize the search for identity by Palestinians as well (#16–17).

Acceptance by *the Evangelical Lutheran Church in America* of the 1974 statement of The American Lutheran Church acknowledges that "it seems clear that there is no consensus among Lutherans with respect to the relation between the 'chosen people' and the territory comprising the present State of

Israel" (see Ditmanson, p. 74). This simply acknowledges the considerable division in the ELCA on this issue, and the 1994 statement of the ELCA regarding Luther does not address this issue.

The Roman Catholic Church in "Nostra Aetate," 4, did not address the issue of the land. The "Guidelines and Suggestions ..." also do not address the land issue. In the Appendix to the report of the *Commission for Religious Relations with the Jews,* in part 6 ("Judaism and Christianity in History," #25), it is stated:

"The existence of the State of Israel and its political options should be envisaged not in a perspective which is itself religious, but in their reference to the common principles of international law.

"The permanence of Israel ... is a historic fact and a sign to be interpreted within God's design. We must in any case rid ourselves of the traditional idea of a people *punished,* preserved as a *living argument* for Christian apologetic. It remains a chosen people...."

It should also be noted that in 1993 formal diplomatic relations were established between the State of Israel and the Holy See. This formal establishment had long been sought by both Jews and many Roman Catholics.

In the *United Church of Christ* statement of 1987, the issue of the land is not addressed directly but the ongoing nature of the covenant is affirmed (see under "III. Resolution," first "Whereas"). See also "A Message to the Churches," *New Conversations,* part 5 under "Affirmations": "We appreciate the compelling moral argument for the creation of modern Israel as a vehicle for self-determination and as a haven for a victimized people; we also recognize that this event has entailed the dispossession of Palestinians from their homes and the denial of human rights.... Christians of the West bear a special responsibility to work for a resolution of the Israeli-Palestinian issue that assures the human rights and dignity of both peoples" (p. 7).

The World Council of Churches, in its 1988 statement on "The Churches and the Jewish People," does not address the issue of land vis-a-vis Israel and the Jewish faith. Jay T. Rock, Director of the Office on Christian/Jewish Relations of the National Council of Churches , quotes at length from the UCC "A Message to the Churches," much of which is quoted above under the UCC entry (see "Christian Understandings of Covenant and the Jewish People," *New Conversations* (Summer, 1990), p. 48).

21. *The Disciples of Christ* "Report From the Commission on Theology" does not address this issue, nor does Joe R. Jones, "Jewish and Christian Theology on Election, Covenant, Messiah, and the Future" (Chapter 7), in Clark Williamson, ed., *The Church and the Jewish People,* pp. 51–58, who talks about the issues but does not address directly the correlative awaiting for the peaceable kingdom and the interim responsibilities attached to each community.

The Episcopal Church, in its "Guidelines," does not address this statement directly either. The closest it comes is in section II ("The Necessity for Christians to Understand Jews and Judaism"), #10, where the focus is on God's election of both communities: "The relationship between the two communities, both worshipping the God of ancient Israel, is a given historical fact, but how it is to be understood and explained theologically is a matter of internal discussion among Christians and Jews in dialogue."

The Evangelical Lutheran Church in America does not address this statement in its 1994 declaration regarding Luther, and the 1974 statement of the American Lutheran Church affirms the solidarity of Christians (especially Lutherans, in this statement) with Jews (Part I, see Ditmanson, pp. 68–69), but the seventh affirmation does not find close parallel.

The Roman Catholic Church, in "Nostra Aetate," 4, addresses affirmation seven somewhat obliquely: "In company with the prophets and the same Apostle, the Church awaits that day, known to God alone, on which all peoples will address the Lord in a single voice and 'serve him with one accord.' ..." (see Abbott, pp. 664–65). In the "Guidelines and Suggestions," it is stated: "Jews and Christians will work willingly together, seeking social justice and peace at every level—local, national, and international" (see Croner, compiler, *Stepping Stones to Further Jewish-Christian Relations,* p. 15).

The United Church of Christ, in its 1987 statement, does not address this affirmation directly, only indirectly by affirming the continuance of "God's covenant with the Jewish people" (as in III, resolution one).

The World Council of Churches has a partial parallel in "The Churches and the Jewish People" (see "C. Affirmations," # 2), where thanks are offered for those "spiritual treasures" shared with the Jewish people, among these "the hope of the coming kingdom."

22. See Ditmanson, p. 722 (found under "II. Confrontation," final paragraph under "Distinctive Ideas, Doctrines, Practices."

23. See Croner, compiler, *Stepping Stone to Further Jewish-Christian Relations,* p. 13 (in the section under "Liturgy").

VII. Conclusion: Improving Jewish-Christian Relations

1. It should be noted that prejudice may also be positive, as the prejudice of a parent for a child, which encourages both the protection and encouragement of the child. This type of prejudice is not what is confronted in antisemitism, for here the prejudice is an irrational perception of the Jew and Judaism apart from any factual data. Negative type of prejudice can potentially lead to harmful actions directed toward the object of the prejudice.

2. Melvin M. Tumin, "What is Antisemitism?" in *Antisemitism in the United States,* ed. Leonard Dinnerstein (New York: Holt, Rinehart and Win-

ston, 1971), pp. 10–11.

    3. Ibid., p. 11.

    4. Bernard Malamud, *The Fixer* (New York: Dell Publishing Co., Inc., 1966), p. 118.

    5. Ibid., pp. 118–19

    6. Tumin, "What is Antisemitism?" p. 11.

    7. According to the *American Jewish Year Book 1992,* vol. 92, ed. David Singer (New York: The American Jewish Committee, 1992), p. 265, the Jewish population constituted 2.3 percent of the total population of the United States.

    8. The one caveat regarding the shared Seder Meal is the absolute necessity that Christians accept the nature and intent of the Seder Meal within its Jewish context. There can be absolutely no usurpation of this ritual by well-intentioned Christians, as we seek to alter the text and message of the Seder to make it a Christian document. An excellent tool to assist Jewish and Christian groups in studying their parallel stories is the book by Michael Goldberg, *Jews and Christians: Getting Our Stories Straight* (Nashville: Abingdon Press, 1985).

    9. See Rabbi David E. Cahn-Lipman, *The Book of Jewish Knowledge* (Northvale, New Jersey: Jason Aronson Inc., 1991), p. 194.

    10. Arthur Hertzberg, "Anti-Semitism and Jewish Uniqueness: Ancient and Contemporary," p. 20, lecture delivered at Syracuse University, April 11, 1973, as a part of The B. G. Rudolph Lectures in Judaic Studies, published c. 1975. Microfiche housed with The Jewish Division of the New York Public Library.

    11. *The Passover Haggadah,* ed. Nahum N. Glatzer (New York: Schocken Books, 1969), is a helpful edition for such use.

Bibliography

The following reading suggestions are not intended to be exhaustive. These volumes are selected to introduce the area concerned and to encourage through the bibliographies of the books listed additional materials that might be explored. At the same time, some areas are more heavily represented than others, particularly in the sections on *Antisemitism—General* and *Jewish-Christian Relations*. This is purposeful, because generally Christians have not read significantly in such areas. Notice also that books rather than journals have been emphasized, because frequently journals are more difficult to obtain, especially if the reader is not directly associated with an academic institution. Regardless, "Of making many books there is no end..." (Eccl 12:12, NRSV), and thus the reader is encouraged to dig deeply into the multiple resources available for enlightening further the important topics discussed in the chapters of this book.

Bible Dictionaries

Achtemeier, Paul J., ed. *Harper's Bible Dictionary*. San Francisco: Harper & Row, Publishers, 1985.

Butler, Trent C., ed. *Holman Bible Dictionary*. Nashville, Tennessee: Holman Bible Publishers, 1991.

Buttrick, G. A., ed. *The Interpreter's Dictionary of the Bible,* 4 vols. New York: Abingdon Press, 1962. Supplementary Volume, Keith Crim, ed., 1976.

Freedman, David Noel, ed. *The Anchor Bible Dictionary,* 6 vols. New York: Doubleday, 1992.

Smith, Jonathan Z., ed. *The HarperCollins Dictionary of Religion*. San Francisco: HarperSanFrancisco, 1995 (NOTE: not a Bible dictionary but the articles are extensive in coverage and quite helpful in numerous areas of inquiry).

Old Testament Introductions

Anderson, Bernhard W. *Understanding the Old Testament,* 4th ed. Englewood Cliffs, New Jersey: Prentice-Hall, 1986.

Crenshaw, James L. *Old Testament Story and Faith: A Literary and Theological Introduction.* Peabody, Massachusetts: Hendrickson Publishers, 1992.

Dearman, J. Andrew. *Religion and Culture in Ancient Israel.* Peabody, Massachusetts: Hendrickson Publishers, 1992.

Humphreys, W. Lee. *Crisis and Story: Introduction to the Old Testament,* 2nd ed. Mountain View, California: Mayfield Publishing Company, 1990.

New Testament Introductions

Kee, Howard Clark. *Understanding the New Testament,* 4th ed. Englewood Cliffs, New Jersey: Prentice-Hall, Inc., 1983.

Perrin, Norman. *The New Testament: An Introduction.* New York: Harcourt Brace Jovanovich, Inc., 1974.

Spivey, Robert A. and D. Moody Smith. *Anatomy of the New Testament,* 5th ed. Englewood Cliffs, New Jersey: Prentice Hall, 1995.

Antisemitism—General

Almog, Shmuel, ed. *Antisemitism Through the Ages.* New York: Pergamon Press, 1988.

Arendt, Hannah. *Antisemitism.* New York: Harcourt, Brace & World, Inc., 1951.

Cohen, Jeremy. *The Friars and the Jews: The Evolution of Medieval Anti-Judaism.* Ithaca: Cornell University Press, 1982.

Daane, James. *The Anatomy of Anti-Semitism and Other Essays on Religion and Race.* Grand Rapids, Michigan: William B. Eerdmans Publishing Company, 1965.

Davies, Alan T. *Anti-Semitism and the Christian Mind.* New York: Herder and Herder, 1969.

Davies, Alan T., ed. *Anti-Semitism and the Foundations of Christianity.* New York: Paulist Press, 1979.

Dawidowicz, Lucy S. *The War Against the Jews, 1933–45.* New York: Holt, Rinehart and Winston, 1975.

Eckardt, Arthur Roy. *Elder and Younger Brothers.* New York: Charles Scribner's Sons, 1967.

Flannery, Edward H. *The Anguish of the Jews.* New York: The Macmillan Company, 1965; New York/Mahwah: Paulist Press, 1985.

Foster, Arnold and Benjamin R. Epstein. *The New Anti-Semitism.* New York: McGraw Hill, 1974.

Gager, John G. *The Origins of Anti-Semitism: Attitudes toward Judaism in Pagan and Christian Antiquity.* New York: Oxford University Press, 1983.

Glassman, Bernard. *Anti-Semitic Stereotypes without Jews: Images of the Jews in England,* 1290–1700. Detroit: Wayne State University Press, 1975.

Glock, Charles Y. and Rodney Stark. *Christian Beliefs and Anti-Semitism.* New York: Harper & Row, Publishers, 1966.

Grosser, Paul E. and Edwin G. Halperin. *Anti-Semitism: Causes and Effects,* 2nd ed. New York: Philosophical Library, 1983.

Heer, Friedrich. *God's First Love: Christians and Jews Over Two Thousand Years,* trans. Geoffrey Skelton. New York: Weybright and Talley, 1970.

Higham, John. *Send These to Me: Jews and Other Immigrants in Urban America.* New York: Atheneum, 1975.

Isaac, Jules. *Has Anti-Semitism Roots in Christianity?* trans. Dorothy and James Parkes. New York: National Conference of Christians and Jews, 1962.

Isaac, Jules. *The Teaching of Contempt: Christian Roots of Anti-Semitism,* trans. Helen Weaver. New York: Holt, Rinehart and Winston, 1964.

Klein, Charlotte. *Anti-Judaism in Christian Theology,* trans. Edward Quinn. Philadelphia: Fortress Press, 1978.

Langmuir, Gavin I. *Toward A Definition of Antisemitism.* Los Angeles: University of California Press, 1990.

Levy, Richard S. *Antisemitism in the Modern World: An Anthology of Texts.* Lexington, Massachusetts: D.C. Heath and Company, 1991.

Lewis, Bernard. *Semites and Anti-Semites: An Inquiry into Conflict and Prejudice.* New York: W. W. Norton & Company, 1986.

Lipset, Seymour Martin. *American Pluralism and the Jewish Community.* New Brunswick, N.J.: Transactions Publishers, 1990.

Lipset, Seymour Martin and Earl Raab. *Jews and the American Scene.* Cambridge, Massachusetts: Harvard University Press, 1995.

Lipstadt, Deborah E. *Beyond Belief: The American Press & the Coming of the Holocaust* 1933–1945. New York: The Free Press, 1986.

Lipstadt, Deborah E. *Denying the Holocaust: The Growing Assault on Truth and Memory.* New York: The Free Press, 1993.

Littell, Franklin H. *The Crucifixion of the Jews: The Failure of Christians to Understand the Jewish Experience.* New York: Harper & Row, Publishers, 1975.

Lookstein, Haskel. *Were We Our Brothers' Keepers? The Public Response of American Jews to the Holocaust 1938–1944.* New York: Hartmore House, 1985.

Morse, Arthur D. *While Six Million Died: A Chronicle of American Apathy.* Woodstock, New York: The Overlook Press, 1983.

Oberman, Heiko A. *The Roots of Anti-Semitism in the Age of Renaissance and Reformation,* trans. James I. Porter. Philadelphia: Fortress Press, 1984.

Parkes, James W. *Antisemitism.* Chicago: Quadrangle Books, 1963.

Parkes, James William. *The Conflict of the Church and the Synagogue.* London: The Soncino Press, 1934.

Parkes, James William. *The Jew and His Neighbour: A Study of the Causes of Antisemitism,* 2nd ed. rev. London: Student Christian Movement Press, 1938.

Penslar, Derek J. *Anti-Semitism: The Jewish Response.* Orange, N.J.: Behrman House, Inc., 1989.

Poliakov, Leon. *The History of Anti-Semitism,* vol. 1, trans. Richard Howard; vol. 2, trans. Natalie Gerardi. New York: Vanguard Press, 1965, 1973.

Rausch, David A. *Fundamentalists, Evangelicals and Anti-Semitism.* Philadelphia: Trinity Press International, 1993.

Ruether, Rosemary. *Faith and Fratricide: The Theological Roots of Anti-Semitism.* New York: The Seabury Press, 1974.

Runes, Dagobert David. *The Jew and the Cross,* 2nd ed. New York: Citadel Press, 1966.

Tobin, Gary A. and Sharon L. Sassler. *Jewish Perceptions of Antisemitism.* New York: Plenum Press, 1988.

Weinberg, Meyer. *Because They Were Jews: A History of Antisemitism.* New York: Greenwood Press, 1986.

Wistrich, Robert S. *Antisemitism: The Longest Hatred.* New York: Pantheon Books, 1991.

Wyman, David S. *The Abandonment of the Jews: America and the Holocaust 1941–1945.* New York: Pantheon Books, 1984.

The New Testament/Christianity and Antisemitism

Baum, Gregory. *Is the New Testament Anti-Semitic?* rev. ed. Glen Rock, N.J.: Paulist Press, 1965.

Cohn-Shebok, Dan. *The Crucified Jew: Twenty Centuries of Christian Anti-Semitism.* London: Harper Collins Religious, 1992.

Freudmann, Lillan C. *Antisemitism in the New Testament.* New York: University Press of America, 1994.

Hare, Douglas R. A. *The Theme of Jewish Persecution of Christians in the Gospel According to St. Matthew.* Cambridge: The University Press, 1967.

Nicholls, William. *Christian Antisemitism: A History of Hate.* Northvale, New Jersey: Jason Aronson Inc., 1993.

Sandmel, Samuel. *Anti-Semitism in the New Testament?* Philadelphia: Fortress Press, 1978.

Sandmel, Samuel. *We Jews and Jesus.* New York: Oxford University Press, 1965.

American Antisemitism

Belth, Nathan C. *A Promise to Keep: A Narrative of the American Encounter with Anti-Semitism.* New York: Schocken Books, 1981. Chances, Jerome A., ed. *Antisemitism in America Today: Outspoken Experts Explode the Myths.* Secaucus, N.J.: Carol Publishing Group, 1995.

Dinnerstein, Leonard. *Antisemitism in America.* New York: Oxford University Press, 1994.

Dinnerstein, Leonard, ed. *Antisemitism in the United States.* New York: Holt, Rinehart and Winston, Inc., 1971.

Gerber, David A., ed. *Anti-Semitism in American History.* Chicago: University of Illinois Press, 1986.

Jaher, Frederic Cople. *A Scapegoat in the New Wilderness: The Origins and Rise of Anti-Semitism in America.* Cambridge, Massachusetts: Harvard University Press, 1994.

Mayo, Louise A. *The Ambivalent Image: Nineteenth-Century America's Perception of the Jew.* Rutherford, N.J.: Farleigh Dickinson University Press, 1988.

Warren, Donald. *Radio Priest: Charles Coughlin, the Father of Hate Radio.* New York: The Free Press, 1996.

Jewish-Christian Relations

Abbott, Walter M., S.J., ed. *The Documents of Vatican II.* New York: Corpus Books, 1966.

Banki, Judith, ed. and compiler. *Christian Statements and Documents Bearing on Christian-Jewish Relations.* New York: Interreligious Affairs Department, The American Jewish Committee, 1972.

Boadt, Lawrence, Helga Croner, and Leon Klenicki, eds. *Biblical Studies: Meeting Ground of Jews and Christians.* New York: Paulist Press, 1980.

Braybrooke, Marcus. *Time to Meet: Towards a Deeper Relationship between Jews and Christians.* Philadelphia: Trinity Press International, 1990.

Brockway, Allan, Paul van Buren, Rolf Rendtorff, and Simon Schoon, commentary. *The Theology of the Churches and the Jewish People: Statements by the World Council of Churches and its Member Churches.* Geneva: WCC Publications, 1988.

Buber, Martin. *Between Man and Man,* trans. Ronald Gregor Smith. London: Kegan Paul, 1947.

Buber, Martin. *I and Thou,* trans. Walter Kaufmann. New York: Charles Scribner's Sons, 1970.

Buber, Martin. *The Way of Response,* ed. Nahum N. Glatzer. New York: Schocken Books, 1966.

Buber, Martin. *Two Types of Faith,* trans. Norman P. Goldhawk. New York: Harper Torchbook, 1961.

Charlesworth, James H., ed. *Jesus' Jewishness: Exploring the Place of Jesus in Early Judaism.* New York: The Crossroad Publishing Company, 1991.

Charlesworth, James H. ed. *Jews and Christians: Exploring the Past, Present, and Future.* New York: The Crossroad Publishing Company, 1990.

Charlesworth, James H., ed. *Overcoming Fear Between Jews and Christians.* New York: The Crossroad Publishing Company, 1992.

Cohen, Arthur A. *The Myth of the Judeo-Christian Tradition.* New York: Harper and Row, Publishers, 1970.

Cohen, Naomi W. *Essential Papers on Jewish-Christian Relations in the United States: Imagery and Reality.* New York: New York University Press, 1990.

Croner, Helga and Leon Klenicki, eds. *Issues in The Jewish-Christian Dialogue: Jewish Perspectives on Covenant, Mission, and Witness.* New York: Paulist Press, 1979.

Croner, Helga, compiler. *More Stepping Stones to Jewish-Christian Relations: An Unabridged Collection of Christian Documents, 1975–1983.* New York: Paulist Press, 1985.

Croner, Helga, compiler. *Stepping Stones to Further Jewish-Christian Relations.* New York: Paulist Press, 1977.

de Corneille, Roland. *Christians and Jews.* New York: Harper and Row, Publishers, 1966.

Ditmanson, Harold H. ed. *Stepping-Stones to Further Jewish-Lutheran Relationships.* Minneapolis: Augsburg, 1990.

Dunn, James D. G. *The Partings of the Ways: Between Christianity and Judaism and their Significance for the Character of Christianity.* Philadelphia: Trinity Press International, 1991.

Eckardt, A. Roy. *Your People, My People: The Meeting of Jews and Christians.* New York: Quadrangle/The New York Times Book Company, 1974.

Evans, Craig A. and Donald A. Hagner, eds. *Anti-Semitism and Early Christianity: Issues of Polemic and Faith.* Minneapolis: Fortress Press, 1993.

Fisher, Eugene J. *Faith Without Prejudice: Rebuilding Christian Attitudes Toward Judaism,* rev. and expanded. New York: The Crossroad Publishing Company, 1993.

Fisher, Eugene J. and Leon Klenicki. *In Our Time: The Flowering of Jewish-Catholic Dialogue.* New York: Paulist Press, 1990.

Fisher, Eugene J., ed. *Interwoven Destinies: Jews and Christians Through the Ages.* New York: Paulist Press, 1993.

Fisher, Eugene J., ed. *Visions of the Other: Jewish and Christian Theologians Assess the Dialogue.* New York: Paulist Press, 1994.

Harrelson, Walter and Randall M. Falk. *Jews and Christians: A Troubled Family.* Nashville: Abingdon Press, 1990.

Kee, Howard Clark and Irwin J. Borowsky, eds. *Removing Anti-Judaism from the Pulpit.* New York: The Continuum Publishing Company, 1996.

Kirsh, Paul J. *We Christians and Jews.* Philadelphia: Fortress Press, 1975.

Klenicki, Leon and Geoffrey Wigoder, eds. *A Dictionary of the Jewish-Christian Dialogue.* New York: Paulist Press, 1984.

Klenicki, Leon and Geoffrey Wigoder, eds. *A Dictionary of the Jewish-Christian Dialogue,* expanded ed. New York: Paulist Press, 1995.

Lodahl, Michael E. *Shekhinah/Spirit: Divine Presence in Jewish and Christian Religion.* New York: Paulist Press, 1992.

Lohfink, Norbert, S.J. *The Covenant Never Revoked: Biblical Reflections on Christian-Jewish Dialogue,* trans. John J. Scullion, S.J. New York: Paulist Press, 1991.

Martin, Vincent. *A House Divided: The Parting of the Ways between Synagogue and Church.* New York: Paulist Press, 1995.

Neusner, Jacob. *Jews and Christians: The Myth of a Common Tradition.* Philadelphia: Trinity Press International, 1991.

Novak, David. *Jewish-Christian Dialogue: A Jewish Justification.* New York: Oxford University Press, 1989.

Oesterreicher, John M. *The New Encounter Between Christians and Jews.* New York: Philosophical Library, 1986.

Parkes, James William. *Prelude to Dialogue: Jewish-Christian Relationships.* New York: Schocken Books, 1969.

Pawlikowski, John T. *Christ in the Light of the Christian-Jewish Dialogue.* New York: Paulist Press, 1982.

Pawlikowski, John T. *What Are They Saying About Christian-Jewish Relations?* New York: Paulist Press, 1980.

Rousmaniere, John. *A Bridge to Dialogue: The Story of Jewish-Christian Relations,* ed. James A. Carpenter and Leon Klenicki. New York: Paulist Press, 1991.

Rubin, Alexis P., ed. *Scattered Among the Nations: Documents Affecting Jewish History,* 49 to 1975. Northvale, New Jersey: Jason Aronson Inc., 1995.

Rudin, A. James and Marvin R. Wilson. *A Time to Speak: The Evangelical-Jewish Encounter.* Grand Rapids, Michigan: William B. Eerdmans Publishing Company, 1987.

Shermis, Michael and Arthur E. Zannoni, eds. *Introduction to Jewish-Christian Relations.* New York: Paulist Press, 1991.

Smiga, George M. *Pain and Polemic: Anti-Judaism in the Gospels.* New York: Paulist Press, 1992.

Spong, John Shelby and Jack Daniel Spiro. *Dialogue: In Search of Jewish/Christian Understanding.* New York: The Seabury Press, 1975.

Stransky, Thomas F., C.S.P. and John B. Sheerin, C.S.P. *Doing the Truth in Charity: Statements of Pope Paul VI, Popes John Paul I, John Paul II, and the Secretariat for Promoting Christian Unity, 1964–1980.* New York: Paulist Press, 1982.

Talmage, Frank. *Disputation and Dialogue: Readings in the Jewish-Christian Encounter.* New York: KTAV, 1975.

Thoma, Clemens and Michael Wyschogrod, eds. *Understanding Scripture: Explorations of Jewish and Christian Traditions of Interpretation.* New York: Paulist Press, 1987.

Wigoder, Geoffrey. *Jewish-Christian Relations Since the Second World War.* New York: Manchester University Press, 1988.

Williamson, Clark M. *Has God Rejected His People?* Nashville: Abingdon, 1982.

Williamson, Clark M., ed. *The Church and the Jewish People: A Study Guide for the Christian Church (Disciples of Christ).* St. Louis, Missouri: Christian Board of Publication, 1994.

Williamson, Clark, ed. *A Mutual Witness: Toward Critical Solidarity Between Jews & Christians.* St. Louis, Missouri: Chalice Press, 1992.

Williamson, Clark M. *When Jews and Christians Meet: A Guide for Christian Preaching and Teaching.* St. Louis, Missouri: CBP Press, 1989.

Wilson, Stephen G. *Related Strangers: Jews and Christians, 70–170 C.E.* Minneapolis: Fortress Press, 1995.

Zannoni, Arthur E., ed. *Jews and Christians Speak of Jesus.* Minneapolis: Fortress Press, 1994.

Understanding Jewish History and Thought

Ariel, David S. *What Do Jews Believe? The Spiritual Foundations of Judaism.* New York: Schocken Books, 1995.

Asheri, Michael. *Living Jewish.* New York: Everest House, 1978.

Ben-Sasson, H. H., ed. *A History of the Jewish People.* Cambridge, Massachusetts: Harvard University Press, 1976.

Blech, Benjamin. *Understanding Judaism: The Basics of Deed and Creed.* Northvale, New Jersey: Jason Aronson Inc., 1991.

Diamant, Anita and Howard Cooper. *Living a Jewish Life: Jewish Traditions, Customs and Values for Today's Families.* New York: HarperPerennial, 1991.

Donin, Hayim Halevy. *To Be A Jew.* New York: Basic Books, Inc., 1972.

Greenberg, Blu. *How to Run a Traditional Jewish Household.* New York: Simon and Schuster, 1983.

Hertzberg, Arthur, ed. *Judaism,* "Great Religions of Modern Man," Richard A. Gard, ed. New York: Washington Square Press, 1962.

Johnson, Paul. *A History of the Jews.* New York: Harper & Row, Publishers, 1987.

Kertzer, Morris N. *What is a Jew?* rev. ed. New York: The Macmillan Company, 1960.

Kugel, James. *On Being A Jew: What Does It Mean To Be A Jew?* New York: HarperSanFrancisco, 1990.

Neusner, Jacob. *Between Time and Eternity: The Essentials of Judaism.* Belmont, California: Dickenson Publishing Company, Inc. 1975.

Neusner, Jacob. *An Introduction to Judaism: A Textbook and Reader.* Louisville, Kentucky: Westminster/John Knox Press, 1991.

Parkes, James William. *A History of the Jewish People,* rev. ed. Baltimore, Maryland: Penguin Books, Inc., 1964.

Roth, Cecil. *A History of the Jews,* rev. ed. New York: Schocken Books, 1970.

Sachar, Abraham Leon. *A History of the Jews,* 5th ed. rev. and enlarged. New York: Alfred A. Knopf, 1967.

Schweitzer, Frederick M. *A History of the Jews.* New York: The Macmillan Company, 1971.

Steinberg, Milton. *Basic Judaism.* Northvale, New Jersey: Jason Aronson Inc., 1987.

Trepp, Leo. *Judaism: Development and Life, 3rd ed.,* Belmont, California: Wadsworth Publishing Company, 1982.

Wylen, Stephen M. *Settings of Silver: An Introduction to Judaism.* New York: Paulist Press, 1989.

American Judaism

Blau, Joseph L. *Judaism in America: From Curiosity to Third Faith,* "Chicago History of American Religion," ed. Martin E. Marty. Chicago: The University of Chicago Press, 1976.

Dimont, Max. *The Jews in America.* New York: Simon and Schuster, 1978.

Feingold, Henry L. *Zion in America,* rev. ed. New York: Hippocrene Books, Inc., 1981.

Feingold, Henry L., ed. *The Jewish People in America,* 5 vols. Baltimore: The Johns Hopkins University Press, 1992.

Feldstein, Stanley. *The Land That I Show You: Three Centuries of Jewish Life in America.* Garden City, New York: Anchor Press/Doubleday, 1978.

Glazer, Nathan. *American Judaism,* 2nd ed. rev., "The Chicago History of American Civilization," ed. Daniel J. Boorstin. Chicago: The University of Chicago Press, 1972.

Hertzberg, Arthur. *Being Jewish in America*. New York: Schocken Books, 1979.

Lipset, Seymour Martin and Earl Raab. *Jews and the New American Scene*. Cambridge, Massachusetts: Harvard University Press, 1995.

Neusner, Jacob. *American Judaism*. Englewood Cliffs, New Jersey: Prentice-Hall, Inc., 1972.

Neusner, Jacob, ed. *Understanding American Judaism*. New York: KTAV Publishing House, Inc., vol. 1, 1975; vol. 2, 1975.

Rosen, Gladys, ed. *Jewish Life in America: Historical Perspectives*. New York: KTAV/Institute of Human Relations Press of the American Jewish Committee, 1978.

Rosenberg, Stuart E. *The New Jewish Identity in America*. New York: Hippocrene Books, 1985.

Rosenberg, Stuart E. *The Search for Jewish Identity in America*. Garden City, New York: Doubleday & Company, Inc., 1965.

Silberman, Charles E. *A Certain People: American Jews and their Lives Today*. New York: Summit Books, 1985.

Waxman, Chaim I. *America's Jews in Transition*. Philadelphia: Temple University Press, 1983.

Indexes

B.   AUTHORS

1 Jn 4:7–8 (127), 4:19–20 (127)

Lk 9:18–22 (37), 9:43b–45 (37), 11:33
    (38), 11:49–51 (41),
    18:31–34 (37), 20:9–19
    (35, 49, 64), 23:34 (41),
    23:46 (42)
Lv 19:27 (125)

Mk 1:1 (20–21), 8:27–33 (37–38),
    8:32 (22), 9:30–32 (37–38),
    10:32–34 (37–38), 10:33
    (38), 12:1–12 (35–37, 49,
    64), 12:9 (36, 65)
Mt 5:14–16 (38), 5:17 (39, 62,
    121), 9:17 (62, 65), 10:5–6
    (39–40), 15:24 (39–40),
    16:13–23 (37), 17:22–23
    (37), 20:17–19 (37),
    21:23–46 (35, 49),
    21:33–46 (64), 21:43

    (36–37), 25:25 (121), 27:1
    (19), 27:25 (172, n 20),
    28:19–20 (39–40)

Num 15:40 (87)

Phil 3:5 (29)
Ps 118:22–23 (36), 103:6 (147)

Rom 3:29–30 (141), 9–11 (30–33,
    49, 64, 170 [n 5], 171 [n
    11]), 9:4–5 (159), 11:1 and
    11 (186 [n 9], 187 [n 17]),
    11:2 (141), 11:17–18 (141),
    11:17–24 (159), 11:25
    (141), 11:28–29 (159, 186
    [n 9], 187 [n 17]), 11:29
    (119, 186 [n 9])
Rv 21:19 (72)

Zech 14:9 (160)

David Burrell and Yehezkel Landau, editors, *Voices from Jerusalem* (A Stimulus Book, 1991).

John Rousmaniere, *A Bridge to Dialogue: The Story of Jewish-Christian Relations;* edited by James A. Carpenter and Leon Klenicki (A Stimulus Book, 1991).

Michael E. Lodahl, *Shekhinah/Spirit* (A Stimulus Book, 1992).

George M. Smiga, *Pain and Polemic: Anti-Judaism in the Gospels* (A Stimulus Book, 1992).

Eugene J. Fisher, editor, *Interwoven Destinies: Jews and Christians Through the Ages* (A Stimulus Book, 1993).

Anthony Kenny, *Catholics, Jews and the State of Israel* (A Stimulus Book, 1993).

Eugene J. Fisher, editor, *Visions of the Other: Jewish and Christian Theologians Assess the Dialogue* (A Stimulus Book, 1995).

Leon Klenicki and Geoffrey Wigoder, editors, *A Dictionary of the Jewish-Christian Dialogue* (Expanded Edition), (A Stimulus Book, 1995).

STIMULUS BOOKS are developed by Stimulus Foundation, a not-for-profit organization, and are published by Paulist Press. The Foundation wishes to further the publication of scholarly books on Jewish and Christian topics that are of importance to Judaism and Christianity.

Stimulus Foundation was established by an erstwhile refugee from Nazi Germany who intends to contribute with these publications to the improvement of communication between Jews and Christians.

Books for publication in this Series will be selected by a committee of the Foundation, and offers of manuscripts and works in progress should be addressed to:

Stimulus Foundation
c/o Paulist Press
997 Macarthur Boulevard
Mahwah, N.J. 07430